Proceedings of the

19th International Congress of Classical Archaeology

Volume 8: Reconstructing Scales of Production

in the Ancient Greek World

Proceedings of the
19th International Congress of Classical Archaeology

Cologne/Bonn, 22 – 26 May 2018
Archaeology and Economy in the Ancient World

Edited by

Martin Bentz and Michael Heinzelmann

Volume 8

ICCA
XIX
AIAC

Edited by

Eleni Hasaki – Martin Bentz

Reconstructing Scales of Production in the Ancient Greek World: Producers, Processes, Products, People

Panel 3.4

Propylaeum
SPECIALIZED INFORMATION
SERVICE CLASSICS

Bibliographic information published by the Deutsche Nationalbibliothek:
The Deutsche Nationalbibliothek lists this publication in the Deutsche Nationalbibliografie; detailed bibliographic data are available on the Internet at http://dnb.dnb.de.

Propylaeum
SPECIALIZED INFORMATION SERVICE CLASSICS

Published at Propylaeum,
Heidelberg University Library 2020.

This publication is freely available under https://www.propylaeum.de (Open Access).
urn: urn:nbn:de:bsz:16-propylaeum-ebook-639-5
DOI: https://doi.org/10.11588/propylaeum.639

Editorial Coordination: Florian Birkner, Ina Borkenstein, Christian Schöne
Editorial Staff: Stefanie Herten, Katharina Zerzeropulos

Layout: Torsten Zimmer, Zwiebelfisch@quarium

Cover illustration: Sociogram courtesy of the Social Networks of Athenian Potters Project. Illustrated by: Yannis Nakas.

ISBN: 978-3-948465-34-6
e-ISBN: 978-3-948465-33-9

Universität zu Köln

UNIVERSITÄT BONN

CONTENTS

PREFACE

On behalf of the 'Associazione Internazionale di Archaeologica Classica (AIAC)' the 19th International Congress for Classical Archaeology took place in Cologne and Bonn from 22 to 26 May 2018. It was jointly organized by the two Archaeological Institutes of the Universities of Cologne and Bonn, and the primary theme of the congress was 'Archaeology and Economy in the Ancient World'. In fact, economic aspects permeate all areas of public and private life in ancient societies, whether in urban development, religion, art, housing, or in death.

Research on ancient economies has long played a significant role in ancient history. Increasingly in the last decades, awareness has grown in archaeology that the material culture of ancient societies offers excellent opportunities for studying the structure, performance, and dynamics of ancient economic systems and economic processes. Therefore, the main objective of this congress was to understand economy as a central element of classical societies and to analyze its interaction with ecological, political, social, religious, and cultural factors. The theme of the congress was addressed to all disciplines that deal with the Greco-Roman civilization and their neighbouring cultures from the Aegean Bronze Age to the end of Late Antiquity.

The participation of more than 1.200 scholars from more than 40 countries demonstrates the great response to the topic of the congress. Altogether, more than 900 papers in 128 panels were presented, as were more than 110 posters. The publication of the congress is in two stages: larger panels are initially presented as independent volumes, such as this publication. Finally, at the end of the editing process, all contributions will be published in a joint conference volume.

We would like to take this opportunity to thank all participants and helpers of the congress who made it such a great success. Its realization would not have been possible without the generous support of many institutions, whom we would like to thank once again: the Universities of Bonn and Cologne, the Archaeological Society of Cologne, the Archaeology Foundation of Cologne, the Gerda Henkel Foundation, the Fritz Thyssen Foundation, the Sal. Oppenheim Foundation, the German Research Foundation (DFG), the German Academic Exchange Service (DAAD), the Romano-Germanic Museum Cologne and the LVR-LandesMuseum Bonn. Finally, our thanks go to all colleagues and panel organizers who were involved in the editing and printing process.

Bonn/Cologne, in August 2019

Martin Bentz & Michael Heinzelmann

Reconstructing Scales of Production in the Ancient Greek World: Producers, Processes, Products, People

Martin Bentz – Eleni Hasaki

Introduction

Scholars have adopted an array of approaches, both traditional and experimental, to approximate the scale of craft production, which has always been central to the study of ancient economies. This panel examines these new methods, for estimating the workshop crew size, the workshop physical space, the time requirements for the chaîne opératoire for each product, the needs of the population for different goods, or the percentage of ancient products surviving to this day. These new approaches, some borrowed from related disciplines, should help us overcome the paucity of archaeological evidence. By employing social network analysis, individual worker's output, architectural energetics, and production-consumption ratios, we aim to improve our understanding of the scale of craft production in the ancient Greek world, both in the Greek mainland and in the Greek colonies in Sicily. Archaeologists and ancient economists are using new approaches to study the ancient economy at a micro-level, taking into consideration several variables, such as raw material procurement, labor investment, cross-craft dependencies, apprenticeship periods, and product demand, to name a few.

Our test cases range chronologically from Prehistoric to Classical times, and geographically from Athens (Hasaki and Cline; Rocco; Sapirstein; Stissi), to the Argolid and central Greece (Jazwa; Fitzsimons), the Aegean (Cecconi) and Selinous in Italy (Bentz). The industries covered are pottery-making, vase-painting, tile works, mosaic construction, and monumental construction. This panel will show how the labor investment for tiling a roof (Jazwa) or for building a monumental tomb in Bronze Age Greece (Fitzsimons) reveals the economic complexity of ancient societies in craft specialization, workforce mobilization, and financing models (Cecconi). Moreover, estimating the sizes of ancient ceramic workshops can lead to better reconstruction of the economic cycles of production and consumption, which in turn helps us understand the range of scales for imported and exported ceramics.

Our discussant, Peter Acton, a business economist, has studied manufacturing operations in Classical Athens. With his micro-level focus he has demonstrated how economic considerations determined enterprise size and profitability in different industries.

Our special thanks to the contributors of this volume for their timely submissions as well as to the reviewers who provided valuable input in a short turnaround. We are also grateful to Florian Birkner, Kendyl Bostic, Karen Donohue, and Megan Mendonca for their assistance in finalizing this volume.

Comparing the Labor Investment and Production of Early and Late Bronze Age Ceramic Roofing Tiles in Mainland Greece

Kyle A. Jazwa

Introduction

In contemporary, romantic images of the Mediterranean, ruddy ceramic tiled roofs crown centuries-old buildings and strike a vivid contrast with the deep blue sea and yellow-green countryside (fig. 1).[1] The modern ubiquity of the tiled roof, however, obscures a multivalent and complex past that, in prehistory at least, was anything but a romantic cliché. On three separate occasions, ceramic roofing tiles were invented in mainland Greece – the Early Bronze Age (Early Helladic 'EH', ca. 3100–2000 BC), the Late Bronze Age (Late Helladic 'LH', or Mycenaean, ca. 1600–1050 BC),[2] and the Archaic period (ca. 700–480 BC). In all three periods, ceramic tiles were initially used only sparingly.[3] Although ceramic roofing tiles offered some functional advantage over their typical vernacular counterparts (flat clay and pitched thatch roofs) with more durability and protection,[4] their greatest impact was as a visually striking architectural feature whose materiality attested to a significant investment of labor and resources. With such qualities, the ceramic tiled roof marked a form of social power and contributed a monumental effect to the buildings that they crowned,[5] even if the buildings were otherwise not considered monumental.

In this paper, I provide a brief economic analysis of Bronze Age tile production to articulate the degree to which these roofs demanded an increased investment of labor relative to the vernacular. This approach can provide a greater understanding of the significance of the tile roofed structures to their communities and the surplus capital and labor available for production. I demonstrate that the production of ceramic roofing tiles, in both periods, required substantially greater time and labor. A comparison of the EH and LH tile production, however, demonstrates differences in the production. Whereas much of the production of EH ceramic roofing tiles could have been performed with the significant help from relatively unskilled laborers, the LH counterparts integrated ceramic specialists for more of the production process.

Tile Production

EH and LH ceramic roofing tiles are easily distinguishable from each other. The EH tiles are thin rectangular pads of fired clay that were hung in a shingle-type arrangement:

Fig. 1: The tiled roofs of Corfu Chora.

each row overlapped approximately 50% of the row below (fig. 2). Typical dimensions are 20–25 × 20–25 × 1.0–1.5 cm.[6] Such tiles have been found at 22 sites in mainland Greece and are mostly concentrated in the Argolid, Corinthia, and Attica (fig. 3). Although the tiles are often discussed alongside the period's corridor houses, EH tiles are in fact associated with a variety of structures: monumental corridor houses, fortifications, and vernacular constructions.

The LH ceramic tiled roof utilized two different tile types and functioned like the later Archaic hybrid roofing system (fig. 4). Pan tiles (ca. 40–50 × 40–50 cm) were placed on the roofing surface, slightly overlapping the pan tiles of the lower row. The raised flanges (ca. 3–7 cm tall) on two sides of the tile abutted the flanges of the neighboring tiles. Semi-cylindrical cover tiles (ca. 40–55 cm length; 13–20 cm diameter) were then placed over these abutting flanges and rested on the upper surface of the flat pan tiles to create a waterproofed exterior. Fewer LH tiles have been recovered relative to their EH counterparts, but the extent of their distribution is generally equivalent (fig. 5).[7] While the publication record of these tiles is not robust enough to assign the tiles to specific structures in many cases, LH tiles have been found at palatial and non-palatial sites alike.[8]

In previous and ongoing studies, I have reconstructed the *chaînes opératoires*, or ordered steps of construction, for each of the tile assemblages by closely examining the visible markings and impressions that are evident on the surfaces of the tiles. Although some variation in production methods between sites has been identified, for this study I reconstruct the production of two representative assemblages: the EH tiles from Mitrou

Fig. 2: EH roofing tile fragments (l) Mitrou, East Lokris (LY784-539-020); (r) Zygouries, Corinthia (Z014).

and the LH tiles from Eleon.[9] With an understanding of the construction processes for these tiles, the economics of production and the tilemakers' relationships to established craft traditions can be better evaluated. In the following, I briefly summarize these *chaînes opératoires* and comment on the economic implications of their production.

The production of Mitrou's EH tiles was recently described as using a "mold-and-cut" method.[10] Moistened clay was placed in a mold and spread within the frame. The mold was then removed and individual tiles were cut along the narrowest width before they were left to dry prior to firing. With this reconstructed *chaîne opératoire*, dedicated training or much specialized equipment by the individuals forming the tiles was not necessary. In fact, the forming methods drew from an established architectural tradition for creating mold-made mud brick. Because every structure required several hundred mud bricks for construction, almost everyone had experience making mud bricks in their personal or communal building projects. The only action that required some specialized knowledge was the firing of clay.[11] Still, the forming of EH tiles was essentially vernacular in its methods and could have been achieved by almost anyone with the time and access to materials.

The production of the LH tiles was more complex, with each type (cover/pan tile) requiring a distinct set of methods and techniques. Pan tiles were exclusively handmade, but had a rather idiosyncratic forming method; a pad of clay was placed on a flat surface and one set of parallel walls was made by bending the edges of the pad upwards.[12] Before drying and firing, further refinements were made by the tilemaker such as finishing the lip of the wall and exerting downward force on the walls for better articulation. The cover tiles were formed as coil-built tubes of clay and finished on the wheel.[13] These

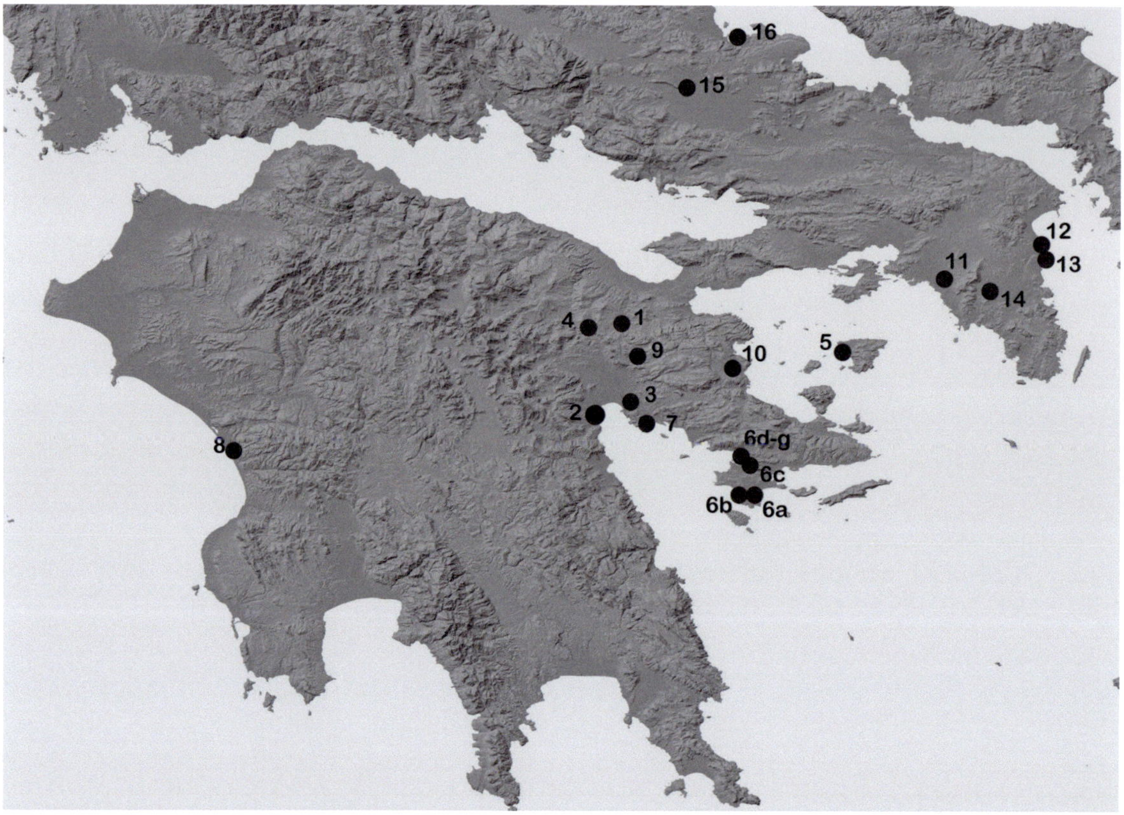

Fig. 3: EH settlements with ceramic roofing tiles: 1. Zygouries; 2. Lerna; 3. Tiryns; 4. Tsoungiza; 5. Kolonna (Aegina); 6. Southern Argolid Exploration [7 sites]; 7. Asine; 8. Ag. Dimitrios; 9. Berbati; 10. Vassa; 11. Rouf; 12. Asketario; 13. Rafina; 14. Koropi; 15. Orchomenos; 16. Mitrou.

Fig. 4: Left: Mycenaean pan (SF0443) and cover tile (SF0230) from the site of Eleon. Right: Mycenaean pan tiles (SF0507; SF0506) and cover tile (SF0230) from the site of Eleon.

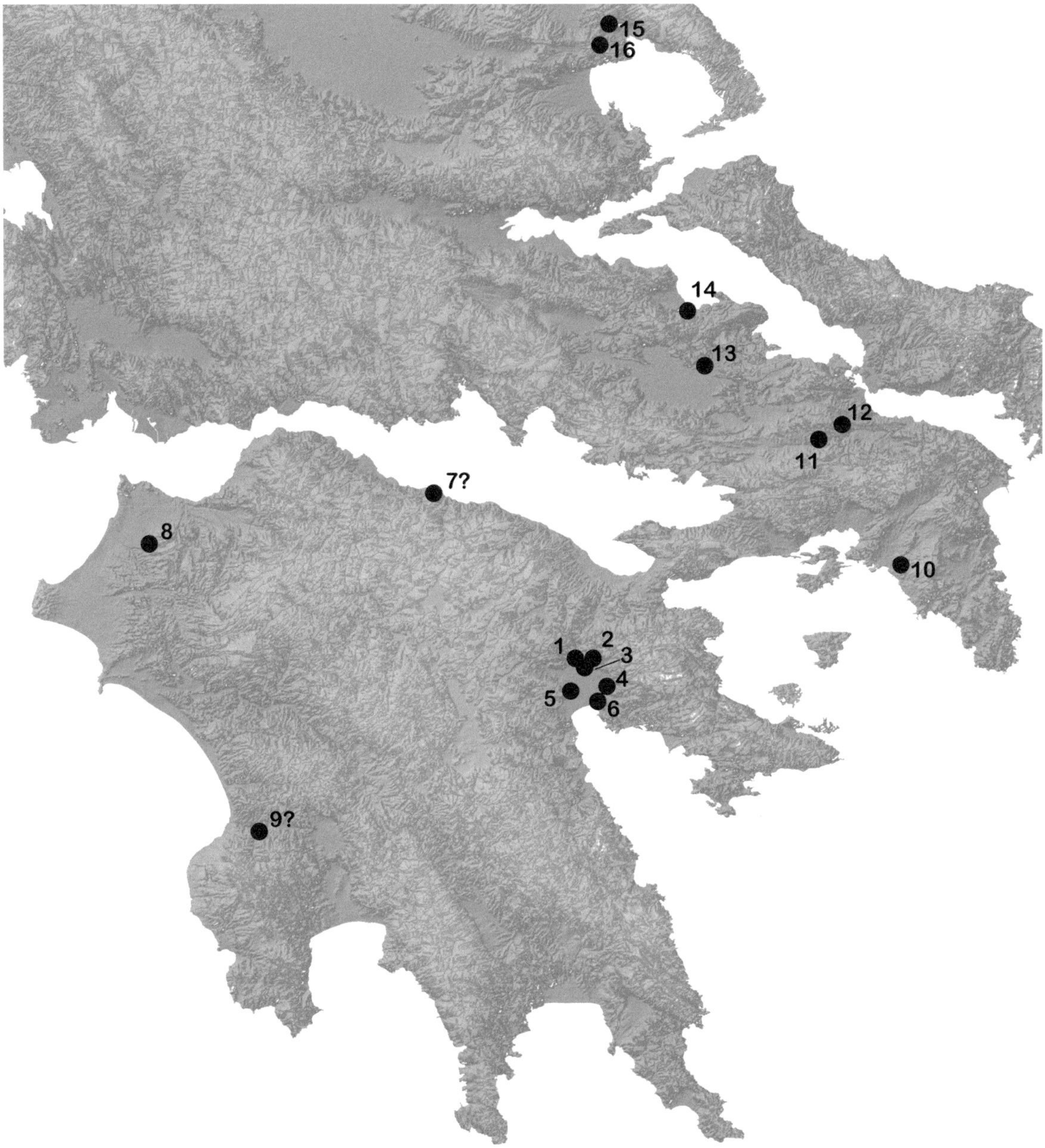

Fig. 5: Mycenaean settlements with ceramic roofing tiles: 1. Mycenae; 2. Berbati; 3. Chania; 4. Midea; 5. Argos; 6. Tiryns; 7. Aigeira (unlikely); 8. Chalandritsa; 9. Malthi (unknown); 10. Athens (unlikely); 11. Thebes; 12. Eleon; 13. Gla; 14. Mitrou; 15. Dimini; 16. Aerino.

tubes were then cut in half to produce two equal cover tiles which were left to dry before firing.[14] Evidence for this production method is found in the undulating remains of the coils on the interior surface of the tile and the rotating smoothing marks on the exterior surface.

Fig. 6: A utilitarian tray from Mitrou (LE795-070-016). This shows the interior wall and a cross-section of the base.

Unlike the EH tiles that have analogs in mud brick production, LH tiles demonstrate a clear dialog with established ceramic craft traditions. The idiosyncratic production of the pan tiles, for instance, has its clearest parallel in hand-made "utilitarian trays" that have been found at several sites in mainland Greece (fig. 6).[15] Both the pan tiles and the utilitarian trays are generally similar in shape and possess a coarse fabric with straw temper and vertical flanges. Utilitarian tray fragments can easily be mistaken for pan tiles, but their curved walls, greater straw temper, and lower firing temperatures help to distinguish them. While it is possible that pan tiles were formed by individual households, the cover tiles certainly required specialist training and habituated movements for their forming and finishing on the wheel. Therefore, the most likely identity of the cover tilemaker is the local potter.

In summary, the production of tiles in EH and LH Greece required distinct abilities. Whereas the EH tiles could have primarily been formed by non-specialists, the construction of the LH tiles demanded at least some trained craftsmen for much more of the production process. This suggests that there were also different economic processes associated with tile production. Unless construction methods were guarded in the EH period, anyone who had access to the materials and basic ceramic firing knowledge potentially had the ability to form their own tiles. While it is quite likely that specialist potters contributed to the firing and clay paste preparation, production was not necessarily exclusive to them with several steps potentially being delegated to non-specialist workers. In contrast, LH ceramic-tiled roofs, in almost all instances, must have demanded a means – economic, cooperative, or coercive – to convince the potters to devote a greater portion of their time to both tile forming and firing. The cover tiles for a large structure would have required a similar amount of time to produce several hundred fine-ware vessels![16] The cost to roof such a structure, therefore, was likely to have been greater than the cost of the equivalent number of ceramic vessels.

Energetic Analysis

To shed further light on the economic impact of a ceramic-tiled roof in each period, I also pursued a comparative energetic analysis of EH tiles, LH tiles, and vernacular roofing construction. Energetic analyses assign labor costs to each step in the production sequence.[17] The cumulative cost of these then provides a quantifiable means with which to evaluate scales of production and compare them between projects. Although the use of finite work rates for such studies has been criticized for their cultural contingency and imprecision,[18] there is still great heuristic value in this approach for understanding relative measures of labor investment. With the application of an energetic analysis to prehistoric roof constructions, I do not seek an accurate representation of labor expenditures. Instead, I offer a means to compare the labor investment among the different roofing systems.

The prevailing vernacular roofing methods against which the tiles' construction are compared are flat clay and pitched thatched roofs.[19] The production methods for both these roof types can vary significantly, from extremely elaborate, multi-stepped methods to rudimentary constructions. This variability makes it difficult to provide accurate energetic analyses for comparison. Archaeological evidence, however, offers some help reconstructing the flat clay roofs. Clay roofing fragments recovered from Bronze Age sites, such as Lerna, often attest to a layer of parallel reeds or small branches spanning crossbeams that formed a suitable bed for the clay roofing material.[20] The clay was then deposited to a depth of a few centimeters (averaging 6–8 cm) on this foundation. This type of flat roof could have conceivably been built by the household in both periods. It seems likely that most thatch roofs in EH Greece were also made using vernacular methods because of the dearth of evidence for centralized and full-time craft specialists in EH Greece. The fundamental need for roofs in every community, as well as their ongoing maintenance would have also made reliance on itinerant craftsmen somewhat prohibitive. In the mature LH period, very few buildings were entirely thatched as suggested by the complex, agglomerative ground plans of the typical structure. Therefore, it is also unlikely that thatch was the predominate roofing technique.

For the energetic analysis, I evaluate the labor investment for each roofing method to cover the same reconstructed building: a 25 × 8 m rectilinear structure with a roof pitched at 36.87°. These precise dimensions are not reconstructed from a single excavated structure but were chosen because they represent the scale of monumental buildings in EH (corridor houses) and LH (palatial megara) periods.[21] They also allow for easy calculations of absolute tile numbers required to cover the surface. The application of an energetic analysis to a hypothetical structure is beneficial by allowing fair comparison among roofing types while producing a relative metric that will not be mistaken as a representation of actual prehistoric labor rates.

Using average tile dimensions for each period, I have reconstructed the number of EH and LH tiles necessary to roof the hypothetical structure and the total volume of clay needed to produce these tiles (Table 1).[22] Ethnographic data from previous energetic analyses offer relevant work rates for excavating and transporting this clay.[23] The transport rates assume that the material was brought by an animal-drawn cart from a source 1 km away. All considered, roofing the same structure would have required 50% more labor for the LH tiles compared to the EH.[24] There certainly would have been significant additions to these estimated times for levigating, mixing, and adding temper to the clay in both periods, but each tile type likely had unique requirements and methods that cannot currently be reconstructed.

Like the tiles, the vernacular flat roof also required the excavation and transport of clay. A roofing fragment from Lerna, RF8, provides a template for calculating the necessary volume of clay.[25] A flat roof with a 6.8 cm thick layer of clay demands the most clay for construction and, as a result, significantly greater labor for extraction and transport, as much as double the requirements for EH roofing tiles!

At first glance, the production of tiles seems to have been a material- and labor-saving activity. However, several important steps of the *chaîne opératoire* for the tiles still remain unaccounted. Significant additional time was necessary for refining the clay, collecting fuel, forming, drying, and firing the tiles, building the wooden roofing supports, as well as placing the tiles on the roof. Whereas labor rates for the complete construction of the support beams and assembly of a flat roof for the hypothetical structures is estimated at only 500 ph,[26] simply firing EH or LH tiles would have required several months of additional time for a single kiln to heat, fire the tiles, and cool.[27] The tiled roof, therefore, required several orders of magnitude of increased labor and time with the construction of a single LH roof perhaps occupying a single potter and his/her kiln(s) for a year's production season.

Among all roofing types, thatch roofs were seemingly the least labor intensive.[28] Although I was unable to find data on prehistoric straw volumes and densities to calculate transport costs for direct comparison, the lesser weight of the straw would have likely demanded significantly less transport time. It is also possible that the straw/thatch used for the roof was an agricultural biproduct that had been acquired at harvest and already available on site.[29]

Ethnographic data for thatched roof construction by professional English thatchers from the turn of the 20th century AD provide additional insight into the labor costs of assembly.[30] Their rate of 10 ph per "square" (10 × 10 ft) of thatch roofing is applied to the hypothetical structure to suggest 269 ph for assembly – almost half the labor investment to complete a flat clay roof. This is perhaps a maximum value because of the likely greater refinement and technical quality of the thatch roofs that were constructed in England at the time. Even after considering the necessary labor to build the structural support of the thatch roof, the labor requirements for the thatch roof likely did not match that of the flat clay roof, much less those of the tiled roofs.

	Length	Width	Roof Pitch	Pitched Surface Area	Flat Surface Area	
Structure	25 m	8 m	36.87°	250 m^2	200 m^2	
	Length	**Width/Diameter**	**Base Thick.**	**Wall Height**	**Wall Thick.**	**Volume/tile**
EH Tile	25	25	1	N/A	N/A	.000625 m^3
LH Pan	50	40	1.5	4	2	.004 m^3
LH Cover	50	14	1.5	N/A	N/A	.00165 m^3
	Total Tiles	**Total Volume**	**Total Weight**			
EH Tile	7800	4.9 m^3	5336.1 kg			
LH Pans	1300	5.2 m^3	5662.8 kg			
LH Covers	1274	2.1 m^3	2286.9 kg			
Flat Roof	N/A	12.0 m^3	13068 kg			
Clay Excavation rate		0.54 m^3/ph				
Clay Transport rate		(kg/2100)*(2*km/1.67)				
	Excavation	**Transport**	**Total**			
EH Tiles	9.07 ph	3.043 ph	**12.11 ph**			
LH Tiles	13.52 ph	4.533 ph	**18.05 ph**			
Flat Roofs	22.22 ph	7.45 ph	**29.37 ph**			

Table 1: A volumetric and energetic analysis of EH tile, LH tile, and flat roof material acquisition. The work rates are taken from Harper 2016. The energetic analysis assumes a standard transport distance of 1 km by animal-powered cart and a volume/weight conversion of clay at 1 m^3 / 1089 kg. All values are in cm unless noted otherwise.

Beyond their greater labor investment, the production of tiles was also a highly conspicuous activity that required a significant surface area for forming and initial drying, 3–6 times greater than the surface area of the building itself.[31] It also would have been prohibitive to produce all the tiles at one time because 9–14 available kilns would have been necessary to fire all the tiles for a single building simultaneously. More realistically, the tiles were likely formed, dried, and fired in batches. In contrast, the vernacular flat and thatch roofs could have been assembled as the materials arrived on site; thus, only a minimal work area beyond the structure itself was needed and the construction could be contained as a single event.

With the tiles produced in batches, the construction process also became an extended event granting even more visibility to and public awareness of the project. A significant amount of materials and tiles in various states of finishing were likely conspicuous for weeks – if not months – at a time. The multi-stage production of the tiles, therefore, would have augmented the time for production and increased the community's awareness. This, in turn, enhanced the monumentality of the tiled roofs by cementing the construction event in the social memory of the local community.

Conclusion

Although the EH and LH tiles shared such a public awareness, the impact of this social memory was likely felt differently in each of the two periods. Because anyone could have possibly participated in EH tile construction, the tiled roof may have served as a marker of communal participation, a symbol of social unity, or an object of conceivable aspiration. LH tiled roofs, in contrast, demanded even greater access to or coercion of specialist craftsmen (potters) and the means to divert their efforts away from pottery production for a longer period. As a result, LH tiled roofs are less likely to have represented the shared efforts of the local community and, instead, signified an elite act of conspicuous consumption or an exercise of socio-political power.

Notes

[1] I would like to thank the organizers of the session, E. Hasaki and M. Bentz, for inviting me to participate in this session, as well as the directors of the Mitrou (A. Van de Moortel, E. Zahou) and Eleon (B. Burke, B. Burns) excavations for allowing me to study the tiles. I also appreciate the helpful comments on the text from Kimberley van den Berg.

[2] Although many have been skeptical of the existence of roofing tiles in LH Greece due to the scarcity of examples (e.g. Blegen 1928, 34 f.; 1945, 41; Sapirstein 2008, 49–54), recent excavations at Eleon have revealed more than 700 tile fragments in a limited area demonstrating their use.

[3] Iakovidis 1990; Winter 1993; Sapirstein 2008, 1–8. 37–56; Jazwa 2018.

[4] Sapirstein 2008, 1; 2009, 197.

[5] With this, I do not mean that tiles are only found on the typical "monumental" buildings of each period but argue that the tiled roof itself was a monumental feature regardless of other qualities of the architecture.

[6] Jazwa 2018.

[7] Marzolff 2017, fig. 2.

[8] Iakovidis 1990.

[9] The identified construction methods for these assemblages are not unique but are shared with several (but not all) assemblages.

[10] Jazwa 2018.

[11] Pullen 1985, 279 suggests that pottery was produced at the household scale but admits that there is not enough evidence to understand craft specialization more broadly in the EH II period. Weiberg (2007, 70–74) also assumes a household level of craftsmanship.

[12] Küpper 1996, 107.

[13] For identification, see Roux – Courty 1998.

[14] Iakovidis 1990, 155 f.; Küpper 1996, 107.

[15] See Jazwa, forthcoming. The precise function of these trays is uncertain. Due to their coarse fabric, uneven firing, and utilitarian function, these objects were likely made by individual households.

[16] This considers that the cover tiles were formed on the wheel with two cover tiles equivalent to one 40–50 cm tall vessel.

[17] For an overview of energetic approaches, see Abrams – Bolland 1999.

[18] See e.g. Voutsaki et al. 2018.

[19] E.g. Darcque 2005, 123–129.

[20] Wiencke 2000, 279–310; Darcque 2005, 123–129.

[21] These were not the only structures in the EH and LH periods to be roofed with tiles; the use of these structures as the model for the energetic analysis is effective because the building forms were adopted at several sites and were among the largest buildings/building units in each period. In reality, the specific type of building used is not of great concern because the study is comparative, evaluating the relative scale of production. The pitch of 36.87° was also chosen for ease of calculations. Although the pitches of EH buildings were certainly shallower (20–30 degrees), Mycenaean pitched roofs have often been reconstructed as steeper than their EH counterparts.

[22] The latter value does not account for clay shrinkage when drying.

[23] All rates are taken from Harper 2016, unless otherwise noted.

[24] All work rates are presented as person-hours ("ph"), the number of hours it would take one person to accomplish this task.

[25] Wiencke 2000, 280. This thickness, 6.8 cm, does not differ greatly from LH examples, see Darcque 2005, 124–126.

[26] Following the formula provided in Harper 2016, 527 of 0.400 m^2/ph. Harper conducted energetic analyses with three significant Mycenaean building projects: the Treasury of Atreus, the Northeast Extension of the citadel wall, and the construction of buildings at Korfos-Kalamianos.

[27] This value is based on the average amount of time to heat a kiln, fire the load, and cool the kiln and the number of batches that could be fired at once. The latter considers the average size of documented kilns in each period (EH: 1.6 m diam.; LH: 2 m diam.) and the number of tiles that could fit in this surface area (EH: 960 tiles, 9 batches; LH: 144 pan and 308 cover tiles, 14 batches, after Hasaki 2002).

[28] Because of the seasonality of the harvest, it is possible that thatch was the best option for houses that were built during the Autumn/Winter seasons – the unfired clay of the drying tiles and flat roofs risked destruction by a rainstorm if produced during the wet season.

[29] Moir – Letts 1999, 58 f.

[30] Rural Development Commission 1988.

[31] This accounts for the number and size of tiles, pitch of the roof, and space between tiles for drying.

Image Credits

Fig. 1. 2. 4–6: by the author. – Fig. 3: after Jazwa 2018, fig. 1. – Table 1: by the author.

References

Abrams – Bolland 1999
E.M. Abrams – T.W. Bolland, Architectural Energetics, Ancient Monuments, and Operations Management, Journal of Archaeological Method and Theory 6, 1999, 263–291.

Blegen 1928
C.W. Blegen, Zygouries: A Prehistoric Settlement in the Valley of Cleonae (Cambridge, MA 1928).

Blegen 1945
C.W. Blegen, The Roof of the Mycenaean Megaron, AJA 49, 1945, 35–44.

Darcque 2005
P. Darcque, L'habitat mycénien. Formes et fonctions de l'espace bâti en Grèce continentale à la fin du IIe millénaire avant J.-C. (Athens 2005).

Harper 2016
C.R. Harper, Laboring with the Economics of Mycenaean Architecture: Theories, Methods, and Explorations of Mycenaean Architectural Production (Ph.D. diss. Florida State University 2016).

Hasaki 2002
E. Hasaki, Ceramic Kilns in Ancient Greece: Technology and Organization of Ceramic Workshops (Ph.D. diss. University of Cincinnati 2002).

Iakovidis 1990
S. Iakovidis, Mycenaean Roofs: Form and Construction, in: P Darcque – R. Treuil (eds.), L'habitat Égéen préhistorique. Actes du la Table Ronde international organisée par le Centre National de la Recherche Scientifique, l'Université de Paris I et l'École française d'Athènes (Athènes, 23–25 juin 1987), BCH Suppl. 19 (Paris 1990) 146–160.

Jazwa 2018
K.A. Jazwa, The Construction of Early Helladic II Ceramic Roofing Tiles from Mitrou, Greece: Influence and Interaction, Mediterranean Archaeology and Archaeometry 18, 2018, 153–173.

Jazwa forthcoming
K.A. Jazwa, Utilitarian Trays from Mitrou: Introducing a New Artifact Class, in: Proceedings of the 5th Archaeological Meeting of Thessaly and Central Greece, 2012–2015, forthcoming.

Küpper 1996
M. Küpper, Mykenische Architektur. Material Bearbeitungstechnik, Konstruktion und Erscheinungsbild (Espelkamp 1996).

Marzolff 2017
P. Marzolff, Beobachtungen am ältesten keramischen Dachdecksystem, in: D. Kurapkat – U. Wulf-Rheidt (eds.), Werkspuren: Materialverarbeitung und handwerkliches Wissen im antiken Bauwesen. Internationales Kolloquium in Berlin vom 13.–16. Mai 2015 veranstaltet vom

Architekturreferat des DAI im Henry-Ford-Bau der Freien Universität Berlin (Regensburg 2017) 179–192.

Moir – Letts 1999
J. Moir – J. Letts, Thatch. Thatching in England 1790–1940 (English Heritage 1999).

Pullen 1985
D. J. Pullen, Social Organization in Early Bronze Age Greece (Ph.D. diss. Indiana University 1985)

Roux – Courty 1998
V. Roux – M.-A. Courty, Identification of Wheel-Fashioning Methods: Technological Analysis of 4th and 3rd Millennium BC Oriental Ceramics, JASc 25, 1998, 747–763.

Rural Development Commission 1988
Rural Development Commission, The Thatcher's Craft, Fourth edition (London 1988).

Sapirstein 2008
P. Sapirstein, The Emergence of Ceramic Roof Tiles in Archaic Greek Architecture (Ph.D. diss. Cornell University 2008).

Sapirstein 2009
P. Sapirstein, How the Corinthians Manufactured their First Roof Tiles, Hesperia 78, 2009, 195–229.

Voutsaki et al. 2018
S. Voutsaki – Y. Van den Beld – Y. De Raaf, Labour Mobilization and Architectural Energetics in the North Cemetery at Ayios Vasilios, Laconia, Greece, in: A. Brysbaert – A. M. Gutiérrez Garcia (eds.), Construction Economics of the Past (Athens 2018) 169–191.

Weiberg 2007
E. Weiberg, Thinking the Bronze Age. Life and Death in Early Helladic Greece (Uppsala 2007).

Wiencke 2000
M.H. Wiencke, Lerna. A Preclassical Site in the Argolid IV. The Architecture, Stratigraphy, and Pottery of Lerna III (Princeton 2000).

Winter 1993
N.A. Winter, Greek Architectural Terracottas from the Prehistoric to the End of the Archaic Period (Oxford 1993).

Crossing Thresholds and Building States: Labor Investment, Tomb Construction, and Early State Formation in the Bronze Age Argolid

Rodney D. Fitzsimons

Introduction

It should go without saying that economics and state formation are inextricably linked: the former, at its most basic level, deals with the production, distribution, and consumption of resources, while the latter is governed, to a large extent, by the acquisition of, access to, and control of said resources. For much of its history, archaeology has explored the process of state formation through the lens of economics, focusing in particular on three types of resources that are well-reflected, both directly and indirectly, in the material record: natural, capital, and intellectual. Studies of early state formation in the Bronze Age Argolid, for example, have tended to focus almost exclusively on the artifacts deposited within the various funerary monuments erected throughout the region, using the quantity, quality, sophistication, and diversity of grave goods as material correlates for the wealth, status, and power of emerging elites.[1] Such a focus is not surprising given that archaeology is, at its core, the study of material objects, and that the material objects recovered from these burials are of such an exquisite and spectacular nature. But there exists a fourth type of resource, one that may leave a much subtler trace in the archaeological record, but which plays just as, if not a more, important role in early state formation: human labor. Human labor in the form of specialized craftspeople has featured prominently in such discussions for decades, but in these instances, it is almost always treated from a qualitative perspective, usually as a reflection of some combination of intellectual, capital, and/or natural resources.[2]

Detailed discussions of non-specialized labor from a purely quantitative perspective, on the other hand, perhaps the most direct reflection of labor as a resource, have, until recently, been relatively rare in archaeological scholarship,[3] in large part because this form of labor is much more difficult to access from the material record in the absence of written documentation. Yet its association with state formation is perhaps even stronger than that of specialized craftspeople, and even to some extent, other resources. Indeed, as anthropologists have long recognized, the ability of a society to amass, organize, and direct large pools of human labor is directly correlated with that society's level of socio-political complexity.[4]

This paper explores the relationship between non-specialized human labor and early state formation in the Argolid by examining two forms of elite funerary construction that dominated the region in the Early Mycenaean Period: the shaft grave and the tholos tomb.[5] Both tomb types served as the primary architectural markers of elite status and competition prior to the erection of the first palace at Mycenae towards the end of the 15th century BC,[6] with the shaft grave serving as the elite sepulchre of choice during the 18th and 17th centuries,

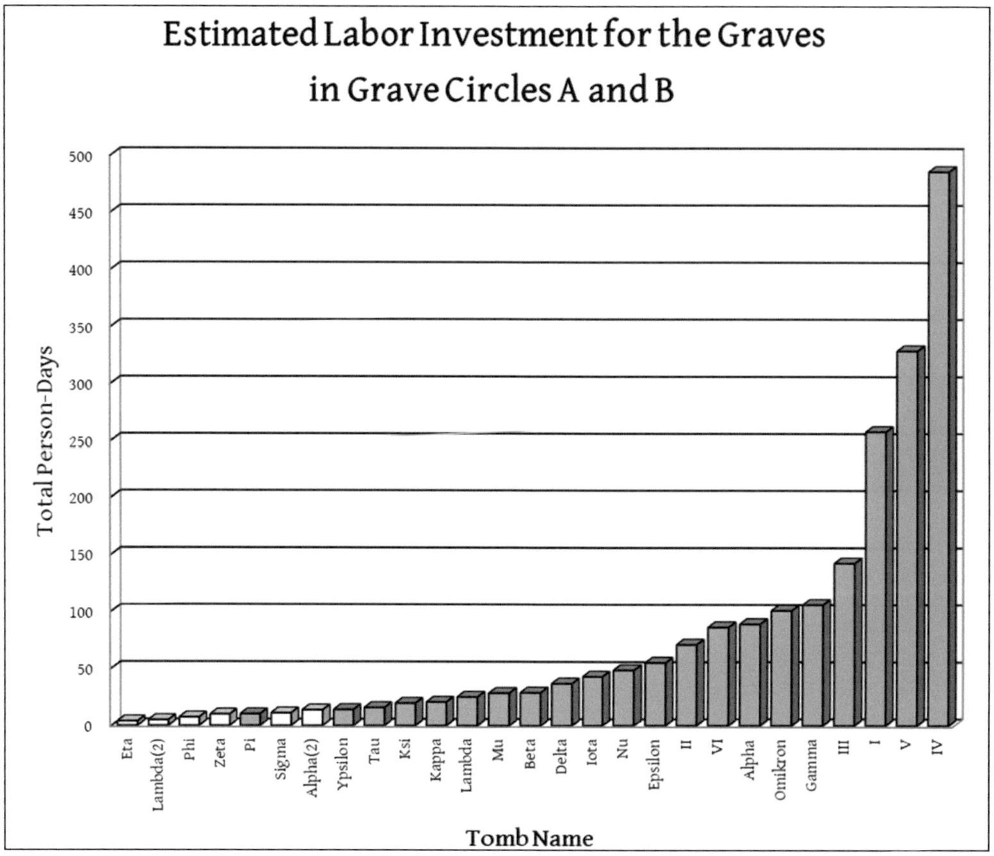

Fig. 1: Bar chart showing estimated labor investment for the construction of cist graves (white) and shaft graves (gray) in Grave Circles A and B.

and the tholos tombs in the 16th and 15th centuries. The analysis presented here combines two theoretical approaches, architectural energetics and social network theory, to explore the relationship between social organization and political power. Further, it proposes that the development of monumental funerary architecture at Mycenae reflects the existence of several discrete stages in the process of early state formation.

Architectural Energetics

As early as the 19th century AD, anthropologists and archaeologists recognized that there is a strong correlation between labor investment, monumentality, and socio-political complexity.[7] Early approaches to quantifying this relationship were based on the premise that the volume of material required for the construction of any monument served as a direct reflection of the size of the workforce necessary for its construction.[8] Since larger pools of labor required increasingly complex organizational systems to manage and direct, it followed that larger and larger monuments must have been the products of societies with

Grave	*Grave Type*	*Person-Days for Excavation*	*Person-Days for Construction*	*Total Labor Investment*
Η	cist	3	1	4
Λ2	cist	2	3	5
Φ	cist	4	3	7
Ζ	cist	7	7	10
Π	shaft	9	1	10
Σ	cist	8	3	11
Α2	cist	12	2	14
Υ	shaft	13	1	14
Τ	shaft	13	3	16
Ξ	shaft	15	5	20
Κ	shaft	19	2	21
Λ	shaft	22	3	25
Μ	shaft	26	2	28
Β	shaft	25	4	29
Δ	shaft	34	3	37
Ι	shaft	40	3	43
Ν	shaft	43	6	49
Ε	shaft	52	3	55
II	shaft	64	7	71
VI	shaft	79	7	86
Α	shaft	86	3	89
Ο	shaft	94	6	100
Γ	shaft	99	7	106
III	shaft	135	8	143
I	shaft	243	14	237
V	shaft	317	11	328
IV	shaft	467	18	485

Fig. 2: Table showing estimated labor investment for the construction of cist graves and shaft graves in Grave Circles A and B.

higher levels of socio-political complexity. Architectural energetics elaborates on these early volumetric studies by adjusting labor cost estimates which were based on the volume of material used by various factors that affect the length and speed of building activities, such as the distance from the building's site to the material's source, the nature of the terrain, and

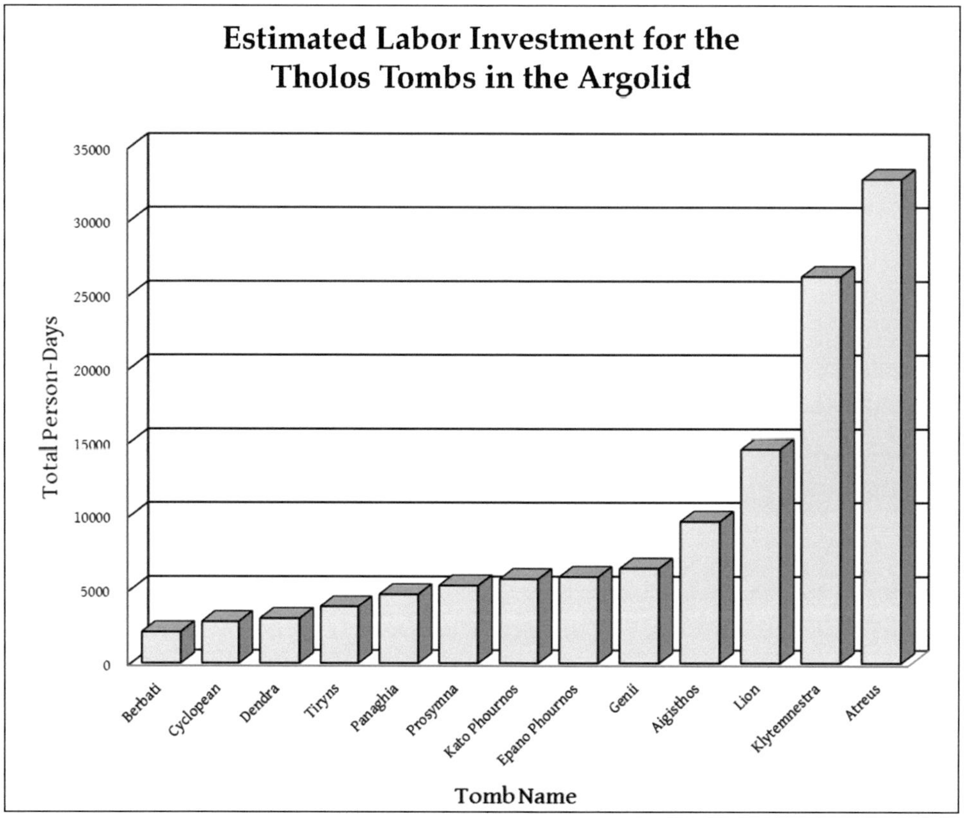

Fig. 3: Bar chart showing estimated labor investment for the construction of tholos tombs in the Argolid.

the difficulty involved in moving, laying, and setting the material.[9] Abundant data on labor estimates associated with these and other building tasks have been made available since the middle of the last century through the publication of labor studies deriving from civil engineering projects undertaken in developing countries in the decades following World War II,[10] as well as numerous ethnographic explorations of the building capabilities of pre-industrial societies,[11] and experimental studies on earthen and stone construction.[12] The publication of these data encouraged further studies in the last decades of the 20th century AD that proved architectural energetics to be a valuable and insightful tool for exploring socio-political complexity.[13]

At its most basic level, architectural energetics estimates the total labor investment required for any building project by multiplying the total volume of each material employed with the observable and reproducible rate of work associated with that material's acquisition, transportation, processing, and construction. The values generated by these calculations, which must be considered minimum values all things considered, can then be converted into standard units of energy, usually expressed as person-hours [p-h] or person-days [p-d] of labor, which serve as quantifiable measurements of the total labor investment required for any constructional undertaking. Moreover, such

Tomb	*Date*	*Largest Lintel Block (tons)*	*Estimated Workforce*	*Total Labor Investment (person-days)*	*Project Time (days)*
Berbati	LH IIB-IIIA:1	1.50	15	2113	141
Cyclopean	early LH IIA	5.07	51	2802	55
Dendra	LH IIB-IIIA:1	3.06	31	3019	97
Tiryns	LH IIA-B	8.39	84	3833	46
Panaghia	LH IIA-B	11.25	113	4670	42
Prosymna	LH IIB-IIIA:1	9.55	96	5270	55
Kato Phournos	LH IIA-B	11.66	117	5705	49
Epano Phournos	early LH IIA	13.31	134	5858	44
Genii	LH IIB-IIIA:1	20.23	203	6423	32
Aigisthos	early LH IIA	8.81	89	9596	108
Lion	LH IIA-B	36.79	368	14496	40
Klytemnestra	LH IIIA:2-B	34.20	342	26198	77
Atreus	LH IIIA:2-B	159.54	1596	32789	21

Fig. 4: Table showing estimated labor investment for the construction of tholos tombs in the Argolid based upon the size of the largest lintel blocks. Sufficient data are not available to produce reliable estimates for the tombs at Kazarma or Kokla. Estimated workforce is calculated by multiplying the mass of the largest lintel block by 10 based on 10 men moving one ton. Project time is calculated by dividing the total labor investment (in person-days) by the size of the estimated workforce. The relatively high values obtained for the tombs at Berbati and Dendra and the Tomb of Aigisthos likely result from the significantly smaller size of their lintel blocks, while those obtained for the Treasury of Atreus and the Tomb of Klytemnestra do not seem to conform to the pattern seen elsewhere (Fitzsimons 2014, 96–98).

values allow for direct and objective comparisons of the workforce size required for the completion of building projects undertaken by multiple inter- or intra-cultural groups, and therefore also allow for similar comparisons between the relative levels of socio-political complexity achieved by those groups.

Labor Investment, Population Thresholds, and Socio-political Complexity

The data on which the current study is based have been presented in detail elsewhere,[14] and are summarized in the accompanying charts and tables (figs. 1–8). Two different methods for calculating labor investment are presented here, the first is based on the premise that in order to move a lintel block it takes ten men for each ton (fig. 4),[15]

Tomb	*Date*	*Project Time (days)*	*Total Labor Investment (person-days)*	*Estimated Workforce*
Berbati	LH IIB-IIIA:1	45	2113	47
Cyclopean	early LH IIA	45	2802	63
Dendra	LH IIB-IIIA:1	45	3019	68
Tiryns	LH IIA-B	45	3833	86
Panaghia	LH IIA-B	45	4670	104
Prosymna	LH IIB-IIIA:1	45	5270	118
Kato Phournos	LH IIA-B	45	5705	127
Epano Phournos	early LH IIA	45	5858	131
Genii	LH IIB-IIIA:1	45	6423	143
Aigisthos	early LH IIA	45	9596	214
Lion	LH IIA-B	45	14496	323
Klytemnestra	LH IIIA:2-B	45	26198	583
Atreus	LH IIIA:2-B	45	32789	729

Fig. 5: Table showing estimated labor investment for the construction of tholos tombs in the Argolid based on an estimated time to completion of 45 days. Sufficient data are not available to produce reliable estimates for the tombs at Kazarma or Kokla. Estimated workforce is calculated by dividing the total labour investment by 45 days (Fitzsimons 2014, 97–98).

and the second is based on an average project length of 45 days (fig. 5),[16] which likely produces more reliable estimates. Approximating the number of households necessary to supply these workforces depends upon the size and composition of the household and which recruitment strategies were employed. Unfortunately, there is little information concerning household size and composition for the Bronze Age Aegean, though five individuals per family, a value supported to some extent by ethnographic research into preindustrial families,[17] seems rather plausible.[18] There is a similar dearth of information concerning the recruitment of workforces in the Bronze Age Aegean, though Abrams and Webster as well as Kirker argue that most households would have contributed one laborer to construction projects.[19] For the current study, therefore, it is posited that each household contributed one laborer, and that a relatively reliable estimate of the total workforce size for each project is produced by assuming a construction period lasting 45 days (figs. 7 and 8).

As social and economic theory demonstrates, direct contact between individuals within any group becomes increasingly difficult as that group's population increases, and internal social and political ties begin to break down after a certain population threshold is met.[20] At that point, unless the horizontal and vertical relationships

Tomb	*Estimated Workforce based on lintels*	*Population based upon:*			
		2 laborers per family of 5	*1 laborer per family of 5*	*laborers representing*	
				30% of the population	*10% of the population*
Berbati	15	38	75	50	150
Dendra	31	78	155	104	310
Cyclopean	51	128	255	170	510
Tiryns	84	210	420	280	840
Tomb of Aigisthos	89	223	445	297	890
Prosymna	96	240	480	320	960
Panaghia	113	283	565	377	1130
Kato Phournos	117	293	585	390	1170
Epano Phournos	134	335	670	447	1340
Genii	203	508	1015	677	2030
Klytemnestra	342	855	1710	1140	3420
Lion	368	920	1840	1267	3680
Atreus	1596	3990	7980	5320	15960

Fig. 6: Table showing estimated size of population pool using a workforce based on the size of the largest lintel blocks. Sufficient data are not available to produce reliable estimates for the tombs at Kazarma or Kokla.

amongst its members are reconfigured, with an increase in socio-political complexity, the system will collapse. Significantly, it is precisely during such periods of political and social stress that large-scale construction projects are often undertaken as a means of maintaining group cohesion.[21]

Drawing upon ethnographic studies and network theory, Kosse has proposed absolute thresholds that signal quantum increases in social complexity once population levels surpass them.[22] One such threshold is met when the population reaches 150 +/- 25 individuals.[23] Up until this point, every member of the group is able to maintain strong face-to-face contact with every other member, and information is easily passed between all individuals. Beyond this level, however, while face-to-face relationships are still maintained between all individuals, but knowledge of most members is more cursory and the information flow tends to be regulated through more formal, ritual channels. Interestingly, this threshold seems to coincide with the switch from the shaft grave to the tholos tomb. It is possible to posit, therefore, that the transition to the latter tomb type, which was marked by a significant increase in labor investment, signaled a corresponding increase in the level of socio-political complexity in the region. While it is conceivable that some elite factions were able to draw upon pools based in settlements

Tomb	*Estimated Workforce based on 45-day project*	*Population based upon:*			
		2 laborers per family of 5	*1 laborer per family of 5*	*laborers representing*	
				30% of the population	*10% of the population*
SG IV	11	28	55	37	110
Berbati	47	118	235	157	470
Cyclopean	63	158	315	210	630
Dendra	68	170	340	227	680
Tiryns	86	215	430	287	860
Panaghia	104	260	520	347	1040
Prosymna	118	295	590	394	1180
Kato Phournos	127	318	635	424	1270
Epano Phournos	131	328	655	437	1310
Genii	143	358	715	477	1430
Aigisthos	214	535	1070	714	2140
Lion	323	808	1615	1077	3230
Klytemnestra	583	1458	2915	1944	5830
Atreus	729	1823	3645	2430	7290

Fig. 7: Table showing estimated size of population pool using a workforce based on a time to completion of 45 days. Sufficient data are not available to produce reliable estimates for the tombs at Kazarma or Kokla.

elsewhere in the Argolid,[24] the fact that the three earliest tholos tombs (the Cyclopean Tomb, the Epano Phournos Tomb, the Tomb of Aigisthos) all appeared at Mycenae itself suggests that their occupants and the workforces they employed were still largely local.

Another such threshold is reached when the population level surpasses 500 +/- 100 individuals, at which point direct face-to-face relationships are impossible to maintain,[25] but it is difficult to associate this threshold with any specific socio-political response. Given the increaslingly large size of the population pools necessary to supply the required labor forces, however, it is plausible that with the introduction of the tholos tomb in the 16th century, Mycenae itself was no longer able to meet the workforce demand. As a result, the factions responsible for the construction of the tholos tombs began to expand their geographical scope beyond the level of individual sites to operate on a regional scale. At the same time, through the process of peer-polity interaction, new, local factions began to emerge at other settlements, their elite emulating the new style of funerary monument (i.e. the tholos tomb), but on a lesser scale owing to the smaller population pools to which their builders had access.

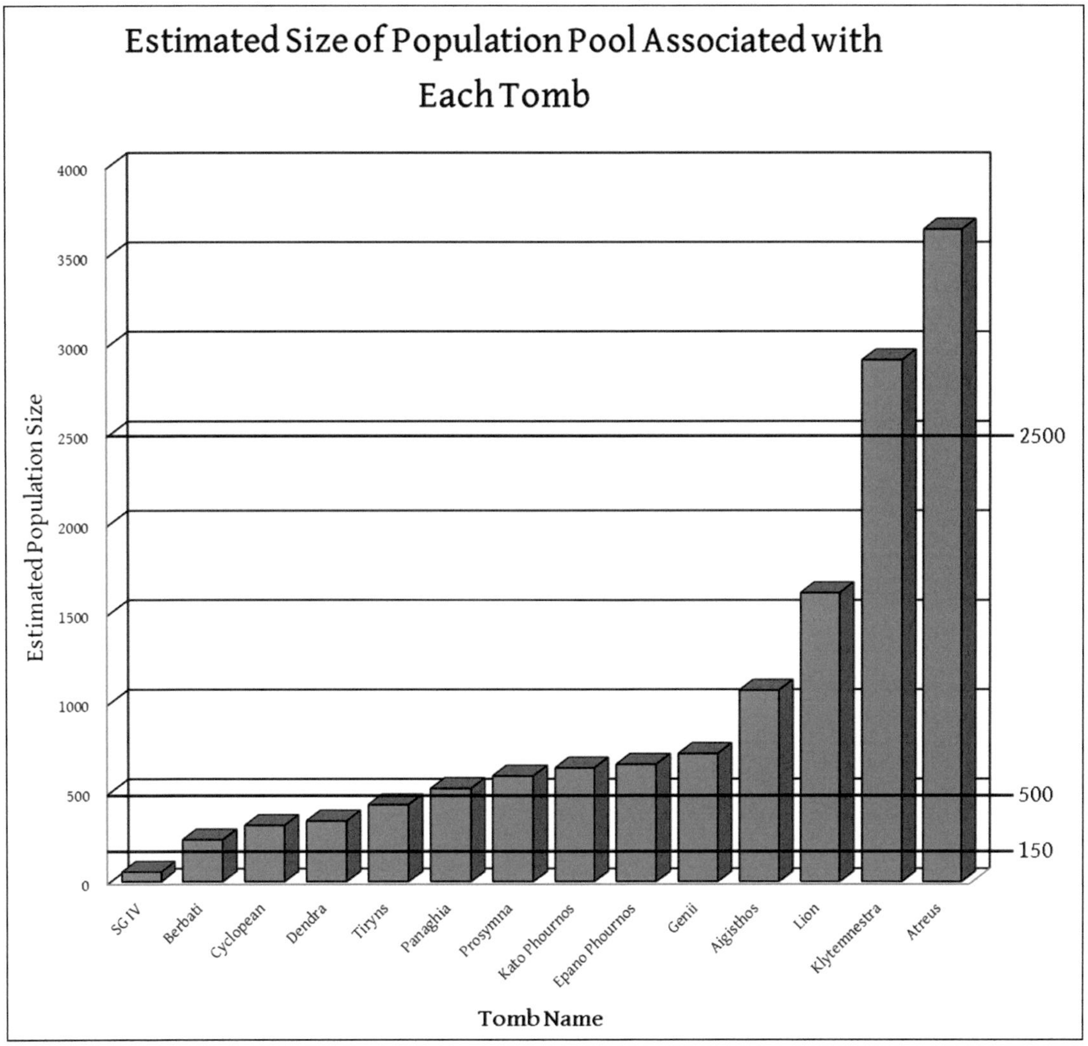

Fig. 8: Bar chart showing estimated size of the population pool associated with each tomb, assuming each household contributed one laborer, as well as Kosse's thresholds.

This discussion of population thresholds and faction size leads us back to the final two tholos tombs constructed in the Argolid, the Treasury of Atreus and the Tomb of Klytemnestra. Following observations made by James C. Wright three decades ago,[26] the author has argued elsewhere that these two monuments stand quite apart from the socio-political system embodied by the other tholoi and belong instead to the fully developed palatial administration of the 14th and 13th centuries.[27] In terms of building technique, both tombs were the only tholoi in the Argolid to have been rendered entirely in ashlar fashion and to have exclusively incorporated conglomerate, a dense stone that likely required specialized masons to work and that was used to emphasize certain key areas of transition in the 13th century palace.[28] In terms of scale, both tombs were constructed on a magnitude far larger than any of the earlier tholoi erected in the region, not only with respect to overall size (fig. 7), but also with respect to the mass of the individual stones employed. And in terms of physical appearance, they not only incorporated elaborate sculptural details,[29] but also may have been designed to mimic the visual effect produced by the contemporary Lion Gate.[30]

To these observations we can now add two further points of support generated by this energetics analysis: first, the total labor investment required for the construction of these two monuments far outstrips that necessary to erect the other Argive examples (fig. 7) – with the Tomb of Klytemnestra nearly doubling, and the Treasury of Atreus more than doubling, the figures calculated for the next largest tomb (the Lion Tomb). Second, and perhaps more significantly, the estimated populations necessary to supply such labor pools exceeds Kosse's next population threshold of 2500 +/- 500, at which point formal hierarchies begin to emerge (fig. 8).[31] It is likely no coincidence, therefore, that these two funerary monuments were constructed several generations after the appearance of the first monumental megaron at Mycenae[32] – the architectural manifestation par excellence of the Late Bronze Age palace state. Moreover, that the state continued to display its authority through the acquisition, organization, and deployment of human labor is illustrated by the creation of a complex system of roads and bridges across the Argolid, remains of which can be seen at a number of points throughout the region, such as Arkadiko, Drakonera, and Lykotroupi, where the remains of three Cyclopean bridges and the roadways they carried are still clearly visible in the landscape.[33] The regional scale of this construction program and the massive amount of manpower it must have required leave little doubt that it was the product of an early state entity that had the ability to mobilize, organize, direct, and support labor pools magnitudes larger than any that had operated in the past.[34]

Conclusion

The above discussion is necessarily summary in nature, but it is hoped that it serves to demonstrate that combining architectural energetics and social network theory can provide a valuable mechanism for understanding early state formation at Mycenae. Further, it allows the possibility of identifying more discrete stages in the process of early state formation, of conducting a more detailed examination of the transitions between these stages, and of producing of a much more nuanced picture of the dynamic period that culminated in the appearance of the Mycenaean palace state.

Notes

[1] The bibliography on early state formation in the Argolid is enormous, but for approaches based upon analysis of the grave goods, see Graziadio 1988, 1991; Voutsaki 1995, 1998, 1999, 2001, 2010.

[2] See, for example, Costin 1991; Henrich – Boyd 2008; Peregrine 1991; Schortman – Urban 2004. For the Aegean, in particular, see, for example, Nakassis 2012, 2015; Nakassis et al. 2016; Parkinson et al. 2013; Pullen 2010.

[3] For the Mediterranean, see for example, Burford 1963, 1965; DeLaine 1997; Cavanagh and Mee 1999; Fitzsimons 2006, 2007, 2011, 2014, 2017; Devolder 2012, 2013, 2015, 2017; Brysbaert 2013, 2015a, 2015b; Cook 2014.

[4] See, for example, Earle 1991; 1997, 85 f. 156 f. 177–179; Fried 1967, 186, 189 f. 207–213; Hayden 1995; Trigger 1990; Wright 1978.

[5] Fitzsimons 2006; 2007; 2011; 2014.

[6] All dates presented in this paper are BC.

[7] See, for example, Udy 1959; Fried 1967; Adams 1975; Wright 1978; Abrams 1984; 1987; 1989; 1994; Trigger 1990; 1995; Webster 1990; Arnold 1993; Hayden 1995; DeMarrais et al. 1996; Abrams – Bolland 1999; Markus 2006.

[8] See, for example, Squier – Davis 1848; Andrews 1877; Morris et al. 1931. For more recent studies, see, for example, Turner et al. 1981; Cheek 1986; Blitz – Livingood 2004. For brief reference to the history of such studies, see Abrams 1994, 5 f.; Abrams – Bolland 1999, 269–272. For a different perspective, see Moore 1996.

[9] Abrams 1984; 1987; 1989; 1994; Mathewson 1987, 321 f.; Carmean 1991; Webster 1991, 840; Abrams – Bolland 1999.

[10] ECAFE 1957; 1961; Indian Ministry of Irrigation and Power 1965.

[11] See, for example, Pulver 1947; Barrau 1958; 1961; Redfield – Villa Rojas 1962; Pospisil 1963; Lerche – Steenburg 1973; Gorecki 1985; Blier 1987.

[12] Atkinson 1961; Erasmus 1965; Coles 1979, 131–158.

[13] See, for example, Puleston 1977; Turner 1983; Golson – Steenburg 1985; Turner – Denevan 1985, 15–16; Abrams 1994, 41–52.

[14] Fitzsimons 2006, 26–194; 2011; 2014.

[15] Fitzsimons 2014, 95–97.

[16] Fitzsimons 2014, 97 f.

[17] Redfield and Villa Rojas 1962, 91; Erasmus 1965, 294; Laslett 1971, 66; Beauroy 1986, 27; Blier 1987, 142; see Pospisil 1963, 59 and Cohen 1975, however, for larger family sizes, and Ruggles 2009 for a review of recent discussions on the preindustrial family.

[18] Webster – Kirker 1995, 374–379; Clare 2010, 250.

[19] Abrams 1987, 493; 1994, 42; Webster – Kirker 1995, 375 f. For reference to labor pools being organized along kinship lines, see Mosely 1975; Sanders – Webster 1978, 274; Abrams 1987, 494–496; Abrams and Bolland 1999, 286 f.

[20] See, for example, Simon 1962; Ember 1963; Carneiro 1967; 1978; Bernard – Killworth 1973; Johnson 1978; 1982; Kosse 1990; 1994; Feinman 1998.

[21] See, for example, McGuire – Schiffer 1983; Oliveira 1986, 106; Abrams 1989, 63; 1994, 92; Trigger 1990, 127; Adams 1992, 216; Kolb 1994, 521. 527–533; 1997, 279; Clare 2010, 250; Fitzsimons 2011, 100; 2014, 100.

[22] Kosse 1990; 1994; 1996; 2000. Interestingly, because these thresholds appear to be related to the limitations of short-term memory and human neurobiology, they are universal rather than culture-specific.

[23] Kosse 1990, 284; 1996; 2000, 62. Kosse (1994, 38) has also proposed an even smaller threshold on the order of 10–12 individuals.
[24] Isotope analyses of some of the skeletal remains from Grave Circle A are less than conclusive, but Nafplioti (2009) has suggested that at least some of the females were non-local, perhaps participants in marriage alliances that were formed between high-status families resident at and beyond Mycenae.
[25] Kosse 1990, 276 f. 281; 1996; 2000, 62 f. See also Carneiro 1978; Feinman 1998, 104–109.
[26] Wright 1987.
[27] Fitzsimons 2006, 190 f.; 2007, 113 f.; 2011, 110 f.; 2014, 95.
[28] Wright 1987, 177. 183; Blackwell 2014; 2018; Fitzsimons 2019.
[29] For the Treasury of Atreus, see Ellis et al. 1968; Younger 1987; Cavanagh – Mee 1999, 98; Fitzsimons 2006, 133. For the Tomb of Klytemnestra, see Wace 1949, 36; Mylonas 1957, 93; Fitzsimons 2006, 142.
[30] Wace 1921–23, 253; 1949, 133; Mylonas 1957, 87 f.; 1966, 122; Wright 1987. Wace and Mylonas were so convinced of the similarity between the Treasury of Atreus and the Lion Gate that they suggested that both were constructed by the same ruler. The similarity between these constructions, which may admittedly be over-emphasized in the literature, is based on both the post-and-lintel construction and the heavy use of coursed, conglomerate ashlar in the flanking walls, a building technique which contrasts rather strongly with the polygonal sections of walling flanking the Lion Gate.
[31] Kosse 1990, 287; 1996; 2000, 62 f.
[32] For a detailed discussion of the date of these tombs, with references, see Fitzsimons 2006, 136 f. 143 f. 228–274. 292–302; 2007; 2011.
[33] Crouwel 1981; Hope Simpson 1998; 2002; Hope Simpson – Hagel 2006; Jansen 1994; 1997; 2002; Mylonas 1966, 86–88. Projects of a similar scale to those listed here include the construction of involved the erection of a stone-lined earthen dike – the so-called Tiryns Dam – and the excavation of a new river channel to divert the course of the Manessi River away from the acropolis at Tiryns and protect it from the periodic, devastating floods that had struck the settlement throughout its history (Balcer 1974; Zangger 1994), the construction of an artificial port near Romanou in Messenia (Davis – Bennet 1999, 106 f.; Zangger et al. 1997, 631 f.), and the construction of a series of drainage channels that drained the Kopaic Basin near Thebes (Knauss 1989; Knauss et al. 1984).
[34] Fitzsimons 2007, 113; 2011, 109 f.

Image Credits

Fig. 1–3: based on data from Fitzsimons 2014. – Fig. 4–7: after Fitzsimons 2014, Table 4. – Fig. 8: by the author.

References

Abrams 1984

E.M. Abrams, Replicative Experimentation at Copan, Honduras: Implications for Ancient Economic Specialization, Journal of New World Archaeology 6, 1984, 39–48.

Abrams 1987
E.M. Abrams, Economic Specialization and Construction Personnel in Classic Period Copan, Honduras, American Antiquity 52, 1987, 485–499.
Abrams 1989
E.M. Abrams, Architecture and Energy: An Evolutionary Perspective, AMedTh 1, 1989, 47–87.
Abrams 1994
E.M. Abrams, How the Maya Built Their World: Energetics and Ancient Architecture (Austin 1994).
Abrams – Bolland 1999
E.M. Abrams – T.W. Bolland, Architectural Energetics, Ancient Monuments, and Operations Management, Journal of Archaeological Method and Theory 6, 1999, 263–291.
Adams 1975
R.N. Adams, Energy and Structure: A Theory of Social Power (Austin 1975).
Adams 1992
R.M. Adams, Ideologies: Unity and Diversity, in: A.A. Demarest – G.W. Conrad (eds.), Ideology and Pre-Columbian Civilizations (Sante Fe 1992) 205–222.
Andrews 1877
E.B. Andrews, Report of Explorations of Mounds in Southeastern Ohio, Tenth Annual Report of the Trustees of the Peabody Museum of American Archaeology and Ethnology 2, 1877, 51–74.
Arnold 1993
J.E. Arnold, Labor and the Rise of Complex Hunter-Gatherers, Journal of Anthropological Archaeology 12, 1993, 75–119.
Atkinson 1961
R.C. Atkinson, Neolithic Engineering, Antiquity 35, 1961, 292–299.
Balcer 1974
J.M. Balcer, The Mycenaean Dam at Tiryns, AJA 78, 1974, 141–149.
Barrau 1958
J. Barrau, Subsistence Agriculture in Melanesia, Bernice P. Bishop Museum Bulletin 219 (Honolulu 1958).
Barrau 1961
J. Barrau, Subsistence Agriculture in Polynesia and Micronesia, Bernice P. Bishop Museum Bulletin 223 (Honolulu 1961).
Beauroy 1986
J. Beauroy, Family Patterns and Relations of Bishop's Lynn Will-Makers in the Fourteenth Century, in: L. Bonfield – R. Smith – K. Wrightson (eds.), The World We Have Gained: Histories of Population and Social Structure (Oxford 1986) 23–42.
Bernard – Killworth 1973
H.R. Bernard – P.D. Killworth, On the Social Structure of an Ocean-Going Research Vessel and Other Important Things, Social Science Research 2, 1973, 145–184.
Blackwell 2014
N.G. Blackwell, Making the Lion Gate Relief at Mycenae: Tool Marks and Foreign Influence, AJA 118, 2014, 451–488.

Blackwell 2018

N.G. Blackwell, Experimental Stone-Cutting with the Mycenaean Pendulum Saw, Antiquity 92, 2018, 217–232.

Blier 1987

S.P. Blier, The Anatomy of Architecture: Ontology and Metaphor in Batammaliba Architectural Expression (Cambridge 1987).

Blitz – Livingood 2004

J.H. Blitz – P. Livingood, Sociopolitical Implications of Mississippian Mound Volume, American Antiquity 69, 2004, 291–301.

Brysbaert 2013

A. Brysbaert, 'Set in Stone'? Socio-Economic Reflections on Human and Animal Resources in Monumental Architecture in Late Bronze Age Tiryns in the Argos Plain, Greece, Arctos 47, 2013, 49–96.

Brysbaert 2015a

A. Brysbaert, 'Set in Stone'? Technical, Socio-Economic and Symbolic Considerations in the Construction of Cyclopean-Style Walls of the Late Bronze Age Citadel at Tiryns, Greece, Analecta Praehistorica Leidensia 45, 2015, 69–90.

Brysbaert 2015b

A. Brysbaert, 'Set in Stone'? Constructed Symbolism Viewed through an Architectural Energetics' Lens at Bronze Age Tiryns, Greece, Analecta Praehistorica Leidensia 45, 2015, 91–105.

Burford 1963

A. Burford, The Builders of the Parthenon, in: Parthenos and Parthenon, Greece and Rome Supplement 10 (Cambridge 1963) 23–35.

Burford 1965

A. Burford, The Economics of Greek Temple Building, Cambridge Classical Journal 11, 1965, 21–34.

Carmean 1991

K. Carmean, Architectural Labor Investment and Social Stratification at Sayil, Yucatan, Mexico, Latin American Antiquity 2, 1991, 151–165.

Carneiro 1967

R.L. Carneiro, On the Relationship between Size of Population and Complexity of Social Organization, Southwestern Journal of Anthropology 23, 1967, 234–243.

Carneiro 1978

R.L. Carneiro, Political Expansion as an Expression of the Principle of Competitive Exclusion, in: R. Cohen – E.R. Service (eds.), Origins of the State: The Anthropology of Political Evolution (Philadelphia 1978) 205–233.

Cavanagh – Mee 1999

W.G. Cavanagh – C. Mee, Building the Treasury of Atreus, in: P.P. Betancourt – V. Karageorghis – R. Laffineur – W.-D. Niemeier (eds.), Meletemata: Studies in Aegean Archaeology Presented to Malcolm H. Wiener as He Enters his 65th Year, Aegaeum 20 (Liège 1999) 93–102.

Cheek 1986

C. Cheek, Construction Activity as a Measurement of Change at Copan, Honduras, in: P.A. Urban – E.M. Schortman (eds.), The Southeast Maya Periphery (Austin 1996) 50–71.

Clare 2010
T. Clare, Megalith Size and the Implications for Our Understanding of Contemporary Society, with Particular Reference to Cumbria, North-West England, OxfJA 29, 2010, 245–252.

Cohen 1975
J.E. Cohen, Childhood Mortality, Family Size and Birth Order in Pre-Industrial Europe, Demography 12, 1975, 35–55.

Coles 1979
J. Coles, Experimental Archaeology (New York 1979).

Cook 2014
P. Cook, The Energetics of Mycenaen Defense Works: Assessing Labour Investment for Fortification Construction during the Late Helladic Period (1600–1200 BC) (Unpublished M.A. Thesis, Trent University 2014).

Costin 1991
C.L. Costin, Craft Specialization: Issues in Defining, Documenting, and Explaining the Organization of Production, Archeological Method and Theory 3, 1991, 1–56.

Crouwel 1981
J. Crouwel, Chariots and Other Means of Land Transport in Bronze Age Crete (Amsterdam 1981).

Davis – Bennet 1999
J.L. Davis – J. Bennet, Making Mycenaeans: Warfare, Territorial Expansion, and Representations of the Other in the Pylian Kingdom, in: R. Laffineur (ed.), Polemos: Le contexte guerrier en Egée à l'âge du Bronze, Aegaeum 19 (Liège 1999) 105–121.

DeLaine 1997
J. DeLaine, The Baths of Caracalla: A Study in the Design, Construction, and Economics of Large-Scale Building Projects in Imperial Rome, JRA Suppl. 25 (Portsmouth 1997).

DeMarrais et al. 1996
E. DeMarrais – L.J. Castillo – T. Earle, Ideology, Materialization, and Power Strategies, Current Anthropology 37, 1996, 15–31.

Devolder 2012
M. Devolder, Labour Costs and Neopalatial Architecture: A Study of the Buildings at Klimataria-Manares and Achladia and the Palace at Gournia, in: D. Panagiotopoulos – U. Günkel-Maschek (eds.), Minoan Realities: Approaches to Images, Architecture, and Society in the Aegean Bronze Age (Louvain 2012) 165–179.

Devolder 2013
M. Devolder, Construire en Crète minoenne: Une approche energétique de l'architecture néopalatiale, Aegaeum 35 (Leuven 2013).

Devolder 2015
M. Devolder, Manpower and Neopalatial Architecture: The Architectural Project as a Meaningful Experience, in: S. Cappel – U. Günkel-Maschek – D. Panagiotopoulos (eds.), Minoan Archaeology: Perspectives for the 21st Century (Louvain 2015) 241–252.

Devolder 2017
M. Devolder, Architectural Energetics and Late Bronze Age Cretan Architecture: Measuring the

Scale of Minoan Building Projects, in: Q. Letesson – C. Knappett (eds.), Minoan Architecture and Urbanism: New Perspectives on an Ancient Built Environment (Oxford 2017) 57–79.

Earle 1991
T. Earle (ed.), Chiefdoms: Power, Economy, and Ideology (Cambridge 1991).

Earle 1997
T. Earle, How Chiefs Come to Power: The Political Economy in Prehistory (Stanford 1997).

ECAFE 1957
Economic Commission for Asia and the Far East (ECAFE), Manual Labor and Its More Effective Use in Competition with Machines for Earthwork in the ECAFE Region, United Nations E/CN.11/conf. 3/L.I. (Manila 1957).

ECAFE 1961
Economic Commission for Asia and the Far East (ECAFE), Earthmoving by Manual Labor and Machines, Flood Control Series No. 17 (Bangkok 1961).

Ellis et al. 1968
S.E. Ellis – R.A. Higgins – R. Hope Simpson, The Façade of the Treasury of Atreus at Mycenae, BSA 63, 1968, 331–336.

Ember 1963
M. Ember, The Relationship between Economic and Political Development in Non-industrialized Societies, Ethnology 2, 1963, 228–248.

Erasmus 1965
C.J. Erasmus, Monument Building: Some Field Experiments, Southwestern Journal of Anthropology 21, 1965, 277-301.

Feinman 1998
G.M. Feinman, Scale and Social Organization: Perspectives on the Archaic State, in: G.M. Feinman – J. Marcus (eds.), Archaic States (Sante Fe 1998) 95–133.

Fitzsimons 2006
R.D. Fitzsimons, Monuments of Power and the Power of Monuments: The Evolution of Elite Architectural Styles at Bronze Age Mycenae (Ph.D. diss. University of Cincinnati 2006).

Fitzsimons 2007
R.D. Fitzsimons, Architecture and Power in the Bronze Age Argolid, in: J. Bretschneider – J.M. Driessen – K. van Lerberghe (eds.), Power and Architecture: Monumental Public Architecture in the Bronze Age East and Aegean. Proceedings of the International Conference Power and Architecture organized by the Katholieke Universiteit Leuven, the Université Catholique de Louvain and the Westfälische Wilhelms-Universität Münster on the 21st and 22nd of November 2002, Orientalia Lovaniensia Analecta 156 (Leuven 2007) 93–115.

Fitzsimons 2011
R.D. Fitzsimons, Monumental Architecture and the Construction of the Mycenaean State, in: N. Terrenato – D.C. Haggis (eds.), State Formation in Italy and Greece: Questioning the Neoevolutionist Paradigm (Oxford 2011) 75–118.

Fitzsimons 2014
R.D. Fitzsimons, An Energetic(s) Approach to Late Helladic Tomb Construction: Funerary

Architecture and State Formation at Bronze Age Mycenae, in: D.W. Rupp – J.E. Tomlinson (eds.), Meditations on the Diversity of the Built Environment in the Aegean Basin and Beyond. Proceedings of a Colloquium in Memory of Frederick E. Winter, Athens 22–23 June 2012, Publications of the Canadian Institute in Greece 8 (Athens 2014) 83–120.

Fitzsimons 2017

R.D. Fitzsimons, Architectural Energetics and Archaic Cretan Urbanisation, in: D.W. Rupp – J.E. Tomlinson (eds.), From Maple to Olive. Proceedings of a Colloquium to Celebrate the 40th Anniversary of the Canadian Institute in Greece, Athens, 10–11 June 2016, Publications of the Canadian Institute in Greece 10 (Athens 2017) 345–383.

Fitzsimons 2019

R.D. Fitzimons, Constructing a Legendary Past: Possible Archaising Elements in the Funerary Landscape of Bronze Age Mycenae, in: E. Borgna – I. Caloi – F.M. Carinci – R. Laffineur (eds.), Mneme: Past and Memory in the Aegean Bronze Age. Proceedings of the 17th International Aegaeum Conference, Udine/Venice, Italy, April 17-21, 2018. Aegaeum 43 (Liège 2019) 261–268.

Fried 1967

M.H. Fried, The Evolution of Political Society: An Essay in Political Anthropology (New York 1967).

Golson – Steenburg 1985

J. Golson – A. Steenburg, The Tools of Agricultural Intensification in the New Guinea Highlands, in: I.S. Farrington (ed.), Prehistoric Intensive Agriculture in the Tropics, BARIntSer 232 (Oxford 1985) 347–384.

Gorecki 1985

P.P. Gorecki, The Conquest of a New 'Wet' and 'Dry' Territory: Its Mechanism and Its Archaeological Consequence, in: I.S. Farrington (ed.), Prehistoric Intensive Agriculture in the Tropics (Oxford 1985) 321–345.

Graziadio 1988

G. Graziadio, The Chronology of the Graves of Circle B at Mycenae: A New Hypothesis, AJA 92, 1988, 343–372.

Graziadio 1991

G. Graziadio, The Process of Social Stratification at Mycenae in the Shaft Grave Period: A Comparative Examination of the Evidence, AJA 95, 1991, 403–440.

Hayden 1995

B.J. Hayden, Pathways to Power: Principles for Creating Socioeconomic Inequalities, in: T.D. Price – G.M. Feinman (eds.), Foundations of Social Inequality (New York 1995) 15–85.

Henrich – Boyd 2008

J. Henrich – R. Boyd, Division of Labor, Economic Specialization, and the Evolution of Social Stratification, Current Anthropology 49, 2008, 715–724.

Hope Simpson 1998

R. Hope Simpson, The Mycenaean Highways, EchCl 42, 1998, 239–260.

Hope Simpson 2002

R. Hope Simpson, The Mycenaean Roads and Mycenaean Chariots, Mouseion 2, 2002, 125–133.

Hope Simpson – Hagel 2006
R. Hope Simpson – D.K. Hagel, Mycenaean Fortifications, Highways, Dams, and Canals, SIMA 133 (Sävedalen 2006).

Indian Ministry of Irrigation and Power
Indian Ministry of Irrigation and Power, Report on the Rates and Costs Committee, Part II (New Delhi 1965).

Jansen 1994
A.G. Jansen, Stations along the Road in the Area of Mycenae: An Analysis of the Mycenaean Road System and Its Relation to the Mycenaean State (Ph.D. diss. University of Pennsylvania 1994).

Jansen 1997
A.G. Jansen, Bronze Age Highways at Mycenae, EchCl 41, 1997, 1–16.

Jansen 2002
A.G. Jansen, A Study of the Remains of Mycenaean Roads and Stations in Bronze Age Greece (Leviston 2002).

Johnson 1978
G.A. Johnson, Information Sources and the Development of Decision-Making Organizations, in: C.L. Redman (ed.), Social Archaeology: Beyond Subsistence and Dating (New York 1978) 87–112.

Johnson 1982
G.A. Johnson, Organizational Structure and Scalar Stress, in: C. Renfrew – M. Rowlands – B.A. Segraves (eds.), Theory and Explanation in Archaeology: The Southhampton Conference (Sheffield 1982) 389–421.

Knauss 1989
J. Knauss, Die Wasserbau-Kultur der Minyer in der Kopais (ein Rekonstruktionversuch), in: H. Beister – J. Buckler (eds.), Boiotika: Vorträge vom 5. internationalen Böotien-Kolloquium zu Ehren von Professor Dr. Siegfried Lauffer (Munich 1989) 269–274.

Knauss et al. 1984
J. Knauss – B. Heinrich – H. Kalcyk, Die Wasserbauten der Minyer in der Kopais: Die älteste Fluregulierung Europas (Munich 1984).

Kolb 1994
M.J. Kolb, Monumentality and the Rise of Religious Authority in Precontact Hawai'i, Current Anthropology 35, 1994, 521–547.

Kolb 1997
M.J. Kolb, Labor Mobilization, Ethnohistory, and the Archaeology of Community in Hawai'i, Journal of Archaeological Method and Theory 4, 1997, 265–285.

Kosse 1990
K. Kosse, Group Size and Social Complexity: Thresholds in Long-Term Memory, Journal of Anthropological Research 9, 1990, 275–303.

Kosse 1994
K. Kosse, The Evolution of Large, Complex Groups: A Hypothesis, Journal of Anthropological Research 13, 1994, 35–50.

Kosse 1996
K. Kosse, Middle-Range Societies from a Scalar Perspective, in: P.R. Fish – J.J. Reid (eds.), Interpreting Southwestern Diversity: Underlying Principles and Overarching Patterns, Anthropological Research Papers 48 (Tempe 1996) 87–96.

Kosse 2000
K. Kosse, Some Regularities in Human Group Formation and the Evolution of Societal Complexity, Complexity 6, 2000, 60–64.

Laslett 1971
P. Laslett, The World We Have Lost: England before the Industrial Age (New York 1971).

Lerche – Steenburg 1973
G. Lerche – A. Steenburg, Observations on Spade-Cultivation in the New Guinea Highlands, Tools and Tillage 3, 1973, 111–124.

Mathewson 1987
K. Mathewson, Estimating Labor Inputs for the Guayas Raised Fields: Initial Considerations, in: W.M. Denevan – K. Mathewson – G.W. Knapp (eds.), Prehispanic Agricultural Fields in the Andean Region, BARIntSer 359 (Oxford 1987) 321–336.

Markus 2006
T.A. Markus, Piranesi's Paradox: To Build Is to Create Asymmetries of Power, in: J. Maran – C. Juwig – H. Schwengel – U. Thaler (eds.), Constructing Power: Architecture, Ideology and Social Practice, Geschichte Forschung und Wissenschaft 19 (Hamburg 2006) 321–335.

McGuire – Schiffer 1983
R.H. McGuire – M.B. Schiffer, A Theory of Architectural Design, Journal of Anthropological Research 2, 1983, 277–303.

Moore 1996
J.D. Moore, Architecture and Power in the Ancient Andes: The Archaeology of Public Buildings (Cambridge 1996).

Morris et al. 1931
E.H. Morris – J. Charlot – A.A. Morris, The Temple of the Warriors at Chichen Itza, Yucatan, Carnegie Institution of Washington Publication no. 406 (Washington 1931).

Moseley 1975
M.E. Moseley, Prehistoric Principles of Labor Organization in the Moche Valley, Peru, American Antiquity 40, 1975, 191–196.

Mylonas 1957
G.E. Mylonas, Ancient Mycenae: The Capital City of Agamemnon (London 1957).

Mylonas 1966
G.E. Mylonas, Mycenae and the Mycenaean Age (Princeton 1966).

Nafplioti 2009
A. Nafplioti, Mycenae Revisited Part 2: Exploring the Local versus Non-Local Geographical Origin of the Individuals from Grave Circle A: Evidence from Strontium Isotope Ratio (87Sr/86Sr) Analysis, BSA 104, 2009, 279–291.

Nakassis 2012
D. Nakassis, Labor Mobilization in Mycenaean Pylos, in: P. Carlier – C. de Lamberterie – M. Egetmeyer – N. Guilleux – F. Rougement – J. Zurbach (eds.), Études mycéniennes 2010. Actes du XIIIe colloque international sur les textes égéens, Sèvres, Paris, Nanterre, 20–23 septembre 2010 (Rome 2012) 269–283.

Nakassis 2015
D. Nakassis, Labor and Individuals in Late Bronze Age Pylos, in: P. Steinkeller – M. Hudson (eds.), Labor in the Ancient Near East (Dresden 2015) 583–615.

Nakassis et al. 2016
D. Nakassis – M.L. Galaty – W.A. Parkinson, Discussion and Debate: Reciprocity in Aegean Palatial Societies: Gifts, Debt, and the Foundations of Economic Exchange, JMedA 29, 2016, 61 132.

Oliveira 1986
D.L. Oliveira, Monuments and Social Complexity: A New Line of Inquiry?, OxfJA 5, 1986, 103–107.

Parkinson et al. 2013
W.A. Parkinson – D. Nakassis – M.L. Galaty, Crafts, Specialists, and Markets in Mycenaean Greece. Introduction, AJA 117, 2013, 413–422.

Peregrine 1991
P.N. Peregrine, Some Political Aspects of Craft Specialization, WorldA 23, 1991, 1–11.

Pospisil 1963
L. Pospisil, Kapauka Papuan Economy (New Haven 1963).

Puleston 1977
D.E. Puleston, Experiments in Prehistoric Raised Field Agriculture: Learning from the Past, Journal of Belizean Affairs 5, 1977, 36–43.

Pullen 2010
D.J. Pullen (ed.), Political Economies of the Aegean Bronze Age, Papers of the Langford Conference, Florida State University, Tallahassee, 22–24 February 2007 (Oxford 2010).

Pulver 1947
H.E. Pulver, Construction Estimates and Costs (New York 1947).

Redfield – Villa Rojas 1962
R. Redfield – A. Villa Rojas, Chan Kom: A Maya Village (Chicago 1962).

Ruggles 2009
S. Ruggles, Reconsidering the Northwest European Family System: Living Arrangements of the Aged in Comparative Historical Perspective, Population and Development Review 35, 2009, 249–273.

Sanders – Webster 1978
W.T. Sanders – D. Webster, Unilinealism, Multilinealism and the Evolution of Complex Societies, in: C.L. Redman – M. Berman – E. Curtin – W. Longhome, Jr. – N. Versaggi – J. Wanser (eds.), Social Archaeology: Beyond Subsistence and Dating (New York 1978) 249–302.

Schortman – Urban 2004
E.M. Schortman – P.A. Urban, Modeling the Roles of Craft Production in Ancient Political Economies, Journal of Archaeological Research 12, 2004, 185–226.

Simon 1962
H.A. Simon, The Architecture of Complexity. Proceedings of the American Philosophical Society 106, 1962, 467–482.
Squier – Davis 1848
E.G. Squier – E.H. Davis, Ancient Monuments of the Mississippi Valley, Comprising the Results of Extensive Original Surveys and Explorations, Smithsonian Contribution to Knowledge 1 (Washington 1848).
Trigger 1990
B. Trigger, Monumental Architecture: A Thermodynamic Explanation of Symbolic Behaviour, WorldA 22, 1990, 119–132.
Trigger 1995
B. Trigger, Architecture, Power, and Politics in Early Civilizations, in: C.C. Davidson (ed.), Anyplace (New York 1995) 210–220.
Turner 1983
B.L. Turner, Constructional Inputs for Major Agrosystems of the Ancient Maya, in: J.P. Darch (ed.), Drained Field Agriculture in Central and South America, BARIntSer 189 (Oxford 1983) 11–26.
Turner – Denevan 1985
B.L. Turner – W.M. Denevan, Prehistoric Manipulation of Wetlands in the Americas: A Raised Field Perspective, in: I.S. Farrington (ed.), Prehistoric Intensive Agriculture in the Tropics, BARIntSer 232 (Oxford 1985) 11–30.
Turner et al. 1981
E.S. Turner – N.I. Turner – R.E.W. Adams, Volumetric Assessment Rank Ordering, and Maya Civic Centers, in: W. Ashmore (ed.), Lowland Maya Settlement Patterns (Albuquerque 1981) 71–88.
Udy 1959
S.H. Udy, Organization of Work: A Comparative Analysis of Production among Nonindustrial Peoples (New Haven 1959).
Voutsaki 1995
S. Voutsaki, Social and Political Processes in the Mycenaean Argolid: The Evidence from the Mortuary Practices, in: R. Laffineur – W.-D. Niemeier (eds.), Politeia: Society and State in the Aegean Bronze Age. Proceedings of the 5th International Aegean Conference, University of Heidelberg, Archäologisches Institut, 10–13 April 1994, Vol I., Aegaeum 12 (Liège 1995) 55–66.
Voutsaki 1998
S. Voutsaki, Mortuary Evidence, Symbolic Meanings and Social Change: A Comparison between Messenia and the Argolid in the Mycenaean Period, in: K. Branigan (ed.), Cemetery and Society in the Aegean Bronze Age, Sheffield Studies in Aegean Archaeology 1 (Sheffield 1998) 41–58.
Voutsaki 1999
S. Voutsaki, Mortuary Display, Prestige and Identity in the Shaft Grave Era, in: V.L. Aravantinos – J.A. Barceló – C. Bockisch-Bräuer (eds.), Eliten in der Bronzezeit: Ergebnisse zweier Kolloquien in Mainz und Athen, Römisch-Germanisches Zentralmuseum Forschungsinstitut für Vor- und Frühgeschichte 43 (Mainz 1999) 103–118.

Voutsaki 2001
S. Voutsaki, Economic Control, Power and Prestige in the Mycenaean World: The Archaeological Evidence, in: S. Voutsaki – J. Killen (eds.), Economy and Politics in the Mycenaean Palace States. Proceedings of a Conference held on 1–3 July 1999 in the Faculty of Classics, Cambridge, Cambridge Philological Society Supplementary Volume 27 (Cambridge 2001) 195–213.

Voutsaki 2010
S. Voutsaki, From the Kinship Economy to the Palatial Economy: The Argolid in the Second Millennium BC, in: D. Pullen (ed.), Political Economies of the Aegean Bronze Age, Papers of the Langford Conference, Florida State University, Tallahassee, 22–24 February 2007 (Oxford 2010) 86–111.

Wace 1921–23
A.J.B. Wace, Excavations at Mycenae. IX - The Tholos Tombs, BSA 25, 1921–23, 283–402.

Wace 1949
A.J.B. Wace, Mycenae: An Archaeological History and Guide (Princeton 1949).

Webster 1990
G.S. Webster, Labor Control and Emergent Stratification in Prehistoric Europe, CurrAnth 31, 1990, 337–366.

Webster 1991
G.S. Webster, Monuments, Mobilization, and Nuragic Organization, Antiquity 65, 1991, 840–856.

Webster – Kirker 1995
G. Webster – J. Kirker, Too Many Maya, Too Few Buildings: Investigating Construction Potential at Copán, Honduras, Journal of Anthropological Research 51, 1995, 363–387.

Wright 1987
J.C. Wright, Death and Power at Mycenae: Changing Symbols in Mortuary Practice, in: R. Laffineur (ed.), Les coutumes funéraires en Égée à l'âge du Bronze. Actes du colloque de Liège, 21–23 avril 1986, Aegaeum 1 (Liège 1987) 171–184.

Wright 1978
T.H. Wright, Toward an Explanation of the Origin of the State, in: R. Cohen – E.R. Service (eds.), Origins of the State: The Anthropology of Political Evolution (Philadelphia 1978) 49–68.

Younger 1987
J.C. Younger, The Elgin Plaques from the Treasury of Atreus: Evidence for a New Reconstruction of the Façade, in: W. Schiering (ed.), Kolloquium zur ägäischen Vorgeschichte, Mannhein 20–22.2.1986, Schriften des deutschen Archäologen-Verbandes 9 (Mannheim 1987) 138–150.

Zangger 1994
E. Zangger, Landscape Changes around Tiryns during the Bronze Age, AJA 98, 1994, 189–212.

Zangger et al. 1997
E. Zangger – M.E. Timpson – S.B. Yazvenko – F. Kuhnke – J. Knauss, The Pylos Regional Archaeology Project, Part II: Landscape Evolution and Site Preservation, Hesperia 66, 1997, 548–641.

Relations among Workshops and Craftsmen in Protoattic Vase-painting: Limits and Perspectives in Quantifying the Production

Giulia Rocco

Introduction

In studying Athenian workshops of the 7th century BC, we encounter the same questions as we do for their successors in the 6th century BC, when the numbers both of painters/potters and of vases had grown considerably, to satisfy the export market. A mere tally of attributions, however, cannot be a starting point for quantifying the scale of production, or of a workforce. It is also necessary to analyze our limits and perspectives in reconstructing an individual craftsman's output and the organization of the work in the ergasteria.[1]

Athenian workshops involved in the production of painted pottery made mainly for ritual purposes seem to be limited in number, in comparison to the last quarter of the 8th century BC when figured vases appealed to a broader clientele. The reduced demand for finely decorated Protoattic pottery probably reflected rather exclusive commissions controlled by a more restricted aristocratic society.[2] These aristocratic groups, often residing in the Attic countryside, had also developed a taste for clay imitations of Near Eastern bronze vases, a prerogative of only few genoi in the Geometric period. We must remember, however, that more than one-half of the output of painted pottery can be attributed to minor artisans, still working in Subgeometric style on smaller shapes, often without a figural decoration. Painted and unpainted pottery, terracottas, and sometimes also storage vases were often made in the same ergasterion; moreover, some craftsmen, working mainly as potters, seem to engage in painting only rarely. In the absence of archaeological data, it is difficult to envision exactly how such a heterogeneous production worked, or to guess at the total number of workshops or their location (not only in Athens, but also in Attica), or to associate them with known painters. Consequently, just as in the Geometric period, the term "workshop" has been used, with all its limitations, to categorize Protoattic vases linked by stylistic elements, and not to represent the production of an ergasterion as a whole.[3]

Collaborations among Craftsmen Belonging to the Same Workshop Tradition

The development of timelines for relationships between Protoattic workshops is often elusive, when compared to the Late Geometric period, but it is useful to approach the dynamics of production through the ideas of "interrelationships" and "interaction."[4] The

Fig. 1: a) Hydria, Melbourne, National Gallery – Victoria D 23/1982 (H. 45.5 cm). b) Hydria, Athens NM VS 63 (H. 43.5 cm). c) Hydria, Baghdad, IM 52041 (not to scale).

importance of apprenticeship and collaboration among craftsmen belonging to the same workshop's tradition means that we must also examine the teacher-pupil relationship. Furthermore, we must keep in mind that we are not always dealing only with painters who share the same training, working for one potter, but also with painters and potters from different ergasteria, sometimes working together; such activities can be detected in their reciprocal influences, as well as in imitations of the work of the leading painter. The migration of potters and painters and the export of their expertise – which was more or less unknown in the previous period – strongly influences not only artistic development, but also production dynamics.

In the study of Protoattic vases, not much attention has been paid to recognizing the distinctive work of a potter, but focusing on the shape allows us to analyze some aspects of their interactions with painters. The potter's eye governed the freehand shaping of proportions, without the use of a template, but the individual styles of the craftsmen who threw the vases are less easily distinguished than those of the painters. From the Geometric period, the selection of vessel types and shapes defined the character of a workshop and of its leading potter, with strong differences in the same period; in Protoattic pottery, however, variations in vase profiles often do not follow a progressive chronological sequence.[5]

The Melbourne hydria painted by the Analatos Painter around 715–710 BC[6] (fig. 1a) in proportions and profile calls to mind those attributed to the Painter of the Stathatos Amphora[7] (fig. 1c), a member of the Workshop of Athens 894, where the

a b

Fig. 2: a) Hydria, Bochum, Kunstsammlungen der Ruhr-Universität S 1067 (H. 42.5 cm).
b) Hydria, Athens, NM 313 (H. 80 cm).

Analatos Painter received his training. Similarly, the hydria by the Mesogeia Painter from Spata (fig. 1b),[8] is close to that old-fashioned model, with ovoid body and large cylindrical neck; one might wonder whether the potter of the Spata hydria, painted in a more advanced style than those from Kalyvia Kouvara by the same painter,[9] was an older craftsman of the workshop.

A slight attenuation of the profile can be detected on very early hydriae by the Analatos Painter in Bad Driburg and in Bochum (fig. 2a), the latter more advanced

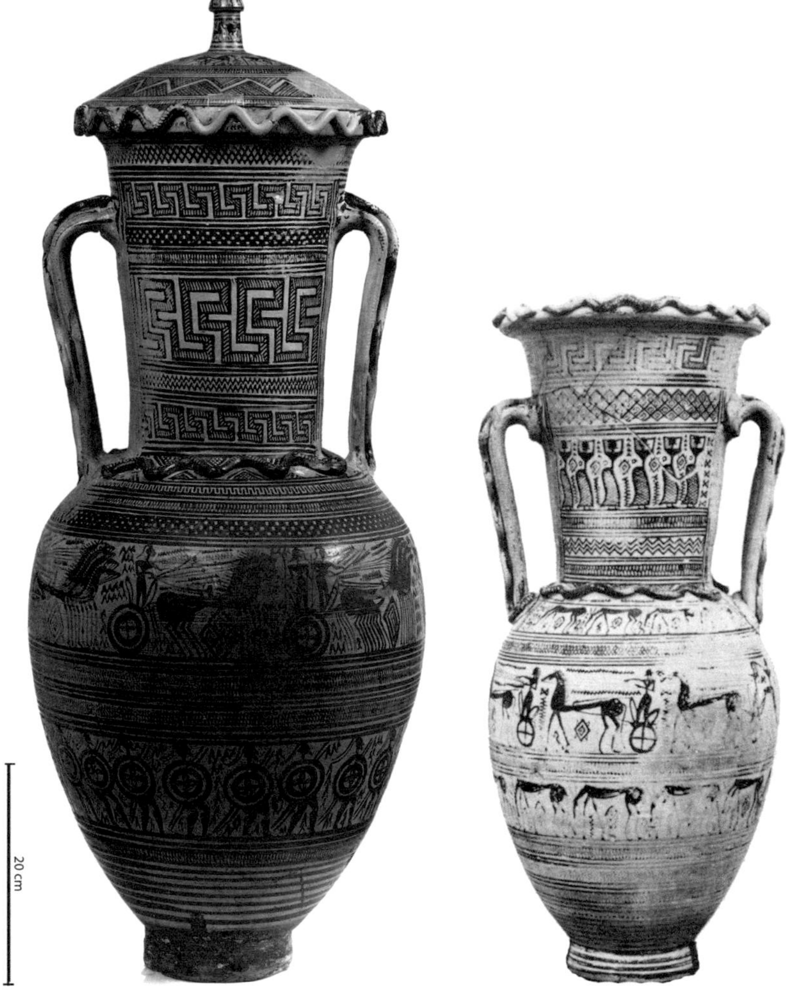

a b

Fig. 3: a) Amphora, Athens NM 894 (H. 77.5 cm). b) Amphora, Athens, NM, St 222 (H. 60 cm).

in design, and then on his name-vase (fig. 2b), which, although larger, maintains the same proportions between neck and body;[10] this trend could betray not a later chronology, but rather the hand of this innovative craftsman also as potter. The name-vase of the Workshop of Athens 894[11] (fig. 3a) has proportions between neck and body close to 1:1:25 like the name-vase of the Painter of the Stathatos Amphora[12] (fig. 3b) and the two amphorae in Oxford (fig. 4a–b). The Oxford amphora from Koropi[13] (fig. 4b) whose attribution to the Analatos or Mesogeia Painter is the subject of much debate, has elongated proportions, but its profile lacks the clear partitions that characterize the early vases of the Analatos Painter. Its decoration, however, is still close to late Geometric, and N. Coldstream was perhaps right to associate it with the apprenticeship of the Analatos Painter. On the other hand, the

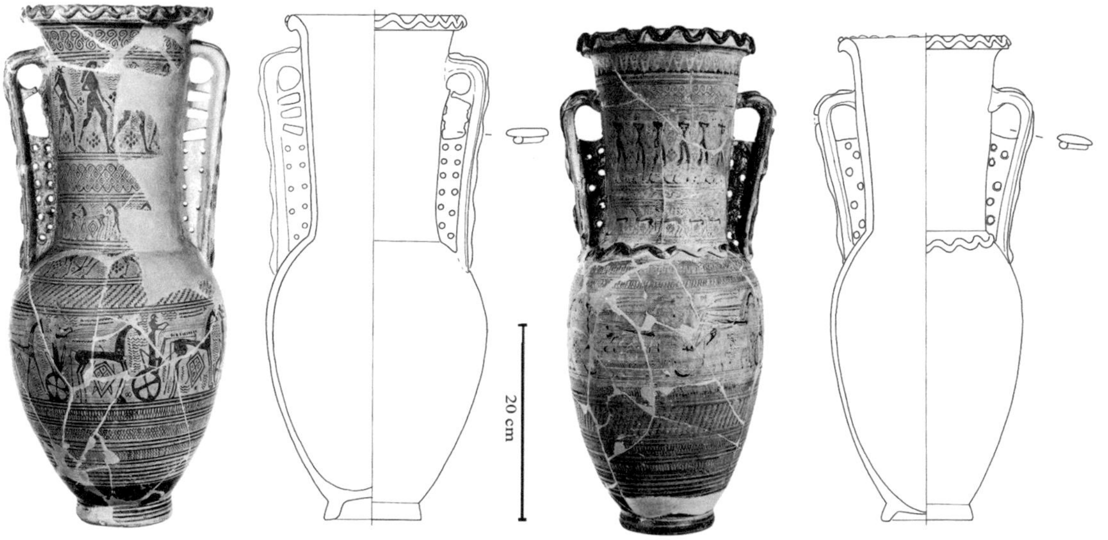

a b

Fig. 4: a) Amphora, Oxford, Ashmolean Museum 1935.19 (H. 51.4 cm). b) Amphora, Oxford, Ashmolean Museum 1936.599 (H. 49 cm).

Oxford amphora from Keratea[14] (fig. 4a), probably by the Mesogeia Painter, with its plump body, is more stiff and less precise in the moulding of foot and lip, with the upper part of the handles closely attached under the lip; we find the same details on the amphorae from Kerameikos, in Houston and San Antonio,[15] painted and perhaps also shaped by the Mesogeia Painter, often with horizontal straps added to the perforated plate of the handles. Thus, it is not just the painted decoration, but also different details in forming the vases that seem to reflect different hands on the two Oxford amphorae. It is likely that two modes could coexist in the workshops producing painted pottery in 7th century Athens: painters throwing their own vases, and master-potters collaborating with painters. Often the two roles had to coincide; the forming of the vases was often entrusted to a more experienced craftsman, sometimes working as painter himself.[16]

Other examples help us trace connections among artisans working together, such as a large number of vases from the offering trenches γ, ζ and δ in the Kerameikos and from Vari, made in the same workshop but painted by different hands that shared the influence of the Parian school (fig. 6 b-c). The I Painter of offering trench γ, a prominent and innovative painter who introduced a kind of rich polychromy like that seen in coroplastic workshops, was probably also working as a potter, modifying some shapes inherited from the late Geometric period in accordance with the new taste for high feet, moulded appliques, and the imitation of bronze vases from the East. The II Painter of offering trench γ could be the early Kynosarges Painter. A third painter (Painter of offering trench ζ), working sometimes in the polychrome technique, decorated vases in the same workshop.[17]

Fig. 5: a) Lid of pyxis, Athens, NM 2491. b) Detail of the high-standed bowl, Athens, Kerameikos Museum 1277. c) Mug, Athens, Kerameikos Museum 93.

Apprenticeship and the Teacher-Pupil Relationship

Identifying relationships among craftsmen in the same workshop could enhance our understanding of how the workers trained in and mastered their craft. We have already mentioned the first hydriae by the Analatos Painter, which show his master-pupil relation with the Painter of the Stathatos Amphora, but his smaller shapes also seem far too advanced to be the efforts of a beginner.[18] Susan Langdon, has recognized on some small vases, however, the work of apprentices or training exercises, which are to be distinguished from the hastily executed decoration by an expert painter;[19] these vases are not trial pieces, scraps or second-quality products, but were fired and used in funerary settings, often related to children. They were also probably made by children; some of them are upside-down painted vases. Sometimes the identification of apprentice work is more complicated, especially when the judging is based on the size of the vessel or on exclusively qualitative criteria. In a group of vases from Kerameikos and Phaleron that can be attributed to the same hand[20] (fig. 5 a– b), the vessel formation is competent and the Geometric decoration on some is complex and accurate, on others uncertain; still, it is difficult to say whether the figures were rendered by a craftsman training on unfamiliar subjects, or by a rushed painter. Closer to the style of training exercises are some cups from the child's grave 10 in Kerameikos[21] (fig. 5c), whose patterns resemble the

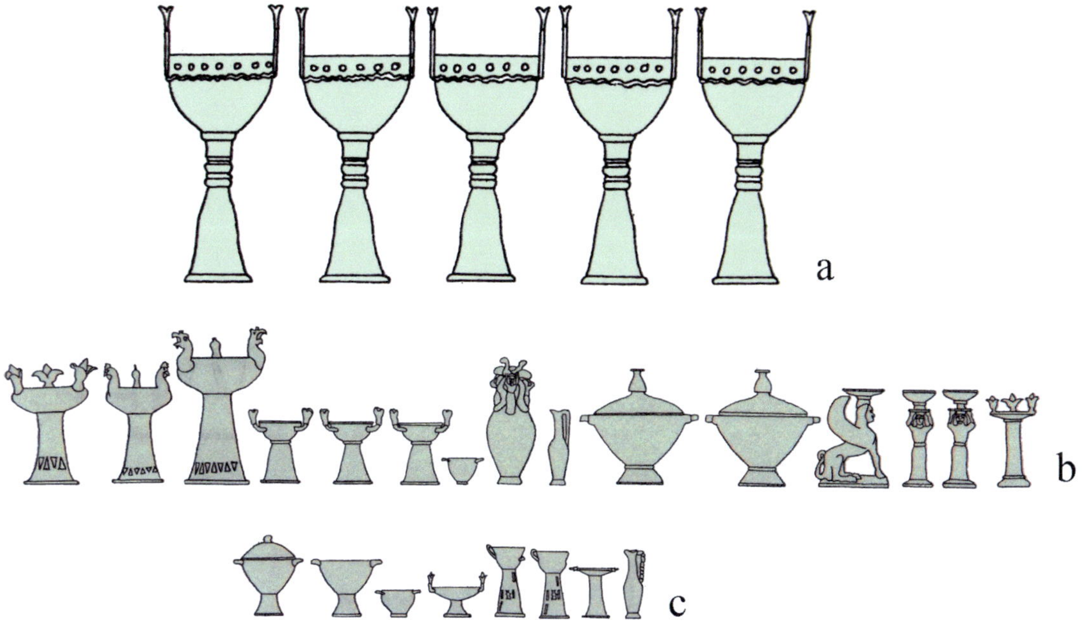

Fig. 6: a) Kraters from an offerig trench, Mainz, Sammlung der Universität; b) Vases from the offering trench γ, Athenian Kerameikos. c) Vases from the offering trench ζ, Athenian Kerameikos.

contemporary Kerameikos Mugs Group (660–670 BC).[22] By contrast, the so-called "Phaleron vases" are usually classified as examples of poor production attributed to "minor" workshops in the area of the old harbor of Athens. If their findspots suggest that their ergasteria were located along the route from Phaleron to Athens, I would argue that a coherent group of them should be associated with one of the most prominent workshops of the beginning of the 7th century, the Würzburg Workshop, and to the circle of its craftsmen, the Vulture, N, and Passas Painters, who were perhaps also working in that area.[23] They should not be considered as second-rate products, but rather as smaller and sometimes miniaturized shapes[24] with ritual purposes, often related to children's graves or sanctuaries. Even if we count these vases among the workshop's products, we are still far from estimating its output, considering the large number of vases with linear decoration that come from the necropoleis of Phaleron, and were probably made by the same craftsmen.[25]

Further, when we look at the lives of artisans, we must consider not only how a career started, but also how long it lasted, and what stages it went through. Groups of vases attributed to different hands could represent instead a development in the style of a single craftsman. From these stages we might follow the transformation from Late Geometric to Protoattic vase painting, and the transfer of skill and knowledge from one artisan to another. The hypothesis that the Analatos Painter's career lasted from 715–710 until 660 BC or later, is unlikely, as it also is in the era of black- and red-figure vase-painting, when careers of even 20 or 30 years are exceptional, given the high mortality rate. Thus, the two louteria from Thebes (one in Athens from an unknown context, the other from the sanctuary of Herakles), along with the one from Incoronata (Metaponto) can be better attributed to a second generation of craftsmen who spread and merged the Athenian tradition of the prolific Analatos Painter's workshop with the new tendencies of the "Wild Style" with its Cycladic flavor, well represented by the Checkerboard Painter.[26] Like the two painters of the vases from the offering place α in the Kerameikos and the painter of the hypokraterion from Argos,[27] these craftsmen were apprentices under the influence of both the Analatos and Mesogeia Painters, whose common training at the beginning of their careers could have built up a long-term collaboration. Although they were influenced by the "Wild Style", they were able to keep the traditions of the Analatos Painter's workshop alive until the second quarter of the 7th century BC.

Collaborations among Painters and Potters Trained in Different Workshops and their Relocation

When we examine the production of 7th century BC Athenian workshops, it is sometimes possible to detect collaboration for the same commission (or, better, for the same potter), by painters trained and employed in independent workshops. This invites us to reflect on the role of painters who moved from one ergasterion to another. The Passas Painter, trained in the Würzburg Group Workshop, painted most of the kraters and hypokrateria in Mainz (fig. 6a), and for this commission the Analatos Painter spent most of his time creating the vases.[28] We cannot say if such occasional collaborations, perhaps necessary for the completion of a large commission in a short time, were the rule, or the exception: this corresponds to a model of activity in which specialized painters were hired by master-potters. The Passas Painter's name-amphora, however, with its perforated handle-plates, is closer to the Analatos Painter Workshop's shapes than to the Würzburg Group's.[29]

We cannot find examples of two painters working on the same vase, as in the Dipylon Workshop.[30] This can perhaps be explained by the abandonment of the labor-intensive Geometric-style decoration and the shift toward a preference for medium and small-sized shapes: the painter of the amphora from Mt Hymettus and the Polyphemus Painter of the amphora from Eleusis decorated their large vases without the help of other craftsmen (and one might also wonder how far away the workshop was located from the actual context of use for such large vases).[31] Workshop organization and scheduling may not have changed so much from the Geometric period, but they no longer involve the work of more than a single painter on the same vase; rather, more painters, sometimes from different workshops, came together to work on a large commission for vases made by the same potter. To what extent this suggests

a

b

Fig. 7: a) Oinochoe, Berlin, Staatliche Museen, Antikensammlung 5826. b) Kotyle, Kythnos, Museum B' 04/Pg12.

a reduced number of craftsmen – and of commissions of painted pottery – in the workshops, and a need for occasional collaborations, is impossible to determine. These examples shed more light on the production model for this period, which has been hypothesized as mainly family-based; in fact, there was probably also a variable number of craftsmen at work in the different stages of production and, perhaps, in the different seasons of the year.[32]

Moreover, small-scale local circulation could be representative of a more complex and widespread trend, involving craftsmen from the same workshop, as well as interactions extending even beyond the borders of Attica – the consequence of potters and painters relocating and thereby exporting their expertise.[33] This phenomenon, while not limited to Attica, is more striking there than in other areas. The lack of a long-lasting tradition inside a single workshop makes it impossible to trace developmental steps and the transfer of skill and knowledge from a workshop to another, as we can see in the late 8th century BC; minor staff members, in particular, seem to come in from elsewhere or to leave for other lands. K. Sheedy supposed that the leading painter of the Parian Ad Group learned to paint pots in the workshop of the Würzburg Group (around 710–700 BC), and adduced this as an explanation for the Atticizing style.[34] An echo of the styles of the Vulture and Analatos Painters can be detected on a group of Cycladic vases by the Parian Painter of the "winged horses", found in the sanctuary at Vryokastro on Kythnos (fig. 7b) and in the Heraion on Delos[35]; in addition a "Phaleron" oinochoe from Aegina, attributed by Denoyelle to the Analatos Painter, seems near the vase-group from Kythnos, that also shares some details with the Passas Painter's production[36] (fig. 7a). The Checkerboard Painter (fig. 8a) and other Athenian pottery of the beginning of the 7th century BC (fig. 8b) seem to have strong ties with the Parian workshop that produced the vases of the Ad Group (fig. 8c), whose influence can be detected also in other craftsmen of the "Wild Style", merging both the Parian and the Subgeometric

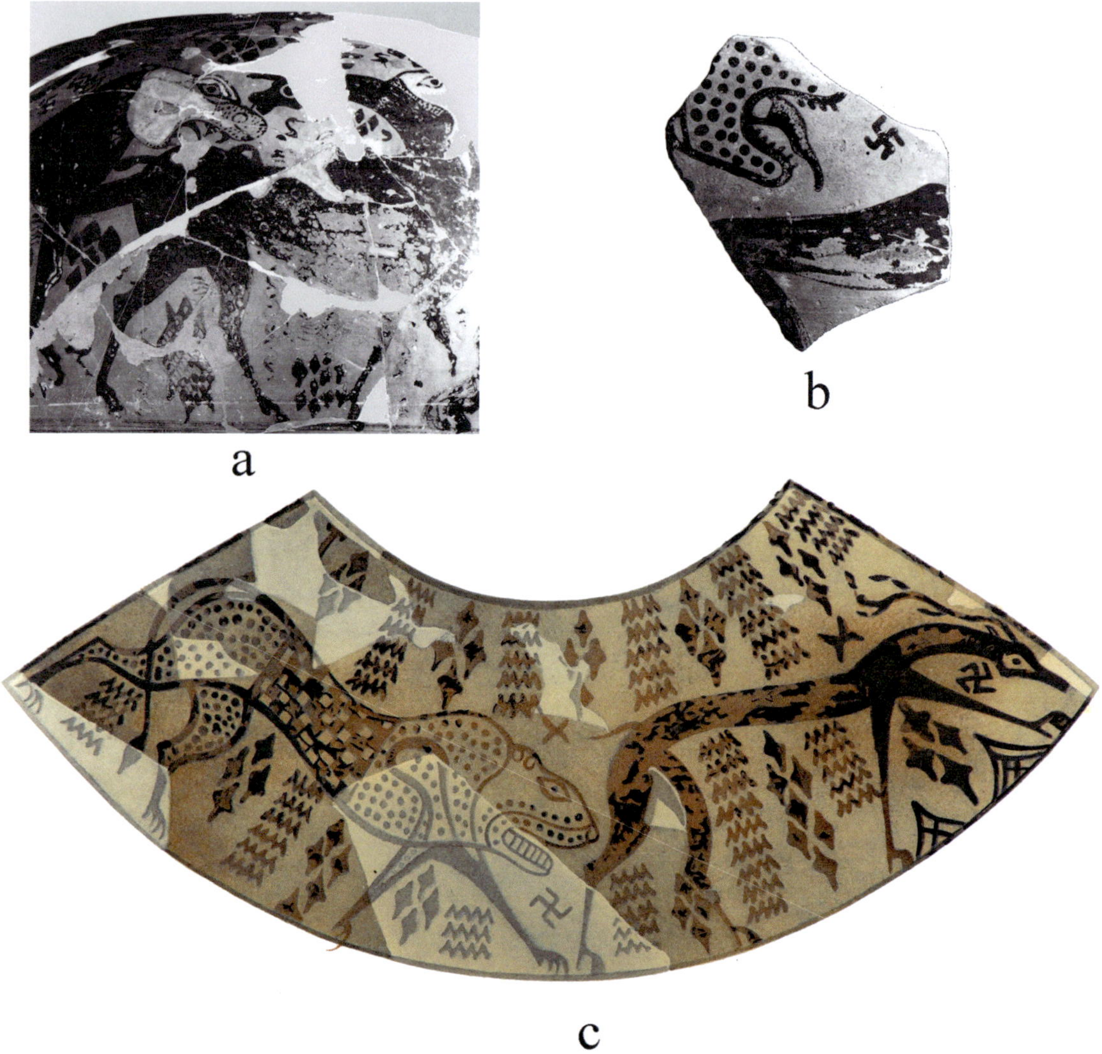

Fig. 8: a) Krater, Berlin, Staatliche Museen, Antikensammlung A 22. b) Fragment of an amphora, Aegina, Museo K 552. c) Drawing from the amphora Delos, Museum Ad 4.

Athenian tradition.[37] Some connections exist also between the Menelaos Painter and vases like the dinos with warriors from Despotiko, showing the creativity and pioneering spirit of the Parian workshops.[38] In the same period, relations between Athens and the Cyclades are documented by a Protoattic amphora of the third quarter of the 7th century BC that was offered as a votive gift in the Apollo sanctuary on Kythnos, related both to the Painter of the Burgon Krater and to the Kynosarges Painter.[39] It is also possible to trace the influence in the other direction: the heritage of the Parian school can be detected in works by the Kynosarges, Pair, and Protome Painters.[40]

Conclusions

Despite the rich exchanges and borrowings between Attica and the Cyclades, when we look at Athenian pottery-shapes, we must recognize that the last great revolution took place in the Late Geometric Workshop of Athens 894: Protoattic potters often keep and perpetuate Late Geometric shapes for ritual and funerary purposes, a tendency inherited also by 6th century workshops. A pyxis dating back to the Protogeometric period is "updated" in the so called ovoid-krater, probably the model for the later standard shape of the lebes gamikos;[41] the hydria comes back into fashion for ritual purposes; from the neck-amphora is developed the amphora-loutrophoros,[42] and old-fashioned shapes such as bowls with high stands become the cultic vases for rituals to Artemis.[43] The workshop of the Analatos Painter improves a krater with a separate lip, almost a forerunner of the later calyx-krater, and develops the kotyle krater, which often fulfills more effectively the use of a pyxis or lekanis.[44] Some shapes are modeled after Oriental bronze vases, or "borrow" from other vase-painting traditions, such as the oinochoe of East-Greek type by the Ram Jug Painter and an olpe of Protocorinthian inspiration decorated with Subgeometric and Protoattic patterns.[45] These are more often the exception than the rule, and did not form a tradition that lasted into the 6th century BC.

These examples lead us to hypothesize that established traditions tended to prevail in the potter's work, in contrast to the swift transformations –in subjects, iconographies, styles, and techniques– in the painter's world. One expression of the conservatism of Protoattic shapes is seen in the cementing of the role of some forms inherited from the Late Geometric workshops in worship and rituals in later ages, which further underscores the prominence of the potters' work in relation to that of the painters. An investigation of the Attic vase-painting industry must begin with the potters.

Notes

* I thank the organizators of this panel of the Congress, M. Bentz and E. Hasaki. As the photos of the vases are taken from different angles, the proportions and the rendering of the profiles may present sometimes some inaccuracies.

[1] For the methodological approach: Bentz – Böhr 2002; Sapirstein 2013; Sapirstein 2014; Pevnick 2016; Stissi 2016. On the ergasteria in 7th century BC Monaco 2000, 24–34; Papadopoulos 2003.

[2] Osborne 1989; Whitley 1994; Alexandridou 2015; D'Onofrio 1997; D'Onofrio 2017; a review of the contexts in Doronzio 2018. For votive dedications on the Akropolis as mirror of the society in Geometric and Archaic Age Gauss and Ruppenstein 1998. A primary funerary destination is not always the rule; both the louterion from Thebes in Athens and the krater attributed to the Pernice Painter show traces of usage on the interior walls, as well as repairs, Rocco 2008, 117–119, LT 9. 156 f., Per 3.

[3] On the limitations of the term "workshop" in discussions of vases that share stylistic elements, see Hasaki 2002, 6–8. 251–257.
[4] Crielaard 1999, 49–81.
[5] Kübler 1970, 150–196; Hünnekens 1987, 108 f. 236 f.
[6] Sheedy 1990b; Rocco 2008, 15. 21–22. 28 An 10 pl. 1, 3.
[7] Davison 1961, 79–82, n° 2. 8 figs. 116a–b. 121; Coldstream 2008[2] 59, 33 (Baghdad IM 52041) 62–63.
[8] Coldstream 2008[2] 85; Rocco 2008, 32. 36. 39 Me 12 pl. 4, 2.
[9] Rocco 2008, 32. 36–39. Me 10–11 pl. 4, 1. 3.
[10] Rocco 2008, 14 f. 16. 27 f. An 8 An 9 An 11.
[11] Davison 1961, 41, n°1 fig. 33; Coldstream 2008[2] 58, n° 4.
[12] Davison 1961, 43. 79–82 n° 1 fig. 115; Coldstream 2008[2] 59, n°15.
[13] Rocco 2008, 14. 27 An 1; Coldstream 2008[2], 63 f. CVA Oxford 4, pls. 16–19.
[14] Rocco 2008, 31. 38 Me 4; Coldstream 2008[2], 145, n° 5; CVA Oxford 4, 12–15.
[15] Rocco 2008, 31 f. 38 Me 3. Me 5.
[16] For the organization of the Dipylon Workshop, Coulié 2010; Coulié 2012–2013; Coulié 2014; Coulié 2015; Vlachou 2015.
[17] Brann 1962, 11. 24 f.; Kübler 1970, 310–312. 328–330. 453–470. 474–481; von Freytag 1975, 49–81; Kistler 1998, 50–54. 64 f. 188–190. 191 f. 206–208; Rocco 2008, 173–186. 190–196.
[18] Rocco 2008, 13.28 An 26 An 27, the krateriskos from Kallithea could be related to a very early stage of the career of the Analatos Painter, Rocco 2008, 15. 30 BAn 9.
[19] Langdon 2013; Langdon 2015.
[20] Rocco 2008, 79 C1–C6.
[21] Kübler 1970, 450–451. pl. 31 ns° 39–41.
[22] Kübler 1970, 427–447; Rocco 2008, 161–165.
[23] Rocco 2008, 47–78. More additions in Palaiokrassa-Kopitsa – Vivliodetis 2015; Palaiokrassa-Kopitsa 2017 252–254.
[24] Ekroth 2003.
[25] Pelekidis 1916; Young 1942; Petrocheilos 1996; Frangopoulou – Zosi 2017; Alexandropoulou 2018.
[26] Denoyelle 1996 (Analatos P.); Giuliano 2005 (Checkerboard P.); Rocco 2008, 117–119; Morris 2014 (Workshop of the Analatos P.). On the sanctuary of Thebes, Aravantinos 2017.
[27] Rocco 2008, 41–46.
[28] Hampe 1960; Kistler 1998, 202 f.; Rocco 2008, 19 f. 33. 67 f.
[29] Rocco 2008, 69 Pa 4; on the amphora from Odos Pireas, Palaiokrassa-Kopitsa 2016. On the amphora's shape in the Analatos and Würzburg Group's workshops, Rocco 2008, 14. 27 An 1–An 5. 29 BAn 1–BAn 2. 31 f. 38 Me 1–Me 8. 47–49. 60 Av 1. 61 Wü 1–Wü 4.
[30] Note 16.
[31] CVA Berlin 1, pls. 43. 44; Mylonas 1968; Rocco 2008, 101 W 2 140 Po 4.
[32] For activity in potter's workshops, Hasaki 2006; Hasaki 2011.
[33] Coulié 2000.
[34] Sheedy 1985; Sheedy 1990a; Rocco 2008, 51–60. See also the Euboean atticizing tradition of some pottery from Oropos, locally made, Charalambidou 2007, 279 f. fig. 5. For the circulation of potters and pots in

the Geometric Age and beyond, Papadopoulos 1997; Papadopoulos 1998; Papadopoulos – Lord Smithson 2002.

[35] Alexandridou et al. 2017, 137 f. figs. 5. 6; Koutsoumpou 2017, 164 f. 171 f. nn° 14–16.

[36] CVA Berlin 1 pl. 45, 2–4; Denoyelle 1996, 81. 86; Rocco 2008, 30 BAn 5.

[37] Rocco 2008, 89–92. 109–116 and on a group of Athenian vases near the Ad Painter, 89.

[38] Kouraghios 2005; Kouraghios 2012, 56. 58.

[39] Alexandridou et al. 2017 138, figs. 9. 10; Koutsoumpou 2017, 165 f.172 n° 17.

[40] Hünnekens 1987, 18 f.; Rocco 2008, 173–181. 187–189. For the "Parian style" Croissant 2007.

[41] Rocco 2017b.

[42] Alexandridou 2014.

[43] Rocco 2017a.

[44] Kistler 1998, 31–38; Rocco 2008, 205.

[45] Coldstream 2007, 81 f.; Rocco 2008, 149 Ar 2. On the olpe, CVA Oxford 4, pl. 29.

Image Credits

Fig. 1a: from Sheedy 1990b. – Fig. 1c: from Davison 1961. – Fig. 1b. 2b. 3a: photo National Archaeological Museum, Athens, G. Patrikianos, © Hellenic Ministry of Culture. Fig. 2a: from CVA Bochum 1. – Fig. 3b: photo National Archaeological Museum, Athens, D. Gialouris, © Hellenic Ministry of Culture. – Fig. 4a. 4b: from CVA Oxford 4; drawings by L. di Blasi. – Fig. 5a: from Böhlau 1887. – Fig. 5b. 5c: from Kübler 1970. – Fig. 6a–c: from Kistler 1998. – Fig. 7a. 8a: from CVA Berlin 1. – Fig. 7b: from Koutsoumpou 2017. – Fig. 8b: from Rocco 2008. – Fig. 8c: from C. Dugas – Ch. Rhomaios, Les vases préhelléniques et géométriques, Exploration Archéologique de Délos, XV (Paris 1934).

References

Alexandridou 2014

A.F. Alexandridou, De l'eau pour les défunts. Les hydries à décor peint en contexte funéraire attique de l'âge du Fer à l'époque archaïque, Pallas, 94, 2014, 17–38.

Alexandridou 2015

A.F. Alexandridou, Shedding Light on Mortuary Practices in Early Archaic Attica: the Case of the Offering Trenches, in: D.C. Haggis – C.M. Antonaccio (eds.), Classical Archaeology in Context. Theory and Practice in Excavation in the Greek World (Berlin–Boston 2015) 121–148.

Alexandridou et al. 2017

A. Alexandridou et al., Pottery and Clay Figurines from the Sanctuary of Kythnos, in: A. Mazarakis Ainian, Les sanctuaires archaïques des Cyclades (Rennes 2017) 135–192.

Alexandropoulou 2018

A. Alexandropoulou, Ein protoattisches Kraterfragment aus Phaleron, in: T. Korkut, B. Özen-Kleine (eds.), Festschrift für Heide Froning. Studies in Honour of Heide Froning (Istanbul 2018) 1–8.

Aravantinos 2017
V. Aravantinos, The Sanctuaries of Herakles and Apollo Ismenios at Thebes: New Evidence, in: Charalambidou – Morgan 2017, 221–230.

Bentz – Böhr 2002
M. Bentz – E. Böhr, Zu den Massen attischer Feinkeramik, in: M. Bentz (ed.), Vasenforschung und Corpus Vasorum Antiquorum: Standortbestimmung und Perspektiven (München 2002) 73–80.

Böhlau 1887
J. Böhlau, Frühattische Vasen, JdI 2, 1887, 33–66.

Brann 1962
E.T.H. Brann, Late Geometric and Protoattic Pottery. Mid 8th to Late 7th Century BC, Agora 8 (Princeton 1962).

Charalambidou 2007
X. Charalambidou, The Fine Pottery from Oropos from the Early Orientalizing to the Archaic Period in: A. Mazarakis Ainian (ed.), Oropos and Euboea in the Early Iron Age: Acts of an International Round Table, University of Thessaly, June 18–20, 2004 (Volos 2007) 275–285.

Charalambidou – Morgan 2017
X. Charalambidou – C. Morgan (eds.), Interpreting the Seventh Century BC: Tradition and Innovation (Oxford 2017).

Coldstream 2007
C. Coldstream, In the Wake of Ariadne: Connections between Naxos and Crete, 1000–600 BC, in: E. Semantoni-Bournia – A.A. Laimou – L.G. Medoni – N. Kourou (eds.), Αμύμονα έργα: τιμητικός τόμος για τον καθηγητή Βασίλη Κ. Λαμπρινουδάκη (Athens 2007) 77–83.

Coldstream 2008²
J.N. Coldstream, Greek Geometric Pottery. A Survey of Ten Local Styles and their Chronology ²(London 2008).

Coulié 2000
A. Coulié, La mobilité des artisans potiers en Grèce archaïque et son rôle dans la diffusion des productions, in: F. Blondé – A. Muller (eds.), L'artisanat en Grèce ancienne. Les productions, les diffusions, Actes du Colloque de Lyon 10–11 décembre 1998 (Lille 2000) 253–262.

Coulié 2012
A. Coulié, I vasi del „Dipylon": dai frammenti alla bottega, AnnAStAnt, 19, 2012, 9–30.

Coulié 2014
A. Coulié, L'atelier du "Dipylon": autour du cratère du Louvre A 522, in: P. Valavanis – E. Manakidou (eds.), Egraphsen kai epoiesen. Essays on Greek Pottery and Iconography in Honour of Professor Michalis Tiverios (Thessaloniki 2014) 35–45.

Coulié 2015
A. Coulié, L'atelier du Dipylon: style, typologie et chronologie relative, in: V. Vlachou (ed.), Pots, Workshops and Early Iron Age Society: Function and Role of Ceramics in Early Greece. Proceedings of the International Symposium Held at the Université Libre de Bruxelles 14–16 November 2013 (Brussels 2015) 37–47.

Crielaard 1999
J.P. Crielaard, Production, Circulation and Consumption of Early Iron Age Greek Pottery (11th to 7th c. BC), in: J-P. Crielaard – V. Stissi – G.J. van Wijngaarden (eds.), The Complex Past of Pottery: Production, Circulation and Consumption of Mycenaean and Greek Pottery (Sixteenth to Early Fifth Centuries BC). Proceedings of the ARCHON International Conference, held in Amsterdam, 8–9 November 1996 (Amsterdam 1999) 49–81.

Croissant 2007
F. Croissant, Aux origines du style parien, in: E. Semantone Bournia – A.A. Laimou – L.G. Medoni – N. Kourou (eds.), Αμύμονα έργα: τιμητικός τόμος για τον καθηγητή Βασίλη Κ. Λαμπρινουδάκη (Athens 2007) 119–133.

CVA Berlin 1
R. Eilmann – K. Gebauer, CVA. Deutschland, 2. Berlin, Antiquarium, 1 (München 1938).

CVA Oxford 4
H.W. Catling – T. Mannack, CVA Great Britain 24. Oxford, Ashmolean Museum 4 (Oxford 2010).

Davison 1961
J.M. Davison, Attic Geometric Workshops (New Haven 1961).

Denoyelle 1996
M. Denoyelle, Le Peintre d'Analatos: essay de synthèse et perspectives nouvelles, AK 36, 1996, 71–87.

D'Onofrio 1997
A.M. D'Onofrio, The 7th Century B.C. in Attica: the Basis of Political Organization, ActaHyp 7, 1997, 63–88.

D'Onofrio 2017
A.M. D'Onofrio, Athenian Burial Practices and Cultural Change: the Rundbau Early Plot in the Kerameikos Revisited, in: Charalambidou – Morgan 2017, 260–280.

Doronzio 2018
A.M. Doronzio, Athen im 7. Jahrhundert v. Chr. Räume und Funde der frühen Polis (Berlin – Boston 2018).

Ekroth 2003
G. Ekroth, Small Pots, Poor People? The Use and Function of Miniature Pottery as Votive Offerings in Sanctuaries in the Argolid and Corinthia, in: B. Schmalz – M. Söldner (eds.), Griechische Keramik im Kulturellen Kontext. Akten des Internationalen Vasen-Symposions in Kiel vom 24.–28. 9. 2001 (Münster 2003) 35–37.

Frangopoulou – Zosi 2017
F. Frangopoulou – E. Zosi, Material Koine and the Case of Phaleron Cups. Conventions and Reality, in: S. Handberg – A. Gadolou (eds.), Material Koinai in the Greek Early Iron Age and Archaic Period, Acts of an International Conference at the Danish Institute at Athens, 30 January – 1 February 2015 (Aarhus 2017) 133–163.

von Freytag 1975
B. von Freytag gen. von Löringhoff, Neue frühattische Funde aus dem Kerameikos, AM 90, 1975, 49–81.

Gauss – Ruppenstein 1998
W. Gauss – F. Ruppenstein, Die Athener Akropolis in der frühen Eisenzeit, AM, 113, 1998, 1–60.
Giuliano 2005
A. Giuliano, Protoattici in Occidente, in: B. Adembri (ed.), Aeimnestos, Miscellanea di Studi per Mauro Cristofani (Firenze 2005) 64–72.
Hampe 1960
R. Hampe, Ein frühattischer Grabfund (Mainz 1960).
Hasaki 2002
E. Hasaki, Ceramic Kilns in Ancient Greece. Technology and Organization of Ceramic Workshops (Ph.D. diss. University of Cincinnati 2002).
Hasaki 2006
E. Hasaki, The Ancient Greek Ceramic Kilns and their Contribution to the Technology and Organization of the Potters' Workshops, in: P. Tasios – C. Palyvou (eds.), Proceedings of the 2nd International Conference on Ancient Greek Technology (Athens 2006) 221–227.
Hasaki 2011
E. Hasaki, Crafting Spaces: Archaeological, Ethnographic, and Ethnoarchaeological Studies on Spatial Organization in Pottery Workshops in Greece and Tunisia, in: M. Lawall – J. Lund (eds.), Pottery in the Archaeological Record: Greece and Beyond (Aarhus 2011) 12–28.
Hünnekens 1987, I–II
L. Hünnekens, Die frühe attische Schwarzfigurige Keramik, I–II (Ph.D. diss. University of Freiburg 1987).
Karl 2016
S. Karl, Die Dipylonwerkstatt – Wer ist der Dipylonmeister? Überlegungen zu Grabkrateren aus dem unmittelbaren Kreis seiner Werkstattkollegen, in: N. Eschbach – S. Schmidt (eds.): Töpfer, Maler, Werkstatt: Zuschreibungen in der griechischen Vasenmalerei und die Organisation antiker Keramikproduktion, CVA Beih. 7 (München 2016) 69–79.
Kistler 1998
E. Kistler, Die „Opferrinne-Zeremonie", Bankettideologie am Grab, Orientalisierung und Formierung einer Adelsgesellschaft in Athen (Stuttgart 1998).
Kouraghios 2005
Y. Kouraghios, Despotiko Mandra: a Sanctuary dedicated to Apollo, in: M. Yeroulanou – M. Stamatopoulou (eds.), Architecture and Archaeology in the Cyclades. Papers in Honour of J.J. Coulton (Oxford University 2005) 105–133.
Kouraghios 2012
Y. Kouraghios, Despotiko. The Sanctuary of Apollo (Athens 2012).
Koutsoumpou 2017
M. Koutsoumpou, Beyond Athens and Corinth. Pottery Distribution in the Cyclades: the Case of Kythnos, in: Charalambidou – Morgan 2017, 160–172.
Kübler 1970
K. Kübler, Kerameikos. Ergebnisse der Ausgrabungen VI, 2. Die Nekropole des späten 8. bis frühen 6. Jahrhunderts (Berlin 1970).

Langdon 2013
S. Langdon, Children as Learners and Producers, in: J. Evans-Grubbs – T. Parkin (eds.), Oxford Handbook of Childhood and Education in the Classical World (Oxford 2013) 172–194.
Langdon 2015
S. Langdon, Geometric Pottery for Beginners: Children and Production in Early Greece, in: V. Vlachou (ed.), Pots, Workshops and Early Iron Age Society: Function and Role of Ceramics in Early Greece. Proceedings of the International Symposium Held at the Université libre de Bruxelles 14–16 November 2013 (Brussels 2015) 21–36.
Mazarakis Ainian 2002
A. Mazarakis Ainian, Recent Excavations at Oropos (Northern Attica), in: M. Stamatopoulou – M. Yeroulanou (eds.), Excavating Classical Culture. Recent Archaeological Discoveries in Greece (Athens 2002) 149–178.
Monaco 2000
M.C. Monaco, Ergasteria. Impianti artigianali ceramici ad Atene ed in Attica dal Protogeometrico alle soglie dell'Ellenismo (Rome 2000).
Morris 2014
S.P. Morris, Artists in Motion: Proto-Attic and Related Pottery of the Seventh Century B.C. in: P. Valavanis – E. Manakidou (eds.), Egraphsen kai epoiesen. Essays on Greek Pottery and Iconography in Honour of Professor Michalis Tiverios (Thessaloniki 2014) 95–104.
Mylonas 1957
G.E Mylonas, Ὁ πρωτοαττικός αμφορεύς της Ελευσίνος (Αθήναι 1957).
Osborne 1989
R. Osborne, A Crisis in Archaeological History? The Seventh Century BC in Attica, BSA 84, 1989, 297–322.
Palaiokrassa-Kopitsa – Vivliodetis 2015
L. Palaiokrassa-Kopitsa – A. Vivliodetis, The Sanctuaries of Artemis Mounichia and Zeus Parnessios. Their Relation to the Religious and Social Life in the Athenian City-State until the End of the 7th Century B.C., in: V. Vlachou (ed.), Pots, Workshops and Early Iron Age Society: Function and Role of Ceramics in Early Greece. Proceedings of the International Symposium held at the Université libre de Bruxelles 14–16 November 2013 (Brussels 2015) 155–180.
Palaiokrassa-Kopitsa 2016
L. Palaiokrassa-Kopitsa, Αμφορέας από την οδό Πειραιώς στην Αθήνα, in: M. Giannopoulou – Ch. Kallini (eds.), Ηχάδιν: τιμητικός τόμος για τη Στέλλα Δρούγου (Athens 2016) 288–310.
Palaiokrassa-Kopitsa 2017
L. Palaiokrassa-Kopitsa, Cult in Attica. The Case of the Sanctuary of Artemis Mounichia, in: Charalambidou – Morgan 2017, 245–259.
Papadopoulos 1997
J.K. Papadopoulos, Innovations, Imitations and Ceramic Styles. Modes of Production and Modes of Dissemination, in: R. Laffineur and P.P. Betancourt (eds.), TECHNE. Craftsmen, Craftswomen and Craftsmanship in the Aegean Bronze Age. Proceedings of the 6th International Aegean Conference, Philadelphia, Aegaeum 16 (Liège 1997) 449–462.

Papadopoulos 1998
J.K. Papadopoulos, A Bucket, by Any Other Name, and an Athenian Stranger in Early Iron Age Crete, Hesperia 67, 1998, 109–123.
Papadopoulos – Lord Smithson 2002
J.K. Papadopoulos – E. Lord Smithson, The Cultural Biography of a Cycladic Geometric Amphora: Islanders in Athens and the Prehistory of Metics, Hesperia 71, 2002, 149–199.
Papadopoulos 2003
J.K. Papadopoulos, Ceramicus redivivus. The Early Iron Age Potters' Field in the Area of the Classical Athenian Agora. Hesperia Suppl. 31 (Princeton 2003).
Pelekidis 1916
S. Pelekidis, Ανασκαφή Φαλήρου, ADelt 2, 1916, 13–64.
Pevnick 2016
S. Pevnick, Le style est l'homme même? On Syriskan Attributions, Vase Shapes, and Scale of Decoration, in: N. Eschbach – S. Schmidt (eds.), Töpfer, Maler, Werkstatt: Zuschreibungen in der griechischen Vasenmalerei und die Organisation antiker Keramikproduktion, CVA Beih. 7 (München 2016) 36–46.
Petrocheilos 1996
I.E. Petrocheilos, Frühe Phaleron-Oinochoen, AM 111, 1996, 45–64.
Rocco 2008
G. Rocco, La ceramografia protoattica: pittori e botteghe (710–630 a.C.), Internationale Archäologie 117 (Rahden 2008).
Rocco 2017a
G. Rocco, Forme vascolari e pratiche rituali in Attica tra la fine dell'VIII e il VII secolo a.C: il caso dei krateriskoi su altopiede, AntK 61, 2017, 3–18.
Rocco 2017b
G. Rocco, Il cratere "ovoide" in Attica, tra conservatorismo e innovazione, in: L. Cappuccini – M. Mohr (eds.), Fragmenta Mediterranea: contatti, tradizioni e innovazioni in Grecia, Magna Grecia, Etruria e Roma: studi in onore di Christoph Reusser (Sesto Fiorentino 2017) 69–90.
Sabetai 2014
V. Sabetai, The Wedding Vases of the Athenians: A View from Sanctuaries and Houses, in: Des vases pour les Athéniens (VI–IV siècles avant notre ère), Dossier de Metis 12, 2014, 51–79.
Sapirstein 2013
P. Sapirstein, Painters, Potters, and the Scale of the Attic Vase-Painting Industry, AJA 117, 2013, 493–510.
Sapirstein 2014
P. Sapirstein, Demographics and Productivity in the Ancient Athenian Pottery Industry, in: J.H. Oakley (ed.), Athenian Potters and Painters III (Oxford 2014) 175–186.
Sheedy 1985
K.A. Sheedy, Three Vase-Groups from the Purification Trench on Rheneia and the Evidence for a Parian Pottery Tradition, BSA 80, 1985, 151–190.

Sheedy 1990a
K.A. Sheedy, Attic and Atticizing Pottery in the Cyclades during the Eighth Century, in: J-P. Descoudres (ed.), Eumousia. Ceramic and Iconographic Studies in Honour of Alexander Cambitoglou (Sydney 1990) 31–40.

Sheedy 1990b
K.A. Sheedy, A Prothesis Scene from the Analatos Painter, AM 105, 1990, 117–151.

Sheedy 1992
K.A. Sheedy, The Late Geometric Hydria and the Advent of the Protoattic Style, AM 107, 1992, 11–28.

Stissi 2016
V. Stissi, Minor Artisans, Major Impact? in: N. Eschbach, S. Schmidt (eds.), Töpfer, Maler, Werkstatt: Zuschreibungen in der griechischen Vasenmalerei und die Organisation antiker Keramikproduktion, CVA Beih. 7, (München 2016) 47–53.

Vlachou 2015
V. Vlachou, From Pots to Workshops: The Hirschfeld Painter and the Late Geometric I Context of Attic Pottery Production, in: V. Vlachou (ed.), Pots, Workshops and Early Iron Age Society: Function and Role of Ceramics in Early Greece. Proceedings of the International Symposium Held at the Université libre de Bruxelles 14–16 November 2013 (Brussels 2015) 49–74.

Whitley 1994
J. Whitley, Protoattic Pottery. A Contextual Approach, in I. Morris (ed.), Classical Greece. Ancient Histories and Modern Archaeologies (Cambridge 1994) 51–70.

Young 1942
R. Young, Graves from the Phaleron Cemetery, AJA 46, 1942, 23–57.

Social Network Analysis and Connoisseurship in the Study of Athenian Potters' Communities

Eleni Hasaki – Diane Harris Cline

Introduction

This article presents a Social Network Analysis (SNA) of the collaborations between Athenian potters and painters of the 7th–5th centuries BC as established by Sir John D. Beazley in the first half of the 20th century AD. In his foundational connoisseurship studies, Beazley identified more than 1.000 potters and painters for over 20.000 black-figured and red-figured vases. His attributions, often critiqued for the opacity of his methodology, have remained largely unchallenged and yet are still central to stylistic analysis of these pots. Our project, entitled *Social Networks of Athenian Potters,* is the first to apply Social Network Analysis to visualize, quantify, and evaluate these associations and interconnections, moving beyond linear lists of painters and potters and encouraging scholars to obtain a synoptic view of the Athenian Kerameikos. The visualizations of the SNA reframe artisans into their roles as facilitators, bridges, and innovators.

Beazley, Connoisseurship, and the Athenian Ceramic Industry

The connoisseurship of Attic vase painting of the Archaic and Classical periods is synonymous with the career of Sir John Davidson Beazley, Lincoln Professor of Classical Archaeology at Oxford University. His pioneering research on Athenian vase-painters needs no lengthy introduction.[1] Over a series of articles in the first decades of the 20th century and often incorporating other scholars' attribution studies, he accomplished the Herculean task of attributing several thousands of Athenian pots decorated in black and red figure techniques to over 1.000 hands that he identified. He summarized his results in two fundamental works, Attic Red-figure Vase-Painters (ARV) and Attic Black-figure Vase-Painters (ABV).[2] Although Beazley was a highly-gifted visual person himself, the volumes have no illustrations nor diagrams to show relationships between artists or the overall organization. Surprisingly no table of contents is included and dates are rarely mentioned.

Beazley shifted the focus from the vases of painters who signed their works to unnamed artists, by discerning distinctive habits to identify the hands of various unrecognized artisans and attribute unsigned pots to them. Without openly stating it, he applied what is called the "Morellian-type" connoisseurship studies, already utilized in Renaissance art, where idiosyncratic renderings of figures (such as faces, hands, feet) capture the essential style of an artist. His kaleidoscope of names for these previously unrecognized artists was most often based on the museum collection of their most representative

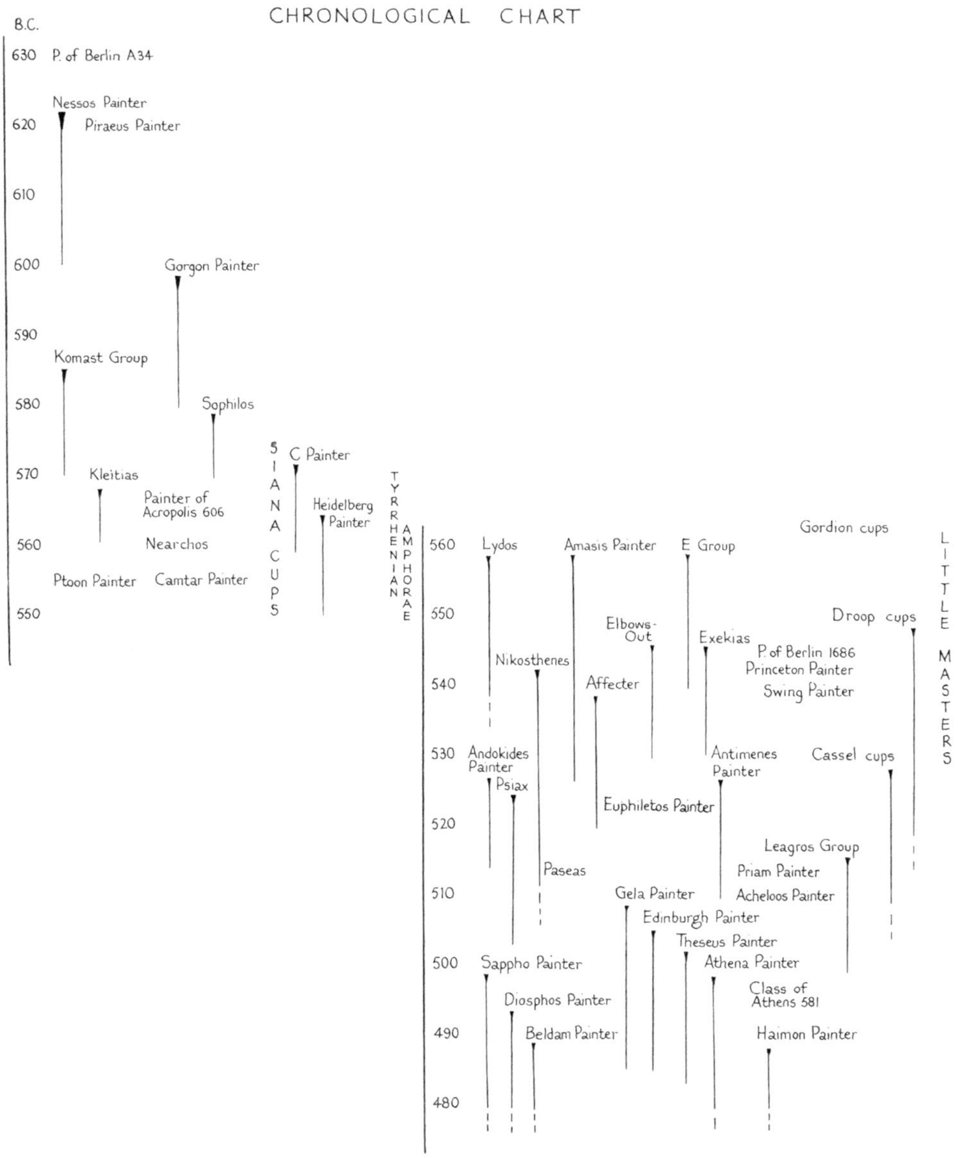

Fig. 1: Chronological chart of Athenian black-figure vase-painters.

vase ("The Painter of London B 76," ABV 85), on their preferred iconography ("The Theseus Painter," ABV 518–521), or on a peculiar feature ("Elbows Out," ABV 248–251). All names were presumed to be male, as are all the surviving signatures of potters and vase-painters, although women must have played a support role in specific tasks, such as painting subsidiary decoration.[3]

It is easy to confuse his stylistic personalities (574 entities: 406 artists and 168 groups for the black figure) with actual people and as a result, Beazley's large number of "hands" (many of them relying on tiny samples)[4] led to reconstructions of industrial scale potters' quarters. It is ironic that his reconstructed *Kerameikos* (potters' quarter) led scholars to believe that the Athenian vase-painting industry was of grand size, when his original intention was precisely to correct the previously-held view, especially in French academic quarters, that imagined a "Kerameikos as a 'small industrial empire' where a few masters who took the trouble to sign their works had command over a whole host of decorators who were inevitably of lowlier status."[5]

Beazley admitted that in several cases he may have identified as two distinct hands what were really just different phases of a single painter's career, so there may actually be fewer artists than we have considered.[6] Moreover, one must not forget that the period under consideration spans more than a century.

The archaeology of ceramic production had not advanced much when Beazley was constructing his connoisseurship-based "potters' quarters" in the pre-World War II years. In a contemporary article, B. F. Cook could list only ca. 60 sites with kilns known from ancient Greece from all periods, whereas today that number has expanded tenfold.[7] Beazley used the term "workshop" only once in ABV, and then only in passing,[8] and we do not have a clear idea how he envisioned a potters' quarter at work. In some cases, spatial imagery seemed to guide his web of artists' relationships: the Painter of "Oinochoai with Large Lips" was thought to work "next door to the Class of Vatican 440" (ABV 442). Proximity in the potters' quarter was likely integral to a painter's stylistic development.

Scholars investigating the scale of pottery production in Archaic and Classical Athens have employed a number of different approaches. They have studied the iconography of potters at work,[9] have estimated the annual output of painters and the length of their careers,[10] have calculated extent of physical workshop space,[11] and have gauged the size of the workforce as well as the number of kilns each workshop could operate efficiently.[12] The ancient evidence is now used often in tandem with ethnographic parallels and ethnoarchaeological data.

The emerging consensus is that a typical pottery workshop was a family-based enterprise, working full-time, year around, with small business capital. With their modestly-sized kilns, they operated on short production cycles and avoided risky business strategies. The mass quantity of Athenian ceramics that reached the Mediterranean ports ought not to be seen as mass production by a few workshops operating at an industrial scale, but the aggregate result of many small units.

The Social Vocabulary of Beazley's *Attic Black-Figure Vase-Painters*

After reading ABV cover to cover, at the macro level we saw an interconnected social world of potters and painters tied to each other through vase shapes and artistic styles. We believed this presented a great opportunity to explore this world further by treating the people and their pots as a data set for Social Network Analysis (SNA). How did Beazley envision the social world of the Athenian Kerameikoi? In ABV, Beazley used social vocabulary to identify the different artistic communities, such as "Lydos and his Companions" (ABV 107) or "The Antimenes Painter and his Circle" (ABV 266). Beazley saw before him individuals who were physically or artistically near to each other, who painted in the manner of others, or were as intimately close as family members could be. Beazley called the Antimenes Painter and Psiax "brothers" (ABV 266), at least in connoisseurship terms, while we also learn from signatures that two Little Master Cup Potters, Tleson and Ergoteles (ABV 162,178), were literally brothers, who signed their names with the patronymic to emphasize their proximity to their famous and successful father, the potter Nearchos.

Beazley used over thirty different qualitative terms in all to relate his derivative painters to major artists.[13] His most common pairing would be "Painter X" and "Near Painter X." Another typical sequence of associations may be seen in the cluster of "The C Painter" (a painter named after the Corinthianizing works he produced), who was followed by the "Manner of the C Painter" and by "Related to the C Painter" (ABV 23–26). Phrases like "not far from", "in imitation of", and "follower of" also occur more regularly than a phrase used once, such as "next door to". While one might wonder what the difference meant to Beazley between "not far from" and "near", we interpreted them as a link, if two entities were linked by Beazley in any qualitative way, we accepted that as a pair.

While a family-based apprenticeship is implied in the father-son specialty in Little Master Cups, in other cases, Beazley was more explicit about direct learning and training.[14] For example, he described the Swing Painter as the teacher of the Princeton Painter (ABV 132) and declared that the Eucharides Painter must have been the pupil of the Nikoxenos Painter (ABV 173). A community of practice develops in all these ways, with artists influencing each other either directly through formal apprenticeship or indirectly through oblique transmission.

His language shows that he had an intertwined community of practice in mind. Beazley put the people – potters and painters – front and center, because their activities and interactions led to the development of the styles and shapes of Attic black figure vase-painting. Artistic styles and shapes may tell us something about the social relationships inside communities of artists. To connect artists who did not sign their pots, we made the assumption that contemporary potters or painters who were working in the same style or making the same shape of pot must be aware of each other, either directly or obliquely. Maybe they saw each other's work in the agora or at the port. Vase shapes often linked these groups of artists, as innovations were adopted and passed forward.

Social Network Analysis (SNA) and Beazley's Athenian Potters' Quarters

To model these communities inside the Athenian potters' quarters, we embarked in our project *Social Networks of Athenian Potters*. We decided to use SNA, which has its roots

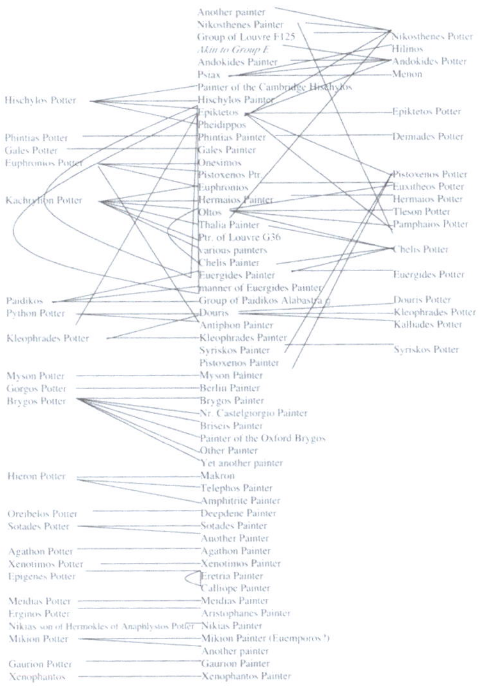

Fig. 2a: Old method of visualizing collaborations among potters and painters of Athenian red-figure pottery.

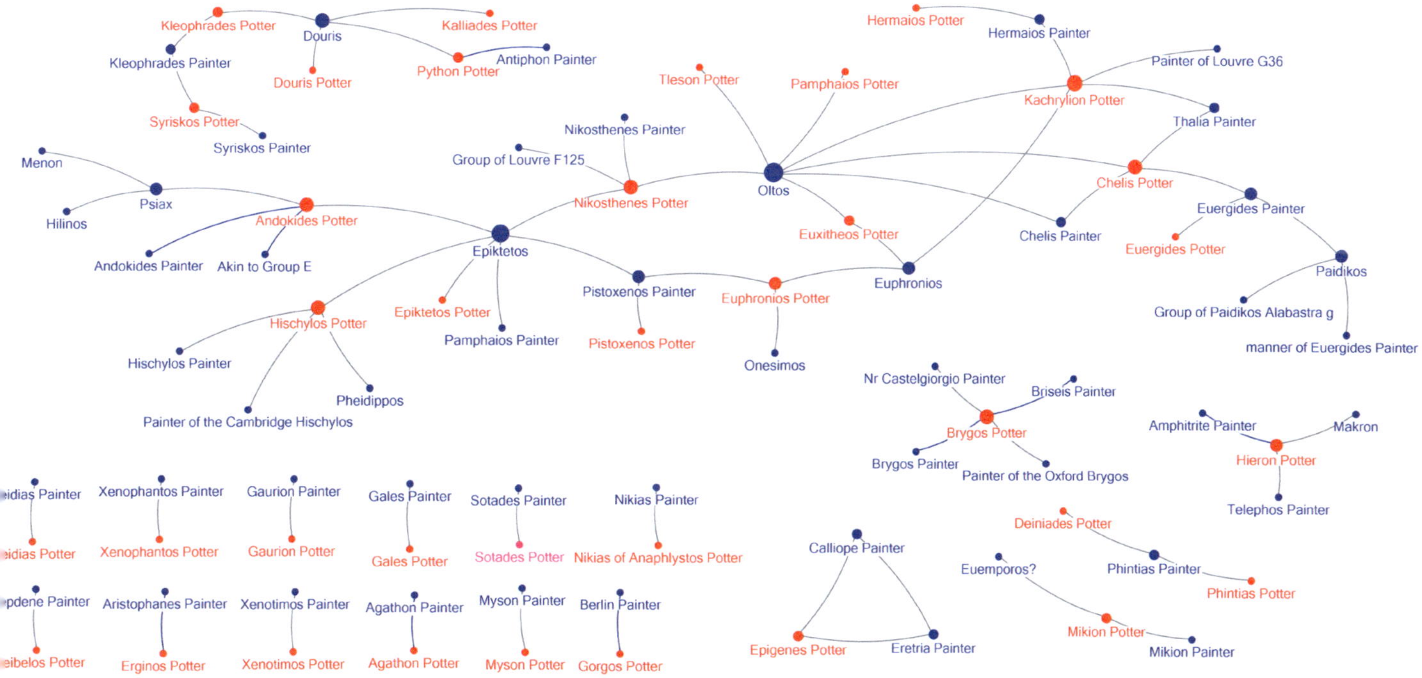

Fig. 2b: New method of visualizing collaborations among potters and painters of Athenian red-figure pottery.

in the combination of mathematics, graph theory, and sociology. Basically SNA is the study of relationships between entities (people, artifacts, institutions). Researchers in dozens of fields use it, and there is a shared language with common tools and methods.[15] Increasingly SNA is being applied in many fields in the humanities, including archaeology and history, and is an analytical technique in the toolbox of the Digital Humanities, the application of quantitative methods to traditional humanities topics.[16]

SNA is ideal for visualizing in their entirety large communities of artists. Previously, Athenian vase-painters were only visually put together in simple timeline graphs without any reference to their relationships. For example, Boardman's chronological chart featured only 45 black-figure artists from 630–480 BC (fig. 1).[17]

A wire diagram by Osborne in 2004 was the most ambitious attempt to capture the complexity of collaborations among Athenian red-figure vase-painters in Beazley's ARV^2 (fig. 2a). His goal to illustrate three modes of collaborations between red-figure painters and potters: a) one potter with one painter; b) one potter with several painters (or one painter with several potters); and c) many potters and many painters working together. Although the visual impression may have fallen short of its goals, it was precisely this wire diagram that inspired us to build the first prototype of applying SNA to Beazley's work.[18]

We took the same data from the wire diagram (fig. 2a) to generate a social network graph, a sociogram (fig. 2b). The method involves reformatting the names of collaborators into two columns as pairs (called an "edge list"). The pairs are then processed by the software, NodeXL. The network visualization is generated from the pairs of names imported into the SNA program, representing the names of the entities as nodes and the ties between them as lines called edges.

As in Osborne's wire diagram, now we can see who worked with whom, but we can also see which artists took on the role of bridges or brokers between areas of the networks. In this sample, there are 88 named artists (excluding the 6 unnamed artists) with 74 ties between them. They are not all connected, however. The largest cluster (around Oltos and Epiktetos) consists of 39 artists who are all linked together in one component, running through the middle of the sociogram. The chain above it (around Douris) has nine interconnected collaborators. There are 19 separate components, most of them (12) with just two members. By color-coding the nodes to indicate whether the craftsman was the potter (red) or a painter of the vase (blue), the scale of collaborations between potters and painters becomes readily visible.

Once we had this prototype and proof of concept, we proceeded to try to graph all of ABV. In our experiment we used the program NodeXL to apply SNA, in order to model and analyze the relationships between artists.[19] We treated the relationships Beazley described in ABV between artists and the shapes of pots they made as a network. The ties between them became the data we used to visualize and analyze this network.[20] This type of network is called bimodal or bipartite because the pairs are not exclusively the same type of entity, like artist with artist.[21] Instead, we sometimes have ties between like entities, but also have ties between artists and the shapes they potted or decorated.

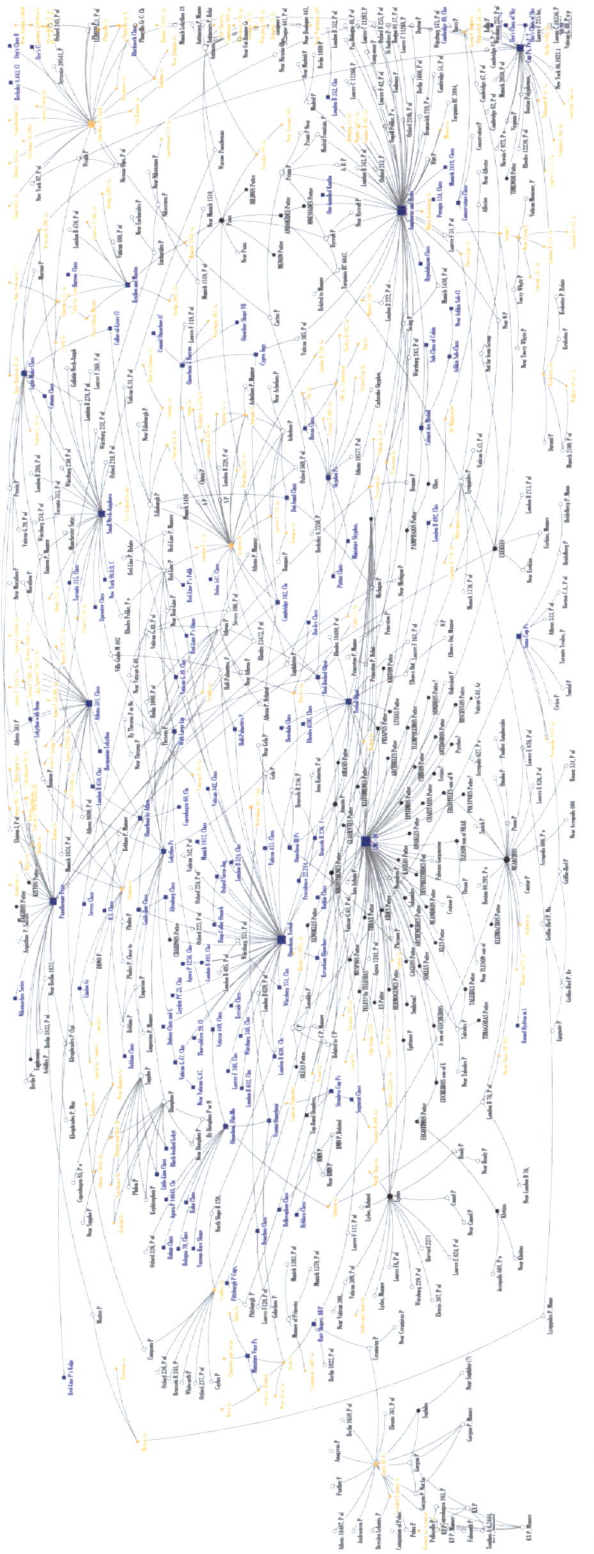

Fig. 3: The SNA Network of Beazley's ABV (incl. Paralipomena). Solid circles represent signed artists; open circles are for attributed artists; diamonds represent "groups"; and squares are for "classes" and shapes.

Classes of vases are tied to other classes or the larger category of shapes, but also to the artists who worked on similar shapes contemporaneously. Sometimes when a dataset seems bimodal, one can avoid this by making direct ties between nodes who share the common entity, such as in this case tying artists to each other when they paint or pot the same shape. We decided not to do this, since some shapes (such as amphorae) survive beyond a generation of craftsmen. In our network, an artist can be associated with a class as well as a shape, and can collaborate with a group of artists as well as individuals. This means it is actually an affiliation network, which one can understand if one imagines that the nodes were individual members of organizations tied to one or more people through membership, but in this case our shapes of pots are the organizations.

Using a statistical package included in all SNA programs, one can measure an individual person's centrality or position relative to others in the network, and describe who should be seen as part of the core and who is peripheral. The network visualizations generated can identify the possible routes of transmission of ideas, new products, and the diffusion of innovation. Once we built the model, we then looked for structural bridges, brokers, and hubs, using measures of centrality and degree, as commonly applied in SNA studies.

In a book as sweeping in scope as Beazley's ABV, it can be difficult to keep all of the connections between the potters and painters in mind at once. The SNA sociograms help us see the relationships from the network perspective, synoptically, allowing us to study unique artists in their contexts. With all artists, groups, and shapes in one visualization, patterns can be observed which can initiate a series of inquiries. We chose SNA for its ability to provide a way to keep track of and display these social relations through a network visualization. SNA is used in many other fields to look for and trace pathways for the diffusion of innovations. Here our social network analyses reframe the relative importance of artists from being based on the influence of their style or the relative perfection of their craftsmanship into a ranking by their roles as facilitators, bridges, and innovators based on their positions in the network.

Using Beazley's ABV as the source of our data, we extracted and harvested social information about the potters and painters working in the black-figure technique in 7th–5th centuries BC.[22] As we looked in ABV for the ties between people working in the Potters' Quarter, we found three main categories: individuals like Exekias; groups of artists given one title (Group E); and vase shapes such as Little Master Cups.[23] We followed Beazley in relying on shapes of vases as nodes to connect artisans to each other.[24] We adopted Beazley's shape-centered taxonomy system to stay true to his original vision, believing that two artists of the same period would not develop this particular shape (for example, Oenochoai, Trefoil, Shapes I–II) without knowing each other's work.

We identified 701 nodes in ABV and Paralipomena consisting of artists (signed and attributed), groups, classes, and shapes. In our multimodal sociogram we differentiated the

101	EXEKIAS	Group E
102	Group E	Near Group E
103	Near Group E	Vatican 347, Gr
104	Near Group E	London B 145, Gr
105	Near Group E	Vatican Mourner, P of
106	Near Group E	London B 174, Gr
107	Near Group E	Towry Whyte P
108	Towry Whyte P	Near Towry Whyte P
109	Group E	Not far from Group E and Exekias
110	EXEKIAS	Not far from Group E and Exekias
111	EXEKIAS	London B 213, P of
112	EXEKIAS	Exekias, Manner
113	EXEKIAS	Near Exekias
114	Exekias, Manner	Near Exekias
115	AMASIS Potter	Amasis P

Fig. 4: Sample edge list of Exekias and Group E.

node types visually, using diamonds, circles, and squares (fig. 3). In this network there are currently 80 individual artists whose real names are known because of their signatures and 326 artists given names through attribution.[25] Furthermore, the network includes 168 of Beazley's artist "groups", and 127 vase shapes including Beazley's "classes".[26]

The network has 863 ties (or "edges" in network terms) linking the nodes, modeling a complex web of interactions between artists working in the Kerameikos of Athens to produce ceramics of various shapes (fig. 3).

We recorded the variety of qualitative distinctions in the styles of artists, such as "near" and "in the manner of" in the edge list. In the example below we show how we recorded ties between artists whom Beazley thought belonged together (Fig. 4). The two columns should be read row by row, and the data shows there is a tie between each pair of nodes. Using the case of Exekias, an individual artist and a cluster of artists called Group E which Beazley thought were close to him, we can see the variety of ties between them. However, for the sociogram we decided to flatten out these subtle differences in Beazley's characterizations of the ties between artists.

One look at the sociogram shows that there are some nodes which appear to be popular, that is, they are a hub for many other nodes, while others have only one connection or tie and are therefore relatively unimportant. Degree centrality is a measure of the relative number of nodes with the most ties. In the sociogram, the entities with the most ties, or highest degree centrality, are shapes and artists (fig. 5). These high-scoring nodes are lit up along with the edges tying them to others. Visually the eye is drawn to these nodes first. These high-degree scorers often serve as a hub for multiple nodes which have only this particular hub as its single tie. In this case, often the highest scoring entity in degree centrality are shapes. Single artists identified by Beazley are tied together by a shape they all make, such as a trefoil oinochoe. The likelihood that these artists would make the shape or paint the decoration independently without knowing of each other's work is nil. They are part of a community of practice, in other words, a social network.

The shapes which connect the largest numbers of potters and painters are the Little Master Cup and Droop Cup Painters, with 61 ties. In second place, with 55 ties,

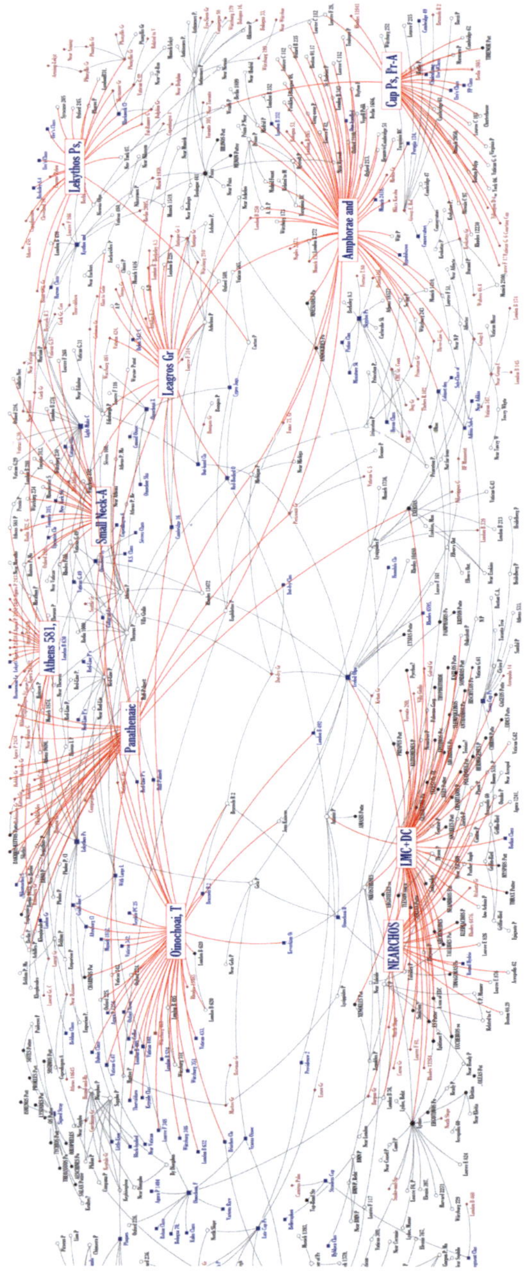

LMC+DC	61
Amphorae and Hydriae Ps	55
Oinochoai, Trefoil I-II Ps	43
Panathenaic Prize Amphora Ps	29
Cup Ps, Pr-A/A	27
Leagros Gr	25
Small Neck-Amphorae Ps	23
Lekythos Ps, Earlier	22
Athens 581, Class	22
NEARCHOS	21
Lydos	15
Trefoil Olpai	15
Early BF Ps	14
Light-Make Class	14
Antimenes P	13
Signed Strays	13
Athena P	12
Lekythos Ps	11
Red-Line P	11
Theseus P	11
Komast Gr	11
Psiax	10

Fig. 5: Degree Centrality of ABV (incl. Paralipomena) featuring the ten nodes which have the most neighbors.

LMC+DC	69931.136
Amphorae and Hydriae Ps	40585.814
Trefoil Olpai	38620.101
Lekythos Ps, Earlier	32679.194
Oinochoai, Trefoil I-II Ps	32224.675
Lekythos Ps	28457.429
Cactus P	24908.595
NIKOSTHENES Potter	24520.056
Panathenaic Prize Amphora Ps	22649.363
Amasis P	21864.772
Leagros Gr	21310.915
Red-Bodied Olpai	20834.843
EXEKIAS	20237.297
Gela P	19901.268
Rare Shapes; All Periods	18671.167
Wraith P	18540.306
Cup Ps, Pr-A/A	18422.000
Athens 581, Class	18154.829
Ceramicus P	16883.000
Early BF Ps	15946.500
Perizoma Gr	15896.494
Nicosia Olpe, P of	15185.604

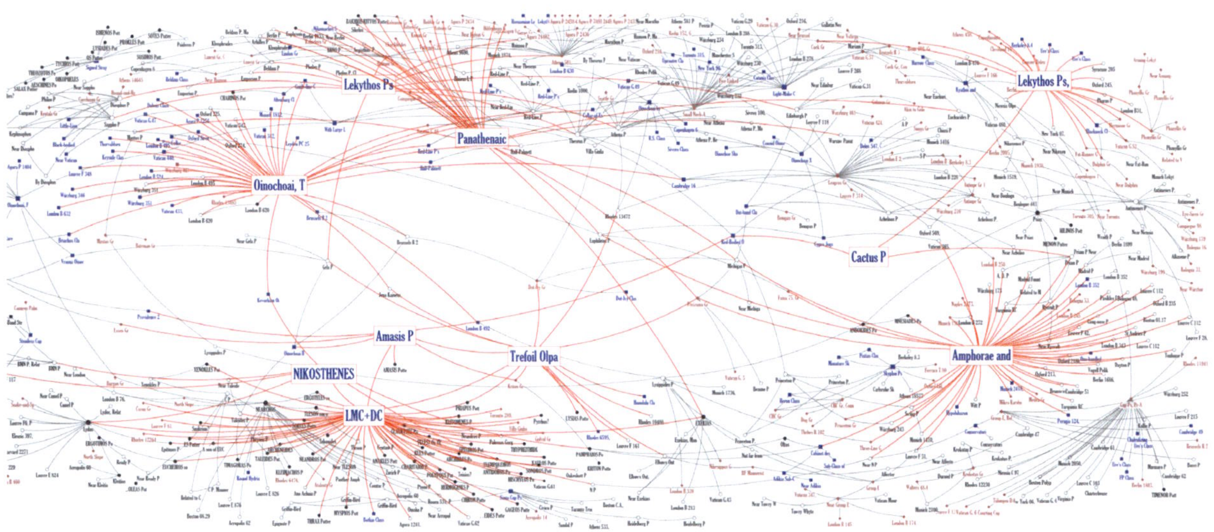

Fig. 6: Betweenness Centrality of ABV (incl. Paralipomena) showing the most important nodes for connecting the network.

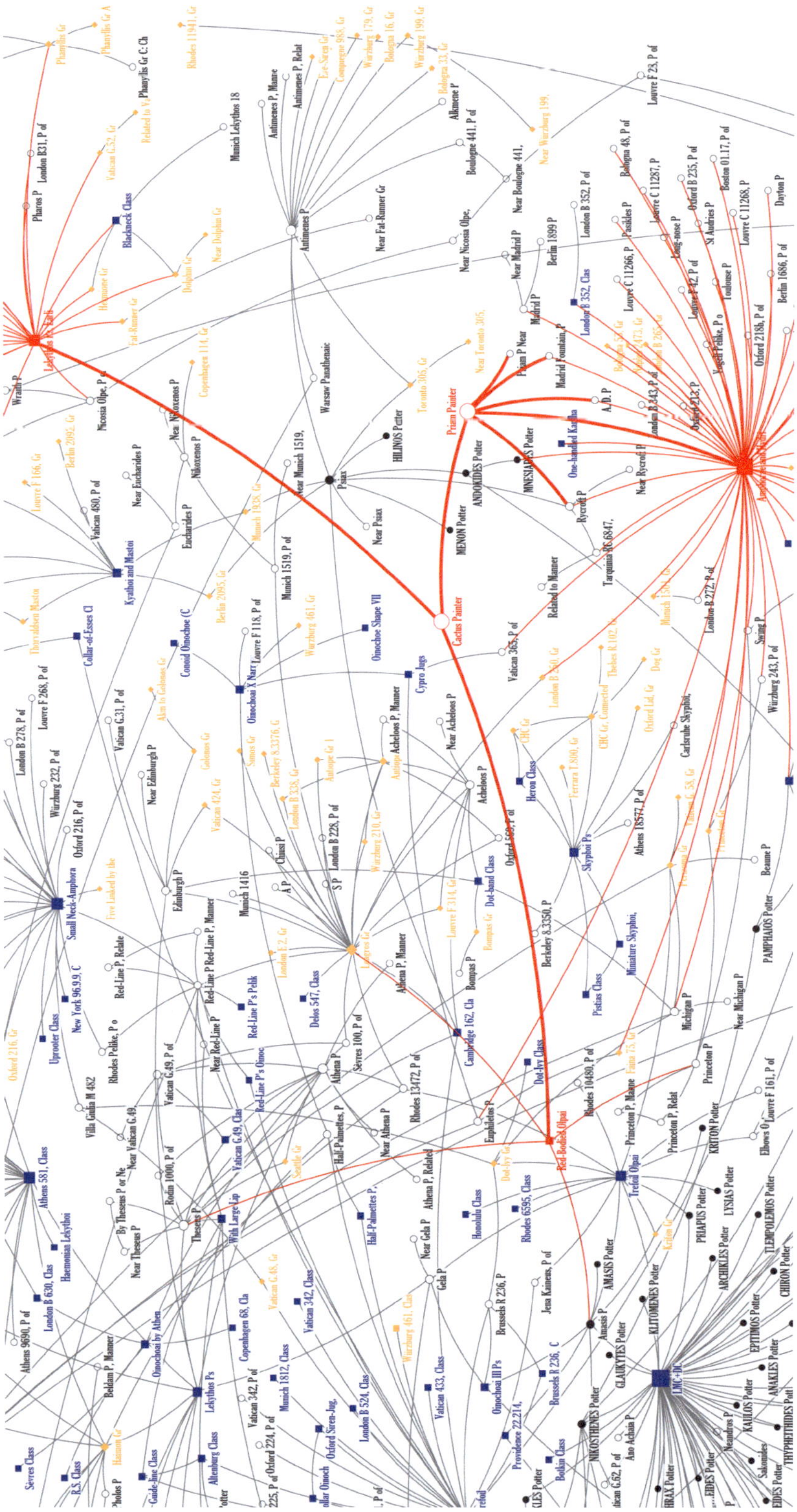

Fig. 7: Detail with Cactus Painter and his ties.

are Oinochoai Painters and then Proto A and A Cup Painters. In terms of individual artists, the top twenty with the highest degree centrality scores (those with the most neighbors) includes the potter Nearchos, Lydos, the Antimenes Painter, the Athena Painter, and the Theseus Painter. The Leagros Group and Komast Group are also in the top twenty.

Our analysis also gave us a ranking of the nodes by their position in the network as a bridge or broker, a network metric called "betweenness centrality".[27] Such nodes are the shortest path between most others in the network, through which information can pass efficiently. Looking for these chains of nodes in a sociogram one can find pathways for the diffusion of stylistic influences and technical innovation. The shapes with the highest betweenness scores are the Little Master and Droop Cup Painters, Amphorae and Hydriae Painters, Trefoil Olpai Painters, The Earlier Lekythos Painters, and the Oinochoai Trefoil I–II Painters. For individual artists, those with high "betweenness centrality" scores are the Cactus Painter, then the Nikosthenes Potter, Amasis Painter, Exekias, the Gela Painter, the Wraith Painter, and the Ceramicus Painter (fig. 6).

Social network statistics are also useful for highlighting anomalies. For instance, consider the Cactus Painter, who scored the highest in betweenness centrality, but is a relatively unknown painter.[28] In a detail showing the right side of the sociogram, we see the pathway from left to upper right from the painters of red-bodied olpai which are in the heart of the network out towards the right side, where the Cactus painter is connected to the Priam Painter, and upwards to the earlier painters of the Lekythos shape (fig. 7). This group is relatively isolated; in fact, the only path any of them have to connect with the rest of the network is through the Cactus Painter. Likewise, taking a second hop on the path, the Earlier Lekythoi Painters could reach the Priam Painter, through whom they have direct access to the second largest cluster, the Amphorae and Hydriae Painters. The high "betweenness centrality" scores for both the Cactus Painter and the Priam Painter comes from their service as a bridge between major shapes.

Conclusions

Through this application of SNA to Athenian vase painting in the *Social Networks of Athenian Potters Project*, undertaken for the first time, Beazley's world of artists can be seen in one visualization, in a synoptic rather than linear way. Our next steps are to add in dates and create time slices in order to filter out those who are not chronological contemporaries, so we can better study the activity inside the social networks of synchronous artists. This is important to do because in a synoptic view as we have here, it would be likely that the earliest artists are going to be less well connected and have fewer ties than later ones. This happens because these artists are elderly or deceased by the time later artists are most active. If there are ties between the earliest artists and later ones, it would be through the common shapes they decorated, which continue beyond the generations of artisans. We also will move forward in time to incorporate the data from Attic Red-Figure Vase-Painters (ARV^2) along with modern scholarship to supplement Beazley's attributions.

In sum, SNA sociograms are not an end in themselves but a way to make discoveries. They are good for finding patterns and anomalies, and also for finding good starting points in terms of prioritizing who or which group to investigate first. We use the sociograms to expand the research agenda for the study of Attic vase painting and potting. Through SNA metrics we can identify the important people, who tend to be connected to more than one shape, acting as bridges and innovators. SNA can identify artists who are worthy of study not because of the high artistic quality of the work or the large quantity of extant samples, but because of the artist's relative position inside the potters' quarter, connecting smaller clusters to the whole network. Studying the chains of linked artists and shapes leads to curiosity about specific nodes that seem to hold central positions inside their corner of the network map. Such high scoring nodes may hold the keys to how innovations flow and catch on. There are many more opportunities to zoom in and study discrete clusters and how they are linked.

Our goal for this innovative and experimental project has been to bring together connoisseurship studies of communities of practice and social network analysis. We hope the sociograms visualizing the connoisseurship-based ties that Beazley established among the Athenian artists will open up wider vistas of analysis of their Kerameikoi in ancient Athens and beyond.

Appendix I

Because of the curious absence of a table of contents in Beazley's ABV, it is not readily apparent that eighteen of his chapters (VIII, XII, XIII, XIV, XX, XXII, XXVI–XXXII, XL–XLIV) are organized around the shape of the vases and the artisans who made them. Twenty-one chapters (III–VII, IX–XI, XV, XVII–XIX, XXIII, XXIV, XXXIII–XXXIX) are focused on an individual artist's personality and those he assigned to be near him. Just four of his chapters (I, II, XVI, XXV) use chronology or decoration technique to organize the artisans he features. In the chart below, we list the ABV chapter titles with the modifications for our project shown in italics. We reduced the original 44 chapters to a total of 34 by merging Chapters III–V as Siana Cup Painters; and Chapters XXXIII–XXXIX as Lekythos Painters.

<table>
<tr><td colspan="2">Ch. I: Earliest Black-Figure</td><td colspan="2">Ch. XXIII: The Leagros Group</td></tr>
<tr><td colspan="2">Ch. II: Early Black-Figure</td><td colspan="2">Ch. XXIV: The Nikoxenos Painter and his Companions (Nikoxenos Painter)</td></tr>
<tr><td>Ch. III: Painters of Siana Cups (PSC): I, The C Painter</td><td rowspan="3">Siana Cup Painters</td><td colspan="2">Ch. XXV: Black-Figure Vases by Red-Figure Painters</td></tr>
<tr><td>Ch. IV: PSC II; The Heidelberg Painter</td><td colspan="2">Ch. XXVI: Some Very Late Standard Neck-Amphorae</td></tr>
<tr><td>Ch. V: PSC III; Others</td><td colspan="2">Ch. XXVII: Panathenaic Prize Amphorae</td></tr>
<tr><td colspan="2">Ch. VI: Kleitias</td><td colspan="2">Ch. XXVIII: Oinochoai, Trefoil, I: Shapes I and II</td></tr>
<tr><td colspan="2">Ch. VII: Nearchos and Others (Nearchos)</td><td colspan="2">Ch. XXIX: Oinochoai, Trefoil or Beaked: Less Common Shapes</td></tr>
<tr><td colspan="2">Ch. VIII: The Tyrrhenian Group</td><td colspan="2">Ch. XXX: Oinochoai, Flat Mouthed (other than Olpai)</td></tr>
<tr><td colspan="2">Ch. IX: Lydos and His Companions (Lydos)</td><td colspan="2">Ch. XXXI: Oinochoai: Olpai</td></tr>
<tr><td colspan="2">Ch. X: Group E and Exekias (Exekias)</td><td colspan="2">Ch. XXXII: Lekythos-Painters, I; Chiefly Earlier</td></tr>
<tr><td colspan="2">Ch. XI: The Amasis Painter</td><td>Ch. XXXIII: Lekythos-Painters, II: The Gela Painter</td><td rowspan="7">Lekythos Painters</td></tr>
<tr><td colspan="2">Ch. XII: Little-Master Cups (and Droop Cups) (LMC+DC)</td><td>Ch. XXXIV: Lekythos-Painters, III: The Edinburgh Painter</td></tr>
<tr><td colspan="2">Ch. XIII: Cups Types Proto-A and A</td><td>Ch. XXXV: Lekythos-Painters IV: The Class of Athens 581</td></tr>
<tr><td colspan="2">Ch. XIV: Some Stemless Cups</td><td>Ch. XXXVI: Lekythos-Painters V: The Sappho and Diosphos Painters</td></tr>
<tr><td colspan="2">Ch. XV: Nikosthenes and Pamphaios</td><td>Ch. XXXVII: Lekythos-Painters VI: The Theseus and Athena Painters</td></tr>
<tr><td colspan="2">Ch. XVI: The Black-Figure Mannerists</td><td>Ch. XXXVIII: Lekythos-Painters VII: The Haimon Group</td></tr>
<tr><td colspan="2">Ch. XVII: The Lysippides Painter</td><td>Ch. XXXIX: Lekythos-Painters, VIII: The Emporion and Beldam Painters</td></tr>
<tr><td colspan="2">Ch. XVIII: The Antimenes Painter and his Circle (The Antimenes Painter)</td><td colspan="2">Ch. XL: Small Neck-Amphorae</td></tr>
<tr><td colspan="2">Ch. XIX: Psiax</td><td colspan="2">Ch. XLI: Kyathoi and Mastoids</td></tr>
<tr><td colspan="2">Ch. XX: Other Pot-Painters (Amphorae and Hydriae Painters)</td><td colspan="2">Ch. XLII: Skyphoi</td></tr>
<tr><td colspan="2">Ch. XXI: Some Signed Strays</td><td colspan="2">Ch. XLIII: Late Cups</td></tr>
<tr><td colspan="2">Ch. XXII: Plaques</td><td colspan="2">Ch. XLIV: Miniature Vases</td></tr>
</table>

Notes

[1] Acknowledgements: Parts of this research were conducted with fellowships in Hellenic Studies at Harvard's Center for Hellenic Studies (Cline and Hasaki); and with the Ailsa Mellon Bruce senior fellowship at the Center for Advanced Study in the Visual Arts, National Gallery of Art in Washington D.C. (Hasaki). We thank both institutions for facilitating our work. We express our deep gratitude to the Oxford Classical Research Center Director Peter Stewart and the Beazley Archive Pottery Database Director Thomas Mannack for their encouragement with this project. We are also indebted to Tyler Jo Smith, Director of The Kerameikos Project (kerameikos.org) and her collaborators Renee Gondek, Ethan Gruber, and Najee Olya, for useful discussions during the early stages of our project. Finally, we thank the two anonymous reviewers for their insightful comments. For surveys with biographical details and professional career of J. D. Beazley, see Kurtz 1983a, 1983b, 1983c, 1985; Von Bothmer 1985, 1997; Robertson 1982; 1991; Rouet 2001; Arrington 2017.

[2] Beazley 1942 (ARV); 1956 (ABV); 1963 (ARV²); 1971 (Paralipomena).

[3] See the sole example of a woman painting the handles of a volute crater depicted on the "Caputi" red-figured Athenian hydria (Vicenza, Banca Intesa Collection, inv. C 278; Williams 2009). For potters' and painters' signatures, see Bolmarcich and Muskett 2016 with earlier bibliography.

[4] Sapirstein (2014) estimated a total of 620 hands (counting only those who had 2 or more works assigned to them); more than half of Beazley's "hands" out of 620 have fewer than ten extant works, whereas only the fifty-four most prolific "hands" (that is ca. 8%) have more than 100 attributed vases.

[5] Rouet 2001, 107.

[6] ABV 330: "I now take the Priam Painter to be the same as what I once called the Painter of London B 332; his earlier phase."

[7] Cook 1961. The WebAtlas of Ceramic Kilns in Ancient Greece (Hasaki web; atlasgreekkilns.arizona.edu; last accessed Nov. 14, 2018) includes over 600 kilns from the Bronze Age to the Post Byzantine Period.

[8] "Oinochoai by the Athena Painter or from his Workshop" (ABV 263; Krokotos Workshop (ABV 98); Workshop of Nikosthenes (Paralipomena 435).

[9] Chatzidimitriou 2005; Williams 2009; Bentz et al. 2010; Hasaki 2013; Hasaki 2020.

[10] Cook 1959; Sapirstein 2013; Stissi 2016; Sapirstein this volume; Stissi this volume.

[11] Hasaki 2011.

[12] Hasaki 2002; Hasaki 2006; Acton 2014, 73–115.

[13] Beazley's fierce critics, although never able to challenge his attributions, condemned the lack of transparency in methodology and in definition of the terms. Robertson (1982) presents them in alphabetical order, masking their frequency or Beazley's hierarchy. For a summary of criticism on Beazley and his vase-painting connoisseurship, see Whitley 1997. The responses by Oakley (1998, 1999) remain a passionate but fitting manifesto for the value of connoisseurship studies. More recently, see Neer 2005.

[14] For craft apprenticeship in the Classical world, see Hasaki 2012.

[15] Wasserman and Faust 2014; Watts 2003; Collar 2013.

[16] For ancient history and classical studies, some samples of data sets analyzed with SNA include analysis of literary sources for Alexander the Great (Cline 2012), Socrates (Cline 2019 web), social relationships in Classical Athens (Cline 2020), and the Amarna Letters of Bronze Age Egypt (Cline 2015; Cline and Cline 2015); epigraphical evidence, such as the inscriptions of family links for Hellenistic sculptors on Rhodes (Larson 2013)

and the inscriptions of the network of theoroi for the Sanctuary of the Great Gods on Samothrace (Blakely 2016; Blakely web), relations between cults in Roman religion (Collar 2013), brick manufacturers along the Tiber (Graham 2006; Ostborn and Gerding 2016); and archaeological evidence for Roman cargoes (Leidwanger 2016), as well as prehistorical maritime networks (Leidwanger et al. 2014), and imports in Bronze Age Italy (Blake 2014). For the more recent surveys of SNA uses in archaeology, see Brughmans 2013; Knappett 2013; Brughmans et al. 2016; Mills 2017.

[17] Boardman 1974, 234 f.

[18] Osborne 2004, 90 fig. 6.8.

[19] We used the term "artists" to maintain the focus on the social dimension of these communities of practice. Sapirstein (2014) has proposed the term "hands," a valid alternative.

[20] For the software, see <https://www.smrfoundation.org/nodexl/> NodeXL, Gephi and UCINET are the most commonly used in historical network research. For NodeXL, see Hansen et al. 2011; for Gephi, see Cherven 2013; and for UCInet, see Borgatti et al. 2013. These excellent handbooks for users of all levels introduce basic concepts and provide step-by-step guidance for constructing and interpreting social networks.

[21] Wasserman and Faust 1994, 291–343.

[22] We updated ABV entries with Paralipomena (Beazley 1971) and Addenda (Burn – Glynn 1982). At this phase of the research we have not included later attributions.

[23] For a general survey of the Beazley Archive Online, see Kurtz 2004; Smith 2005.

[24] For full titles of the ABV chapters and our modifications for the SNA study, see Appendix I.

[25] This number includes both the attributed artists (235) and 91 derivative ones linked to signed or attributed artists with the terms "near", "follower", "not far from", "close", "related", "in the manner of".

[26] Beazley's term "group" refers to vases related through a likeness in drawing. His term "class" is for vases he put together for likeness of potter-work – in other words, their shape (Robertson 1982, xiv–xv).

[27] Newman 2005.

[28] Beazley Archive Pottery Database lists only 8 vases attributed to him (last accessed Dec. 15, 2018)

Image Credits

Fig. 1: adapted from Boardman 1974. – Fig. 2a: from Osborne 2004 – Fig. 2b: by the authors. – Fig. 3–7: by the authors. The sociograms in figs. 2, 3, 5–7 are also available on the *Social Networks of Athenian Potters* website (snap.sbs.arizona.edu).

References

Acton 2014

P. Acton, Poeisis: Manufacturing in Classical Athens (Oxford 2014).

Arrington 2017

N.T. Arrington, Connoisseurship, Vases and Greek Art and Archaeology, in: J.M. Padgett (ed.), The Berlin Painter and His World. Athenian Vase-Painting in the Early Fifth Century BC (New Haven 2017) 21–39.

Beazley 1942

J.D. Beazley, Attic Red-Figure Vase-Painters (Oxford 1942).

Beazley 1956

J.D. Beazley, Attic Black-Figure Vase-Painters (Oxford 1956).

Beazley 1963

J.D. Beazley, Attic Red-Figure Vase-Painters [2](Oxford 1963).

Beazley 1971

J.D. Beazley, Paralipomena. Additions to Attic Black-Figure Vase-Painters and to Attic Red-Figure Vase-Painters (Oxford 1971).

Bentz et al. 2010

M. Bentz – W. Geominy – J.M. Müller (eds.), TonArt. Virtuosität antiker Töpfertechnik (Petersberg 2010).

Blake 2014

E. Blake, Social Networks and Regional Identity in Bronze Age Italy (Cambridge 2014).

Blakely 2016

S. Blakely, Beyond Braudel: Network Models and a Samothracian Seascape, in: C. Concannon – L.A. Mazurek (eds.), Across the Corrupting Sea. Post-Braudelian Approaches to the Ancient Eastern Mediterranean (Abington 2016) 17–38.

Blakely web

S. Blakely, web. "Samothracian Networks". Retrieved from <https://scholarblogs.emory.edu/samothraciannetworks/the-samothracian-social-network/> (last accessed Oct. 30, 2017).

Boardman 1974

J. Boardman, Athenian Black Figure Vases: A Handbook (London 1974).

Bolmarcich – Muskett 2016

S. Bolmarcich – G. Muskett, Artists' Signatures on Archaic Greek Vases from Athens, in: K. Seaman – P. Schultz (eds.), Artists and Artistic Production in Ancient Greece (Cambridge 2016) 154–176.

Borgatti et al. 2013

S.P. Borgatti – M.G. Everett – J.C. Johnson, Analyzing Social Networks (Los Angeles 2013).

Brughmans 2013

T. Brughmans, Thinking Through Networks: A Review of Formal Network Methods in Archaeology, Journal of Archaeological Method and Theory 20, 2013, 623–662.

Brughmans et al. 2016

T. Brughmans – A. Collar – F. Coward (eds.), The Connected Past: Challenges to Network Studies in Archaeology and History (Oxford 2016)

Burn – Glynn 1982

L. Burn – R. Glynn (eds.), Beazley Addenda. Additional References to ABV, ARV[2], and Paralipomena (Oxford 1982).

Chatzidimitriou 2005

A. Chatzidimitriou, Παραστάσεις εργαστηρίων και εμπορίου στην εικονογραφία των αρχαϊκών και κλασικών χρόνων (Athens 2005).

Cherven 2013
K. Cherven, Network Graph Analysis and Visualization with Gephi (Birmingham 2013).
Cline 2012
D.H. Cline, Six Degrees of Alexander: Social Network Analysis as a Tool for Ancient History, Ancient History Bulletin 26, 2012, 59–70.
Cline 2015
D.H. Cline, The Amarna Letters: A Web of Interaction, Journal of Ancient Egyptian Interconnections 7, 2015, 58–60.
Cline 2019 web
D.H. Cline, The Social Network of Socrates, CHS Research Bulletin 7, 2019 <http://nrs.harvard.edu/urn-3:hlnc.essay:ClineD.The_Social_Network_of_Socrates.2019> (last accessed Dec. 20, 2019)
Cline 2020
D.H. Cline, Athens as a Small World, Journal of Historical Network Research 4, 36–56.
Cline – Cline 2015
D.H. Cline – E. Cline, Text Messages, Tablets, and Social Networks in the Late Bronze Age Eastern Mediterranean: The Small World of the Amarna Letters, in: J. Myrnarova et al. (eds.), Egypt and the Near East: Crossroads II. Proceedings of an International Conference on the Relations of Egypt and the Near East in the Bronze Age (Prague 2015) 17–44.
Collar 2013
A. Collar, Religious Networks in the Roman Empire: The Spread of New Ideas (Cambridge 2013).
Cook 1959
R.M. Cook, Die Bedeutung der bemalten Keramik für den griechischen Handel, JdI 74, 1959, 114–123.
Cook 1961
R.M. Cook, The 'Double-Stoking Tunnel' of Greek Kilns, BSA 56, 1961, 64–67.
Graham 2006
S. Graham, Ex figlinis: The Network Dynamics of the Tiber Valley Brick Industry in the Hinterland of Rome, BARIntSer 1486 (Oxford 2006).
Hansen et al. 2011
D. Hansen – B. Shneiderman – M.A. Smith, Analyzing Social Media Networks with NodeXL: Insights from a Connected World (Burlington 2011).
Hasaki 2002
E. Hasaki, Ceramic Kilns in Ancient Greece: Technology and Organization of Ceramic Workshops. (Ph.D. diss. University of Cincinnati 2002). On-line publication <http://etd.ohiolink.edu/view.cgi?acc_num=ucin1023219003> (last accessed Oct. 30, 2017)
Hasaki 2006
E. Hasaki, The Ancient Greek Ceramic Kilns and their Contribution to the Technology and Organization of the Potters' Workshops, in: P. Tasios – C. Palyvou (eds.), Proceedings of the 2nd International Conference on Ancient Greek Technology (Athens 2006) 221–227.
Hasaki 2011
E. Hasaki, Crafting Spaces: Archaeological, Ethnographic, and Ethnoarchaeological Studies on

Spatial Organization in Pottery Workshops in Greece and Tunisia, in: M. Lawall – J. Lund (eds.), Pottery in the Archaeological Record: Greece and Beyond (Aarhus 2011) 12–28.

Hasaki 2012

E. Hasaki, Workshops and Technology, in: T.J. Smith – D. Plantzos (eds.), A Companion to Greek Art (Oxford 2012) 255–274.

Hasaki 2013

E. Hasaki, Craft Apprenticeship in Ancient Greece: Reaching beyond the Masters, in: W. Wendrich (ed.), Archaeology and Apprenticeship: Acquiring Body Knowledge in the Ancient World (Tucson 2013) 171–202

Hasaki 2020

E. Hasaki, Potters at Work in Ancient Corinth. Industry, Religion and the Penteskouphia Pinakes, Hesperia Suppl. 51 (Princeton 2020).

Hasaki web

E. Hasaki (ed.), Web. The WebAtlas of Ceramic Kilns in Ancient Greece.

Knappett 2013

C. Knappett (ed.), Network Analysis in Archaeology. New Approaches to Regional Interaction (Oxford 2013).

Kurtz 1983a

D.C. Kurtz, The Berlin Painter (Oxford 1983).

Kurtz 1983b

D.C. Kurtz, Beazley and the Connoisseurship of Greek Vases, Greek Vases in the J. Paul Getty Museum 2, 1983, 237–250.

Kurtz 1983c

D.C. Kurtz, Gorges' Cup, an Essay in the Connoisseurship of Greek Vases, JHS 103, 1983, 68–86.

Kurtz 1985

D.C. Kurtz, Beazley and Oxford (Oxford 1985).

Kurtz 2004

D. Kurtz, Archaeologia e Calcolatori 15, 2004, 497–508 <www.beazley.ox.ac.uk> (last accessed Oct. 30, 2017)

Larson 2013

K.A. Larson, A Network Approach to Hellenistic Sculptural Production, JMedA 26, 2013, 235–260.

Leidwanger 2016

J. Leidwanger, From Time Capsules to Networks: New Light on Roman Shipwrecks in the Maritime Economy, AJA 121, 2016, 595–619.

Leidwanger et al. 2014

J. Leidwanger – C. Knappett – P. Arnaud – P. Arthur – E. Blake – C. Broodbank – T. Brughmans – T. Evans – S. Graham – E.S. Greene – B. Kowalzig – B. Mills – R. Rivers – T.F. Tartaron – R. – Van de Noort, A Manifesto for the Study of Ancient Mediterranean Maritime Networks, Antiquity 342, 2014, <http://journal.antiquity.ac.uk/projgall/leidwanger342> (last accessed Dec. 12, 2018).

Mills 2017
B.J. Mills, Social Network Analysis in Archaeology, Annual Review of Anthropology 46, 2017, 379–397.
Neer 2005
R. Neer, Connoisseurship and the Stakes of Style, Critical Inquiry 32, 2005, 1–26.
Newman 2005
M. Newman, A Measure of Betweenness Centrality based on Random Walks, Social Networks 27, 2005, 39–54.
Oakley 1998
J.H. Oakley, Why Study Greek Vase-Painter? A Response to Whitley's "Beazley as Theorist", Antiquity 72, 1998, 209–213.
Oakley 1999
J.H. Oakley, 'Through a Glass Darkly'' I: Some Misconceptions about the Study of Greek Vase-Painting in: R.F. Docter – E.M. Moormann (eds.), Classical Archaeology towards the Third Millenium: Reflections and Perspectives. Proceedings of the XVth International Congress of Classical Archaeology, Amsterdam, July 12–17, 1998 (Amsterdam 1999) 286–290.
Osborne 2004
R. Osborne, Workshops and the Iconography and Distribution of Athenian Red-figure Pottery: A Case Study, in: S. Keay – S. Moser (eds.), Greek Art in View: Essays in Honour of Brian Sparkes (Oxford 2004) 78–94.
Östborn – Gerding 2016
P. Östborn – H. Gerding, Brick makers, Builders and Commissioners as Agents in the Diffusion of Hellenistic Fired Bricks: Choosing Social Models to Fit Archaeological Data, Journal of Greek Archaeology 1, 2016, 233–270.
Robertson 1982
C.M. Robertson, Beazley's Use of Terms, in: L. Burn – R. Glynn (eds.), Beazley Addenda. Additional References to ABV, ARV^2, and Paralipomena (Oxford 1982) xi–xviii.
Robertson 1991
C.M. Robertson, Adopting an Approach, in: T. Rasmussen – N. Spivey (eds.), Looking at Greek Vases (Cambridge 1991) 1–12.
Rouet 2001
P. Rouet, Approaches to the Study of Attic Vases: Beazley and Pottier (Oxford 2001).
Sapirstein 2013
P. Sapirstein, Painters, Potters and the Scale of the Attic Vase-Painting Industry, American Journal of Archaeology 117, 2013, 493–510.
Sapirstein 2014
P. Sapirstein, Demographics and Productivity in the Ancient Athenian Pottery Industry, in: J. Oakley (ed.), Athenian Potters and Painters III (Oxford 2014) 175–186.
Smith 2005
T.J. Smith, Beazley Archive: Inside and Out, Art Documentation 24, 2005, 22–25.

Stissi 2016
V. Stissi, Minor Artisans, Major Impact? in: N. Eschbach – S. Schmidt (eds.), Töpfer, Maler, Werkstatt: Zuschreibungen in der griechischen Vasenmalerei und die Organisation antiker Keramikproduktion, CVA Beih. 7 (Munich 2016) 47–53.

von Bothmer 1985
D. Von Bothmer, Beazley the Teacher in: D.C. Kurtz (ed.), Beazley and Oxford (Oxford 1985) 5–17.

von Bothmer 1987
D. Von Bothmer, Greek Vase-Painting: Two Hundred Years of Connoisseurship, in: M. True (ed.), Papers on the Amasis Painter and His World (Los Angeles 1987) 184–204.

Wasserman – Faust 1994
S. Wasserman – K. Faust, Social Network Analysis: Methods and Applications (Cambridge 1994).

Watts 2003
D. Watts, Six Degrees: The Science of a Connected Age (New York 2003).

Whitley 1997
J. Whitley, Beazley as Theorist, Antiquity 71, 1997, 41–47.

Williams 2009
D. Williams, Picturing Potters and Painters, in: O. Palagia – J. H. Oakley (eds.), Athenian Potters and Painters II (Oxford 2009) 307–317.

Productivity of Athenian Vase-painters and Workshops

Philip Sapirstein

Introduction

This paper examines the organization of the ancient Athenian pottery industry from a statistical perspective. My foundational research published in 2013 established a previously unrecognized pattern among vases attributed to Attic painters active between 600–400 BC by J.D. Beazley and later scholars.[1] A regularity in the numbers of extant vases for each year a painter was active, defined as the *annual attribution rate* (henceforth AR), is a new tool for studying the economics of ancient painting. The current paper aims to clarify the relationship of the AR, which is based on tallies of firmly attributed works, to the actual lifetime productivity of an ancient artisan, and what this reveals about the total number of painters simultaneously active in the Kerameikos. The conclusions apply the AR concept to whole workshops rather than individual painters.

Attribution Rates

The inspiration for the AR is the 1959 economic study by R.M. Cook, who posited that Attic vase-painters worked at consistent rates which could be used to estimate total employment in the Kerameikos.[2] If one artisan had decorated 3–4 vases per year out of the total of perhaps 40.000 pots that were known at Cook's time, then about 70 painters must have been active, at least on average, over the 200 years of production. Because Beazley had also designated a large number of individual hands – about 500 from the 5th century BC – Cook thought the population should be higher by the Classical era, perhaps 100–125 painters. Next, adding the potters and staff needed to shape and fire the vases would bring the total population of the Kerameikos to 400–500, with less than half that number in the 6th century.

Since Cook did not document how he derived the underlying figures, my previous studies sought to establish annual productivity in a more transparent fashion and to include the ensuing 50 years of research. An initial exploration revealed that the AR, defined as the total number of vases for a hand divided by years of activity, is frequently close to 8 pots/year.[3] Building on that finding, a more comprehensive study incorporated all the attributions published through 2011 for a larger cohort of painters, following a rigorously defined methodology.[4] Because the choices of *which* painters were included in that study impact the relevance of the AR in other scenarios, they should be reviewed here.

First, only *long-lived* painters can be assessed meaningfully by the AR due to the imprecision in our ability to date individual vases. For example, assuming 8 pots/year of

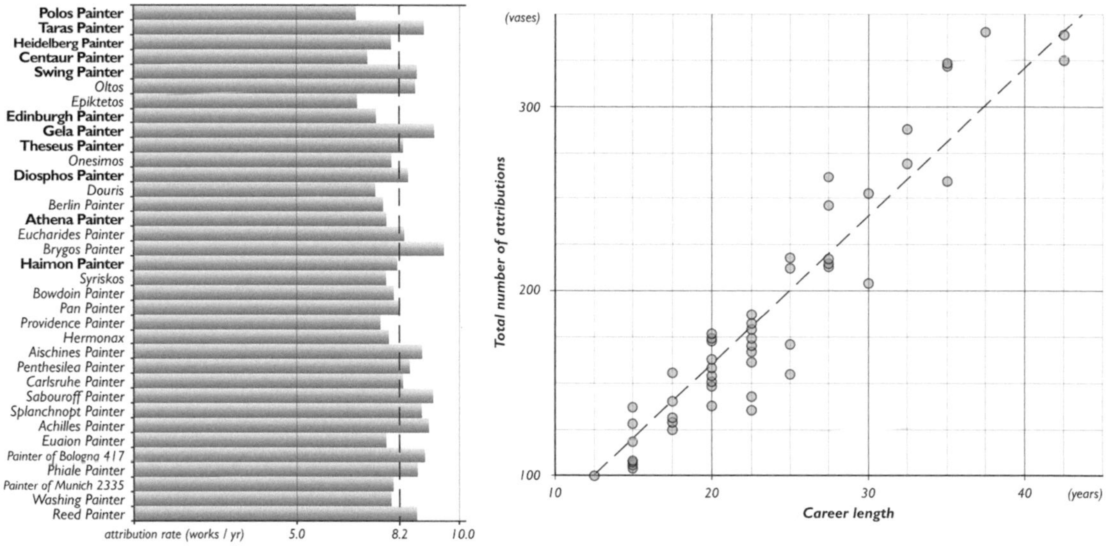

Fig. 1: Left: annual attribution rate of prolific Attic painters (more than 150 vases), excluding Makron. Names in bold painted in the black-figure technique; those in italics specialized in red-figure. Right: career length vs. total number of vases for all painters with at least 100 vases.

activity as the norm, a hand with 8 vases from a 1-year career would fall below the 5–10-year resolution at which Athenian vases are typically dated. If we dated this hand to the minimum detectable 5-year period, the AR would be greatly skewed: 1.6 instead of the actual 8. As a starting point, the painters with many surviving works are likely to have been long-lived. After compiling every hand with at least 150 attributions, amounting to 36 artisans in 2011, the AR was between 6.8–9.5 for all but one case (fig. 1).[5] Most of this variation is to be expected from the imprecision in dating individual careers, and such regularity is unusual with archaeological materials.[6] The AR of the whole set of painters, cumulatively active over more than 930 years and responsible for more than 7.500 vases extant today, can be determined at 8.2 works per year, although for individual cases we should expect variations of at least ca. ±1 in the AR, and more for those with short or poorly known dates of activity.

Are there long-lived painters with fewer works? While they are more difficult to identify, several carefully studied hands active more than 15 years, such as Exekias and the Codrus Painter, belong to another cohort with as few as 2–3 works per year of activity.[7] Some of these painters preferred large or complex compositions that took more time to complete than the typical Attic vase, and so they left us fewer, albeit unusually impressive works per year – as was surely the case with the intricately painted François vase by Kleitias.[8] However, other hands with a low AR created unremarkable paintings. A more comprehensive explanation for the less productive artisans is that they did not paint full time. I focused on hands whose vases were signed by a *poietes* –indicating the potter – or where the potter-work was consistent, both situations which could mean

Specialist painter model

Oltos	**8.7**	**8.0**	P. Munich 2335
Epiktetos	**6.8**	**8.0**	Antimenes P.
Douris	**7.4**	**8.3**	Theseus P.
Hermonax	**7.8**	**8.3**	Eucharides P.
Sabouroff P.	**9.2**	**8.0**	Bowdoin P.
Euergides P.	**9.1**	**8.3**	Carlsruhe P.
Triptolemos P.	**7.4**	**5.4**	Calliope P.
Achilles P.	**9.1**	**7.7**	Eretria P.
Phiale P.	**8.7**	**7.9**	Washing P.
Providence P.	**7.6**		

8.02 works / yr

Consistent potter-work

Exekias	**2.0**	**4.1**	Amasis P.
C P.	**7.4**	**3.7**	Nikosthenes (P. N)
KY P.	**6.0**	**5.9**	The Affecter
Heidelberg P.	**7.9**	**6.5**	Red-Line P.
Red-black P.	**3.7**	**4.1**	Sappho P.
Griffin-bird P.	**5.8**	**6.2**	Niobid P.
Tleson P.	**5.5**	**5.7**	Shuvalov P.
Centaur P.	**7.2**		

5.05 works / yr

partial evidence

Gela P.	**9.2**	**9.5**	Brygos P.
Onesimos	**7.9**	**7.6**	P. Paris Gigantomachy
Berlin P.	**7.6**	**8.5**	Penthesilea P.
Athena P.	**7.7**	**8.9**	Splanchnopt P.
Haimon P.	**8.1**	**8.9**	P. Bologna 417
Pan P.	**8.2**	**6.0**	P. London D 12
Villa Giulia P.	**8.0**	**6.9**	Veii P.

8.13 works / yr

Euphronios	**3.4**	**8.7**	Swing P.
Syriskos	**7.7**	**8.4**	Diosphos P.
Polos P.	**6.8**	**7.4**	Edinburgh P.
Taras P.	**8.9**	**7.1**	Beldam P.
Malibu P.	**3.9**	**8.0**	Altamura P.
Hermogenes P.	**2.2**	**3.6**	Codrus P.

6.55 works / yr

Fig. 2: Left: attribution rates of painters with independent evidence for specialization; right: evidence consistent with both painting and potting. The study of the potter-work is incomplete or ambiguous for the names below the line.

that the painter of a vase had also shaped it.[9] One should expect these *potter-painters* to have decorated fewer vases. The less productive artisans might also have engaged in other workshop jobs – such as mixing paint, firing the kiln, speaking to clients – or worked on and off outside the Kerameikos, but only those who also potted are likely to be archaeologically and epigraphically detectable.

A clear division emerges between the most productive specialists, who often worked with several different potters, and the less productive hands, many of whom appeared to have been potter-painters (fig. 2).[10] Most studies of Attic production and trade build on a reasonable expectation that large tallies of vases are representative of trends in actual ancient production, but my work demonstrates that statistical analysis is viable even at finer resolutions, down to the work of certain individual painters. Furthermore, the results lend support to Beazley's fundamental assumption that the vases he linked to a hand were indeed the work of an individual – an idea that has been affirmed by later generations of scholars despite some lingering skepticism of the validity of attribution.[11] But if it were merely an arbitrary guessing game, or if many of Beazley's hands were actually the products of a collective, we would not expect to find a correlation between the AR and the independent evidence for either specialization or part-time potting. Because the strong correlation shown in Figure 2 is very unlikely to have come about by pure chance, this confirms the general validity of attribution as a method to identify individual painters.[12]

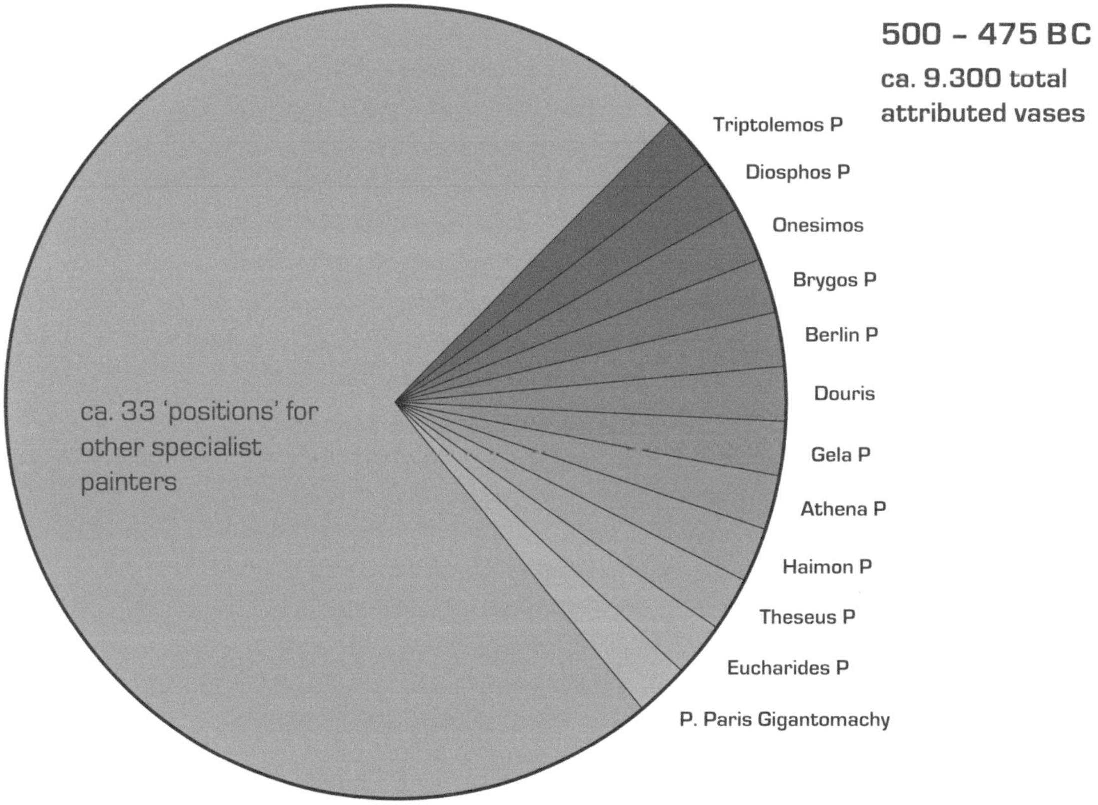

Fig. 3: Minimum number of full-time specialists responsible for the extant Attic vases from the first quarter of the 5th century BC. In reality, more individuals would have been involved in the painting of these works.

Nonetheless, some important caveats accompany these findings. First, it is quite possible for a known artisan to have painted some vases which are not specifically attributed, and so the list of *firmly* attributed works cannot comprise every extant work by that individual.[13] Second, the approach is intended for categories of attribution that are likely to belong to an individual – which is the case for most of Beazley's "hands" — while groups, classes, and other more general forms of classification must be treated as the products of collectives. Furthermore, for meaningful statistical analysis of an individual hand, he or she must have been active at least 15 years, or else the AR is too susceptible to error to be reliable. Third, the painter's corpus should be well-preserved and not overrepresented by a single findspot. An instructive example is the Painter of the Athens Dinos, all but two of whose ca. 50 identified works are from the debris of a kiln in Athens.[14] The many tiny sherds would not have been assigned to this hand had they not been found together in this remarkable context, which makes them statistically unlike the widely distributed, better-preserved, and stylistically distinctive vases of more prominent artisans like Epiktetos or Douris.[15]

Period	Beazley attributions	Potter-painters		Specialist painters
600-575	760	11	+	0
575-550	1.600	16	+	2
550-525	3.170	29	+	5
525-500	5.180	36	+	12
500-475	9.260	41	+	30
475-450	9.390	43	+	30
450-425	7.510	45	+	20
425-400	1.960	10	+	6
Total	**38.830**			

Fig. 4: Estimated employment in the Kerameikos, 600–400 BC. The total production is expanded from Beazley's attribution counts, while the population of simultaneously active potter-painters and painting specialists is an approximation, since the actual ratio of potter-painters to specialists is uncertain by the middle of the 6th century.

Industry Population

One aspect of my work that has stirred controversy is the estimated population of painters in the Kerameikos. Since more vases had been discovered and published after Cook's 1959 study, I needed to reassess not just the AR but also the total number of extant pots. Near the peak of Attic production in 500–475 BC, there are fewer than 10.000 such figure-decorated vases, equivalent to the production of 45 artisans working simultaneously at the speed of the most prolific hands (fig. 3). By tallying vases in 25-year intervals, one observes production rise among a small group of potter-painters in the early 6th century, and then collapse during the Peloponnesian War (fig. 4).[16] This minimum number of painters is useful for gauging how many other workers were employed full time in the production of figure-decorated pottery – perhaps 200–300, somewhat fewer than proposed by Cook.

This low estimate moves against a tendency since Cook's time to argue for higher populations.[17] V. Stissi recently entertained an industry potentially employing thousands of painters, with perhaps 3.000–4.000 Kerameikos workers in all, and criticized Cook's method as expanded in my recent work.[18] His central claim is that minor artisans had a major impact on Attic production, painting huge numbers of vases not recognized by the AR because the individuals were not long-lived. Thus, it is critical to review the reasons why the two estimates differ by more than an order of magnitude.

First, a distinction must be drawn between *continuously employed* painters, the roughly 45 "positions" available at any time during 500–475 BC (fig. 3), and the number of individuals who ever painted a vase during this period. Those who see high populations at the Kerameikos typically conflate continuous employment with tallies of individual hands. It is as if we assess the population of teachers in Canada not as those currently employed teaching, but as every person who had taught a class at some point during the last 25 years – which obviously is a much larger number, but one irrelevant to assessing the scale of employment.

We must account for *turnover* also in order to compare raw tallies of individuals with the population of simultaneously employed workers. Stissi argues from the 130 hands connected to Little Master and related cups, the Tyrrhenian Group, and the Nikosthenes workshop, that 40–50 different painters were simultaneously active around the middle of the 6th century BC, higher than allowed in Figure 4.[19] This high estimate relies on an assumption that each hand, regardless of productivity, had an average career of 5 years (equivalent to 40 extant vases at the standard AR for specialist painters). Only 26 of the 130 hands have at least 20 attributions, and many of the other just 1–2; the total of roughly 2.500 vases suggests the output of no more than 10 full-time specialists, which is in keeping with the 7 prolific hands that dominate this set of vases.[20] Since we have no reliable means by which to estimate actual turnover in antiquity, such simplistic conversions of the total number of designated hands can lead to wildly variable estimates of population. For example, we could imagine that turnover ranged between 2–20 years, which would allow for anywhere from 60 to 560 individuals to have filled the 45 full-time "positions" available over the quarter century shown in Figure 3.[21]

Still, nonspecialist painters may not only have painted less often, but also at slower rates than specialists, thereby increasing the actual population of artisans who considered painting an important part of their job. Indeed, we might even propose a third mode, *occasional painters*, such as a potter painting one batch of vases herself while her preferred painter was unavailable, an apprentice who ceased painting after a short period due to a lack of aptitude, and other scenarios where the painter might have worked quite slowly.[22] However, the data suggest the economic impact of minor figures was modest. Ranking Beazley's hands from the most productive to the least – a style shared by just two pots – results in the lopsided distribution seen in Figure 5. Douris alone was responsible for more attributed vases than the bottom 140 hands all together, while the top 53 hands produced as many as the bottom 582. In light of the natural aptitude and lengthy period of training to develop the skills required for Attic figured painting, I find it unsurprising that seasoned experts would have dominated production.

While the hands with occasional or sporadic production did not have much economic impact, their presence would bring down the average AR of 8.2 attained by specialists for

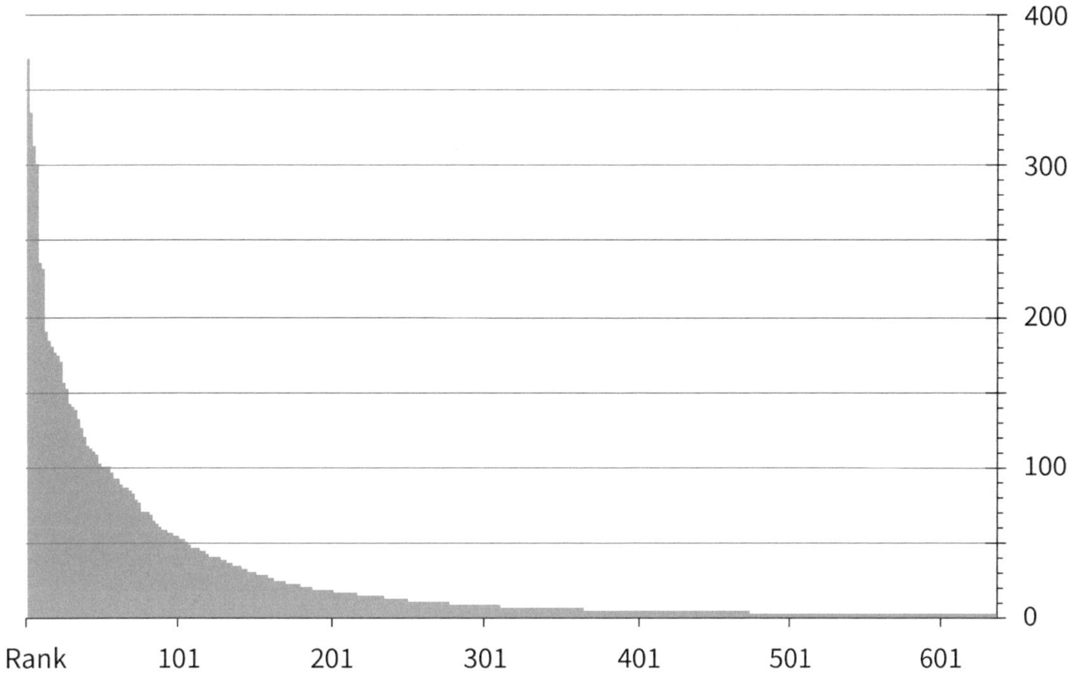

Fig. 5: Attributions per painter as designated by Beazley. The vertical axis shows the total number of attributions for every hand with at least two works ranked in descending order on the horizontal axis (e.g., Makron, the most productive, is the first on the left). Groups, classes, and other kinds of non-individual entities have been excluded.

the industry as a whole. A more realistic scenario allows for ca. 70 "positions" including potter-painters and trainees, who worked less efficiently than their specialized peers and would have modestly reduced the average rate of painting across the industry as a whole (fig. 4). Since the actual productivity of nonspecialists is hard to assess, one could plausibly argue for a range of 50–100 employed figure-painters at the apogee of Attic production. The important conclusion is that this population cannot have been massively greater than if the industry were almost exclusively staffed by high-output specialists like Douris.

Total Numbers of Attic Vases

The only other way to restore a much larger population of painters is to argue that Beazley and later scholars overlooked a large number of unattributed vases. My estimate for the total number of pots for each period – close to 400 per year at the height of production, and totaling fewer than 39.000 between 600–400 BC – is key to reconstructing the population (fig. 4). If there were actually many more extant pots, we would open up more "positions" for full-time painters – but only if the AR remained at 8.2.

Stissi argues that we should use the total number of Attic vases that have ever been excavated, which he put near 1.1 million, as the basis for calculation. Over 250 years, an AR of 5–8 vases per artisan would indeed equate to thousands of painters during peak production. This total is based on the 110.000 records (in 2015) in the Beazley Archive Pottery Database (BAPD), and an estimate that only 10% of excavated Attic pottery has yet to be published and entered into the database.[23]

While doubtlessly there are many additional Attic sherds, it is fundamentally inappropriate to apply the AR to a new, vastly larger population which has yet to be fully studied and published. Were this material incorporated, the typical specialist AR would certainly rise above 8 because at least some of these unpublished sherds would be attributed to prominent painters. In other words, as the total number of published vases grows with future study, we would certainly find many new works by Nikosthenes, Douris, and other well-known hands in the expanding corpus. The new attributions to known hands would of course increase the AR, which is the number of extant works (a growing quantity) divided by the artisans' years of activity (a fixed quantity). For example, if the corpus had expanded to five times larger than it is now, the AR of ca. 5–8 would probably grow to roughly 25–40 vases per year.

The other question is how to count known vases. While a tremendously useful research tool, the whole BAPD – which now exceeds 115.000 records – does not provide a reliable tally of Attic figural pottery from 600–400 BC, since it includes non-Athenian wares, earlier and later material, nonfigural and black gloss vases, and other extraneous entries numbering in the tens of thousands. Furthermore, the counts are inflated by pieces from overrepresented contexts. For example, the Painter of the Athens Dinos has 64 separate BAPD records, mostly inscrutable sherds from the aforementioned kiln deposit, that would be equivalent to no more than a few intact vases by a prolific hand if we employed a fair basis for comparison, such as preserved surface area. Any reader wishing to apply the AR to another problem may review the methods developed for controlling the impact of unusually rich contexts, which result in an industry-wide tally of comparable figural vases near 40.000.[24]

Finally, we must ask whether the unpublished figural sherds, perhaps numbering in the hundreds of thousands, will turn out to have been dominated by minor hands rather than the specialists, thus implying a greater population in the Kerameikos. Assuming the corpus is unbiased, we should know the productivity of a prominent painter like Douris within ca. 14%, and the overall AR for the industry should be more accurately determined, since it is based on many hands.[25] Bias against minor hands, however, might result in more of their work appearing among the unpublished material. Beazley claimed that he attended to all figural vases regardless of quality, and his catalogues do include low-quality work such as the masses of sloppily painted 'Haimonian' lekythoi or the 23 vases by the unfortunate 'Worst Painter'.[26] Since Beazley's death in 1970, scholars of monographs on individual painters and workshops have striven to locate new works.[27] The corpora have grown apace with the publication of museum holdings and archaeological discoveries over the last

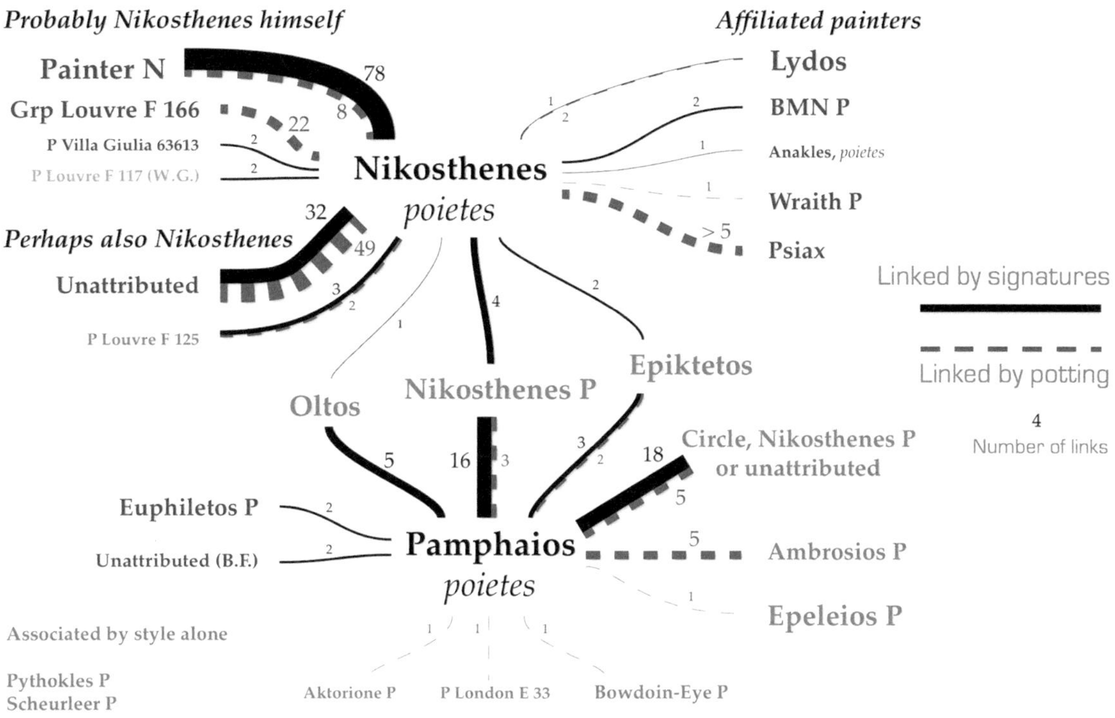

Fig. 6: Painters affiliated with Nikosthenes and Pamphaios, whose connection is recognized through the three painters who worked with both potters. The thickness of the pairs of lines showing affiliation increases according to the number of links, which is written next to the lines.

50 years – by about 15% for red figure, though up to 50% for early black-figure.[28] The modest bias against early black-figure, probably due to the ABV not having been expanded as thoroughly as the ARV^2, was already factored into the tabulations underlying Figure 4. Nothing in the data support the 900% expansion of work by minor hands which would be required to sustain Stissi's population estimates.

Many of the unpublished vases may be similar to the hordes of Little Master and related cups, some of which Beazley rightly ignored due to their lack of figural decoration. These vases are of course important evidence for Attic production, but they did not take as much skill or time to paint. In the end, a population of no more than 50–100 full-time painting "positions" who worked alongside a few hundred other workers in the Kerameikos could have produced all of its figural pottery. In addition to those engaged in forming vases, some workers may have assisted painters by adding border patterns or mixing paints, but this cannot have been a very large group.[29] Neither is it likely that new evidence will radically alter this picture. We can envisage additional workshops which produced other types of pottery – plainware, cooking pots, pithoi, to mention a few – perhaps staffed by dozens or even hundreds of other workers, but we would need to examine this body of evidence separately.

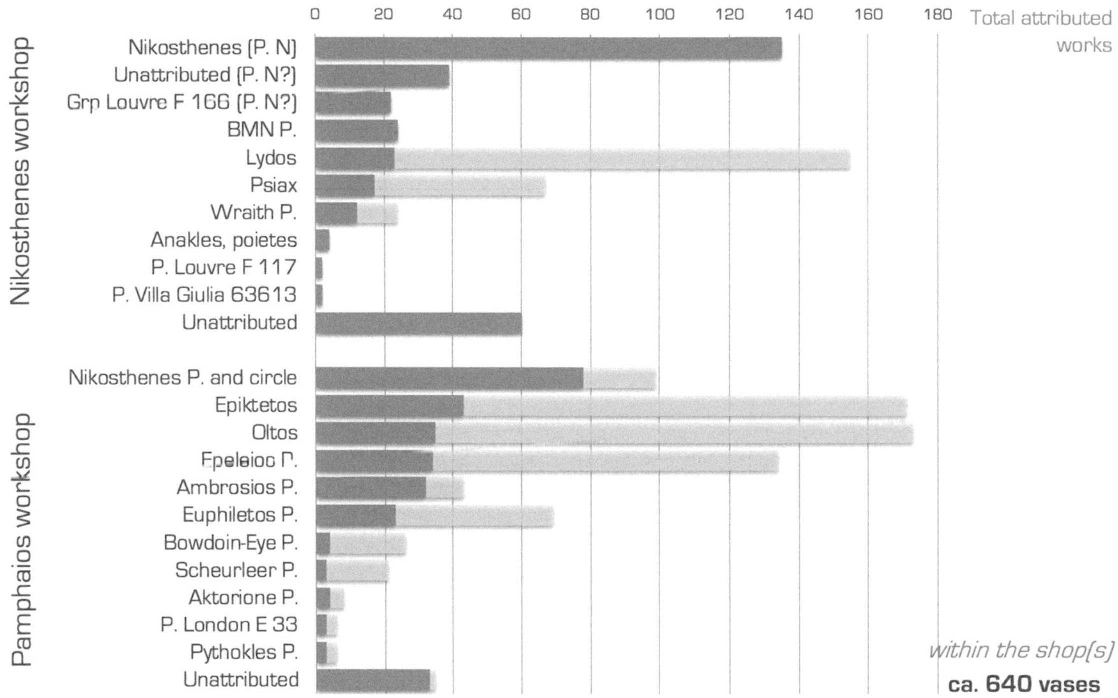

Fig. 7: Attributions to painters and groups around Nikosthenes and Pamphaios. The complete length of the bar indicates the total number of attributions for each painter. The darker portion of each bar shows the approximate number of works for the potter in question, according to the evidence that each painter had (or had not) worked in other shops.

Small Workshops

A closing example illustrates how workshops might be approached using the AR. We know from signatures that late Archaic painting specialists often worked with many different *poietes* – meaning the corpora of vases attributed to most prolific painters are divided among several different potters and workshops. The case of Nikosthenes affords us a more secure footing, since his many signatures and distinctive potterwork demarcate the workshop, which possibly was inherited by Pamphaios.[30] Figure 6 plots their associations, including estimates for partial contributions by Epiktetos and others who spend more time painting in other workshops.

The workshop is usually assumed to be the largest in Athens producing black-figure. The many associated hands once prompted large estimates for the staff, up to dozens of workers.[31] More recent scholarship has observed that just a few hands – Painter N, and the Nikosthenes Painter – dominate the extant vases.[32] The AR supports this picture of a small operation, with specialist painters moonlighting in the workshop as estimated in Figure 7. Assuming Nikosthenes was Painter N, he need only have employed one other painter, either apprentices or specialists like Lydos, to decorate some of the vases which he had thrown but did not have time to paint. The quantities of extant workshop vases are simply inadequate to have sustained more full-time staff. Pamphaios may have hired two red-figure painters, but even so the two workshops need not have employed more than five people, at least their equivalent in full-time positions equivalents, including the other jobs besides potting and painting.[33]

Conclusions

In review, the AR can be used to examine the production of individual painters, but only under the circumstances where it is statistically relevant. It can be extended to workshops such as those around Nikosthenes or Pamphaios, but additional precautions are necessary to control for the possibility that the painters worked for other shops during their careers. When we examine the surviving vases painted by individuals or workshops, rather than the misleadingly high numbers of hands, it becomes clear that the permanent staff of many other Attic workshops was fairly small. These enterprises are entirely consistent with the portrait drawn from ethnographic sources: Athenian ceramic production was a pre-modern industry built upon family-run workshops.

Notes

[1] Beazley 1956 (ABV); 1963 (ARV[2]); 1971 (Paralipomena). Sapirstein 2013a; 2013b; 2014.

[2] Cook 1959, 119–121.

[3] Sapirstein 2008, 184–189.

[4] Sapirstein 2013a, 494–497; 2013b, 2–8.

[5] Makron, with more than double the next highest rate, is an outlier. His AR is inflated by large numbers of small sherds in the corpus, in part due to unusual collection practices: Sapirstein 2013b, 26 f.

[6] For a hand with 200 vases over 25 years, incorrect dating by ±5 years would change the AR to 6.7–10.

[7] Mackay 2010; Avramidou 2011.

[8] Hirayama 2010.

[9] Sapirstein 2013a, 497–501.

[10] Sapirstein 2013a, 501–503.

[11] Beazley 1922, 83–90; Oakley 1999; 2016; Arrington 2017, 22–28. 36.

[12] The odds of such a distribution occurring by accident are less than 1:10,000: Sapirstein 2013a, 501 n. 31. 508.

[13] cf. Arrington 2017, 30–32.

[14] Oakley 1992; Bentz et. al. 2010, 150–162. 170–204. Of 54 catalogued sherds, some could have come from the same vessel, but other unattributed sherds from the context could also have been by this painter.

[15] Buitron-Oliver 1995; Paléothodoros 2004. As with many of the other prominent painters, their lists include sherds, but the majority of their attributions are largely intact – i.e., where at least half of the vase is represented.

[16] Sapirstein 2013a, 506–508.

[17] Webster 1972, 2 f.; Stissi 2002, 30–34; cf. Arafat – Morgan 1989, 327.

[18] Stissi 2016, 48–52.

[19] Stissi 2016, 50 f. Table 1; the same figures are repeated in his chapter in this volume.

[20] Brijder 1983; 1991; 2000 (dominated by the C, Taras, Heidelberg, and Griffin-Bird Painters); Tosto 1999 (Painter N); Kluiver 2003 (no prolific hand); Heesen 2009 (Tleson and Centaur Painters).

[21] For the ca. 9.260 attributed vases from the first quarter of the 5th century (Figure 4), with an AR of 8.2, the output is equivalent to the annual production of more than 1.100 painters, i.e.: 9.260 vases ÷ 8.2 vases / painter-year = ~1.129 painter-years. If we assume a short average career length of just 2 years, then the total number of individuals who would have worked at some point over the 25-year period is 1.129 painter-years ÷ 2 years / painter = ~564 painters. With a 20-year career, the number of painters is much lower: 1.129 ÷ 20 = ~56. The actual turnover was probably somewhere between, but it can only be estimated from the number of individual hands we recognize – e.g., more hands indicates a shorter average period of activity and a higher turnover.

[22] Williams 2016, 61–64; perhaps also the Painter of the Athens Dinos: above, note 14. On the evidence for apprenticeship in Greek workshops in general, Hasaki 2013.

[23] Stissi 2002, 24 n. 77; similar estimates are repeated in Stissi's chapter in this volume. On the AR calculation, see Stissi, 48–50: 1.1 Ma ÷ 250 years ÷ 5–8 vases / painter = 550–880 painters.

[24] Sapirstein 2013b, 3–6. Stissi's estimate (in this volume) of an original Athenian production in the tens of millions is also wildly inflated because of how it applies the survival rate to his proposed collection of over a million extant vases. As with the AR, the survival rate is also increased by new finds – i.e., the rate of 0.25–1.0%, which was estimated from a corpus of about 50.000 vases known then, would expand in proportion to the number of new discoveries. If the corpus has indeed grown 20 times larger, then the survival rate has also increased to 5–20%. Otherwise the rate would need to be recalculated afresh by means of some other proxy evidence.

[25] Levy – Leveshow 1999, 61–64. 70–75; contra Stissi 2016, 53 n. 18. Assuming we already have 10.000 attributed vases from 500–475, and 205 from this period belong to one specialist painter (from the standard AR of 8.2), we can estimate the 95% confidence interval for the whole population. If 1% of vases have been recovered—which is debatable but close enough for estimating the sampling error—the painter would have 177–233 additional vases 95% of the time whenever 10.000 new vases were sampled, equivalent to an AR of 205±27.5 (13.5%). Since close to a quarter of extant vases were assessed for determining the AR (about 2.500 instead of 205), it theoretically could have been determined within ±1%. A preference to study well-preserved pots would not introduce meaningful bias, but if Beazley and later scholars had routinely ignored certain types of Attic painting, bias would be more of an issue. In any case, actual errors are probably somewhat higher.

[26] Robertson 1985, 27 f.; Volioti 2014; Jubier-Galinier 2016; Haspels 1936 (ABL) 130–141. 241–249. 368; ABV, 538–583. 705–708. 716; Paralipomena 269–289; ARV^2 1353 f.

[27] Recently, see Oakley 2016; Padgett 2018.

[28] Sapirstein 2013b, 8.

[29] Lezzi-Hafter identifies separate hands of ornament painters in the circle of the Shuvalov and Eretria Painters, perhaps indicating that one of the figure-painters was responsible for most of the ornament in

her or his workshop: Lezzi-Hafter 1976, 41–51. 95 f.; 1988, 133–135. This arrangement may have been unusual, and Beazley (1922, 88) wrote "there is no reason to suppose that the patterns were not regularly executed by the same hand as the figures; the labour may sometimes have been divided, though I do not for a moment believe that it was often so."

[30] Immerwahr 1984; Tosto 1999.

[31] Webster 1972, 1–41 (10–20 staff); Eisman 1974, 48 f. (30 painters); Valavanis 1997, 86 f. (ca. 20 staff).

[32] Scheibler 1983, 110–118; 1984, 130–134 (6–8 staff); Tosto 1999, 193–200; Hasaki 2011, 27.

[33] Scheibler 1984; Tosto 1999, 193–200; Sapirstein 2008, 182 f. 198–205; Lüdorf 2010; Hasaki 2011, 24–28; Williams 2016.

Image Credits

All images by the author.

References

Arafat – Morgan 1989
K. Arafat – C. Morgan, Pots and Potters in Athens and Corinth. A Review, OxfJA 8, 2016, 311–346.

Arrington 2017
N.T. Arrington, Connoisseurship, Vases, and Greek Art and Archaeology, in: J.M. Padgett (ed.), The Berlin Painter and His World. Athenian Vase-Painting in the Early Fifth Century B.C. (New Haven 2017) 21–39.

Avramidou 2011
A. Avramidou, The Codrus Painter. Iconography and Reception of Athenian Vases in the Age of Pericles (Madison 2011).

Beazley 1922
J.D. Beazley, Citharoedus, JHS 42, 1922, 70–98.

Beazley 1956
J.D. Beazley, Attic Black-Figure Vase-Painters (Oxford 1956).

Beazley 1963
J.D. Beazley, Attic Red-Figure Vase-Painters ^{2}(Oxford 1963).

Beazley 1971
J.D. Beazley, Paralipomena. Additions to Attic Black-Figure Vase-Painters and to Attic Red-Figure Vase-Painters (Oxford 1971).

Bentz et. al. 2010
M. Bentz – W. Geominy – J.M. Müller (eds.), TonArt. Virtuosität antiker Töpfertechnik (Petersberg 2010).

Brijder 1983
H.A.G. Brijder, Siana Cups I and Komast Cups, Allard Pierson Series 4 (Amsterdam 1983).
Brijder 1991
H.A.G. Brijder, Siana Cups II. The Heidelberg Painter, Allard Pierson Series 8 (Amsterdam 1991).
Brijder 2000
H.A.G. Brijder, Siana Cups III. The Red-black Painter, Griffin-bird Painter and Siana Cups resembling Lip-cups, Allard Pierson Series 13 (Amsterdam 2000).
Buitron-Oliver 1995
D. Buitron-Oliver, Douris. A Master-Painter of Athenian Red-Figure Vases, Kerameus 9 (Mainz 1995).
Cook 1959
R.M. Cook, Die Bedeutung der bemalten Keramik für den griechischen Handel, JdI 74, 1959, 114–123.
Eisman 1974
M.M. Eisman, A Further Note on ΕΠΟΙΕΣΕΝ Signatures, JHS 94, 1974, 172.
Hasaki 2011
E. Hasaki, Crafting Spaces: Archaeological, Ethnographic, and Ethnoarchaeological Studies of Spatial Organization in Pottery Workshops in Greece and Tunisia, in: M.L. Lawall – J. Lund (eds.), Pottery in the Archaeological Record: Greece and Beyond (Aarhus 2011) 12–28.
Hasaki 2013
E. Hasaki, Craft Apprenticeship in Ancient Greece: Reaching beyond the Masters, in: W. Wendrich (ed.), Archaeology and Apprenticeship: Acquiring Body Knowledge in the Ancient World (Tucson 2013) 171–202.
Haspels 1936
C.H.E. Haspels, Attic Black-figured Lekythoi (Paris 1936).
Heesen 2009
P. Heesen, Athenian Little-Master Cups (Ph.D. diss. University of Amsterdam 2009).
Hirayama 2010
T. Hirayama, Kleitias and Attic Black-Figure Vases in the Sixth-Century B.C. (Tokyo 2010).
Immerwahr 1984
H.R. Immerwahr, The Signatures of Pamphaios, AJA 88, 1984, 341–352.
Jubier-Galinier 2016
C. Jubier-Galinier, Les attributions des vases à figures noires tardives en question, in: N. Eschbach – S. Schmidt (eds.), Töpfer, Maler, Werkstatt: Zuschreibungen in der griechischen Vasenmalerei und die Organisation antiker Keramikproduktion, CVA Beih. 7 (Munich 2016) 130–138.
Kluiver 2003
J. Kluiver, The Tyrrhenian Group of Black-Figure Vases. From the Athenian Kerameikos to the Tombs of South Etruria (Amsterdam 2003).
Levy – Lemeshow 1999
P.S. Levy – S. Lemeshow, Sampling of Populations. Methods and Applications 3 (New York 1999).
Lezzi-Hafter 1976
A. Lezzi-Hafter, Der Schuwalow-Maler. Eine Kannenwerkstatt der Parthenonzeit, Kerameus 2 (Mainz 1976).

Lezzi-Hafter 1988
A. Lezzi-Hafter, Der Eretria-Maler. Werke und Weggefährten, Kerameus 6 (Mainz 1988).
Lüdorf 2010
G. Lüdorf, Zur Größe athenischer Töpferwerkstätten des 6. und 5. Jhs. v. Chr. Familienunternehmen oder zentralisierte Massenproduktion? in: H. Lohmann – T. Mattern (eds.), Attika. Archäologie einer „zentralen" Kulturlandschaft (Wiesbaden 2010) 151–159.
Mackay 2010
E.A. Mackay, Tradition and Originality. A Study of Exekias, BARIntSer 2092 (Oxford 2010).
Oakley 1992
J.H. Oakley, An Athenian Red-Figure Workshop from the Time of the Peloponnesian War, in: F. Blondé – J.Y. Perreault (eds.), Les ateliers de potiers dans le monde grec aux époques géométrique, archaïque et classique. Actes de la Table Ronde organisée à l'École française d'Athènes – 2 et 3 octobre 1987, BCH Suppl. 23 (Paris 1992) 195–203.
Oakley 1999
J.H. Oakley, 'Through a Glass Darkly' I: Some Misconceptions about the Study of Greek Vase-painting, in: R.F. Docter – E.M. Moormann (eds.), Classical Archaeology towards the Third Millenium: Reflections and Perspectives. Proceedings of the XVth International Congress of Classical Archaeology, Amsterdam, July 12–17, 1998 (Amsterdam 1999) 286–90.
Oakley 2016
J.H. Oakley, Changing Personalities – What New Attributions Can Tell Us, in: N. Eschbach – S. Schmidt (eds.), Töpfer, Maler, Werkstatt: Zuschreibungen in der griechischen Vasenmalerei und die Organisation antiker Keramikproduktion (Munich 2016) 25–35.
Padgett 2018
M.J. Padgett (ed.), The Berlin Painter and His World. Athenian Vase-Painting in the Early Fifth Century B.C. (New Haven 2018).
Paléothodoros 2004
D. Paléothodoros, Épictétos, Collection d'Études Classiques 18 (Louvain 2004).
Robertson 1985
M. Robertson, Beazley and Attic Vase Painting, in: D. Kurtz (ed.), Beazley and Oxford. Lectures delivered in Wolfson College, Oxford, 28 June 1985 (Oxford 1985) 19–30.
Sapirstein 2008
P. Sapirstein, The Emergence of Ceramic Roof Tiles in Archaic Greek Architecture (Ph.D. diss. Cornell University 2008).
Sapirstein 2013a
P. Sapirstein, Painters, Potters, and the Scale of the Attic Vase-Painting Industry, AJA 117, 2013, 493–510.
Sapirstein 2013b
P. Sapirstein, Methodology, Bibliography, and Commentary for the Painters in the Study, AJA 117, 2013, online 1–47.
Sapirstein 2014
P. Sapirstein, Demographics and Productivity in the Ancient Athenian Pottery Industry, in: J.H. Oakley (ed.), Athenian Potters and Painters III (Oxford 2014) 175–186.

Scheibler 1983
I. Scheibler, Griechische Töpferkunst. Herstellung, Handel und Gebrauch der antiken Tongefässe (Munich 1983).

Scheibler 1984
I. Scheibler, Zur mutmasslichen Grösse attischer Töpfereien des 6. Jahrhunderts v. Chr., in: H.A.G. Brijder (ed.), Ancient Greek and Related Pottery. Proceedings of the International Vase Symposium – Amsterdam (12–15 April, 1984), Allard Pierson Series 5 (Amsterdam 1984) 130–134.

Stissi 2002
V.V. Stissi, Pottery to the People. The Production, Distribution, and Consumption of Decorated Pottery in the Greek World in the Archaic Period (650–480 BC) (Ph.D. diss. University of Amsterdam 2002).

Stissi 2016
V.V. Stissi, Minor Artisans, Major Impact? in: N. Eschbach – S. Schmidt (eds.), Töpfer, Maler, Werkstatt: Zuschreibungen in der griechischen Vasenmalerei und die Organisation antiker Keramikproduktion, CVA Beih. 7 (Munich 2016) 47–53.

Tosto 1999
V. Tosto, The Black-figure Pottery Signed ΝΙΚΟΣΘΕΝΕΣΕΠΟΙΕΣΕΝ, Allard Pierson Series 11 (Amsterdam 1999).

Valavanis 1997
P. Valavanis, Βάκχιος, Κίττος και παναθηναϊκοί αμφορείς. Σκέψεις για τη δομή των αττικών κεραμικών εργαστηρίων του 4ου αι. π.Χ., in: J.H. Oakley – W.D.E. Coulson – O. Palagia (eds.), Athenian Potters and Painters, Oxbow Monograph 67 (Oxford 1997) 85–95.

Volioti 2014
K. Volioti, Dimensional Standardisation and the Use of Haimonian Lekythoi, in: A. Kotsonas (ed.), Understanding Standardization and Variation in Mediterranean Ceramics. Mid 2nd to Late 1st Millennium BC, BABesch Suppl. 25 (Leuven 2014) 149–168.

Webster 1972
T.B.L. Webster, Potter and Patron in Classical Athens (London 1972).

Williams 2016
D. Williams, Peopling Athenian kerameia. Beyond the Master Craftsmen, in: N. Eschbach – S. Schmidt (eds.), Töpfer, Maler, Werkstatt: Zuschreibungen in der griechischen Vasenmalerei und die Organisation antiker Keramikproduktion, CVA Beih. 7 (Munich 2016) 54–68.

From Counting Pots to Counting People: Assessing the Scale of Athenian Pottery Production and Its Impact on Workshop Staff

Vladimir Stissi

Introduction

Production of Greek table wares, particularly Athenian painted pottery, is usually considered refined craft, requiring highly skilled artisans, almost artists, carefully producing their masterpieces.[1] There are some reasons to question this image, however: the amount of preserved pots is staggering, and what we can see of ancient workshops, shows more than just masters. In this paper I want to explore the scale of Athenian figured pottery production, and the way this question is connected with the scale, organization and modus operandi of workshops.

Numbers: Production and Producers

Let me begin with scale: the digital Beazley archive now contains more than 86.000 Athenian figured pots.[2] Depending on one's estimate of the survival rate,[3] these represent between 8.600.000 (at 1%) and 34.400.000 (at 0,25%) pots originally made. However, the Beazley archive is far from complete. No good estimates are available, but (starting from some exemplary cases I checked) it seems to cover about 5–15% of the known material, at least that in major collections and publications – with both the corpus and the archive growing. That would imply an original production between ca. 57.300.000 and 688.000.000, mostly produced during a period of around 250 years (discounting the earliest and latest production, which was relatively marginal). This amounts to an average yearly output of between ca. 230.000 and over 2.750.000 – surely less during the first half of the 6th century and the 4th century BC, and more during the heyday of Athenian export in the decades around 500 BC. If we discount the extremes, a yearly output of 1.000.000–2.000.000 seems a fair guesstimate, certainly for the period between 550 and 400 BC.

If we then turn to the human side: the Beazleyan corpus contains about 1.300 possible individuals or groups of individuals (e.g., hands, groups, classes and related entities).[4] Dividing 250 years in ten generations of 25 years, this would imply an average of 130 active hands or groups at any given time – again, probably fewer in the early and late years of production, and more during the heyday. However, 25-year generations may be quite long in view of life expectancy, interruptions by war service, illness and famine, and considering the rather low amount of surviving items for most hands, though perhaps not for collective categories. On the other hand, at 130 hands or groups (etc.) even the lowest average total output I just provided would imply an average output of about 1.770 items a year, which seems on the high side as a lower margin for painted vessels,[5] at least for individuals; the highest would lead to a surely impossible yearly production of more than 21.150 items. Also taking into consideration the conclusions of Sapirstein, who noted that the Beazleyan corpus is based on a (smaller) core of potter/painters who left us about 5 pots for each active year (so an actual production of 500–2.000), and specialized painters usually producing around 8 surviving pots (so an actual output of 800–3.200, which has, however, to be shared with potters), the inevitable conclusion must be that we are wholly or partly missing many of the makers – not even counting assisting staff, preparing clay, loading, firing and unloading kilns.

If we (arbitrarily, just for the sake of argument) assume a normal yearly output of 2.000 for each maker, 1–2 million pots would require a group of 500–1.000 makers – or rather more as potter-painters were slower and specialized painters decorated work of often 'invisible' potters. We would thus only recognize ca. 10–20% of the hands, at the very best, since the many hands that are known from just a handful of pots, or even less, must have had more lost counterparts than the relatively productive ones, which dominate the oeuvre lists. It is moreover likely that most groups and classes and other collective units comprise several individuals. Taking a different approach, if we assume (theoretically, of course) every fully productive hand would on average last 10 years, which is probably on the optimistic side, and produce 2.000 pots a year, there would be 50–100 new hands needed every year, leading to a total number of 12.500–25.000 hands employed over 250 years, 5–10% of which made it into Beazley's lists. Since, as we have mentioned, productive painters with long careers are much less likely to have escaped Beazley, we can assume that proportionally many more 'major' painters are represented in our lists, but very few of the minor hands – as we indeed seem to see in practice.

All this is not exactly a surprise if, as we can safely assume, the Beazleyan corpus only represents between 0.0125% (a 0,25% survival rate, with 5 % of existing material in the Beazley corpus) and 0.066% (1% survival with 15% in the corpus) of the original output, or something in that order of magnitude. This brings us to some core problems. In order to convert quantitative data based on attributions to a social reality, it is important to evaluate whether such a miniscule proportion is still somehow representative. We also need to contextualize our data in two ways: first, the numbers have to be meaningful and the workshop setting has to be realistic. In other words, we need to place hands, groups and other related entities in a credible working environment: a workshop organization with a certain division of labor, producing at a certain scale, in the spatial and technological context known to us from other types of evidence.

In order to do so, we have three or perhaps four main sources of information: excavations, depictions, and the workshop output – these vases we have counted, catalogued and classified in large numbers and great detail. In addition, ethnographic research can help us understand the archaeological record. For the Athenian vase industry, however, where the high quality in shaping and painting was crucial, very few ethnographic parallels are available.

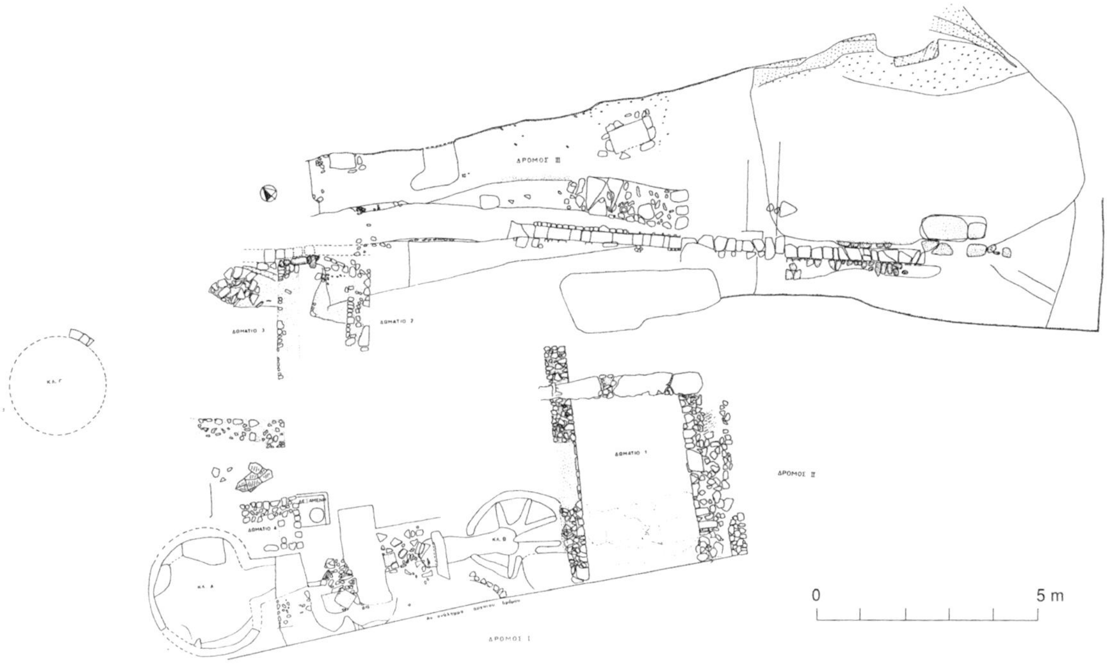

Fig. 1: The Classical pottery workshop excavated at Lenormant/Konstantinoupoleos Street, Athens: site plan.

From Numbers to the Social Reality of Workshops: Excavated Remains

Excavated pottery workshops offer the most direct way to study potters' workplaces. Remains of at least seven Athenian workshops producing black- and red figure pottery have been unearthed, plus a few sites with workshop wasters. In addition, architectural remains and dumps point to ten more Athenian workshops from the Archaic and Classical periods, which were producing other types of ceramics. The total number of Archaic and Classical workshops known from the entire Greek world is over 250.[6] Even though most workshop sites in Athens and elsewhere are poorly preserved and the state of publication also leaves much to desire, the available data offer a good impression of the scale and organization of work in workshops all over the Greek world.

One insight which may come unexpected is that all known Athenian workshops are quite a bit smaller than some very large workshops mostly producing undecorated ceramics in places like Selinous (see Bentz in this volume) and Corfu, which are not known as major pottery producers.[7] This may perhaps imply that on the level of the single workshop, the scale of production of plain pottery was higher than that of the labor intensive and more exclusive production of decorated fine wares. On the other hand, the single excavated Athenian workshop of black and red figure where kilns remained shows two rather large kilns, with a diameter of over 2 meters, operating at the same time (fig. 1).[8]

Fig. 2: Depiction of a potter's workshop. Hydria, Munich, Staatliche Antikensammlungen and Glyptothek 1717. Ca. 520–510 BC; Leagros Group.

Finally, the extensive series of production sites uncovered during rescue excavations in the Kerameikos cemetery near the Dipylon Gate and as far as the 'Plato's Academy', about 2 kilometers from the city walls, is indeed impressive, but perhaps not surprising when compared to similar extension of the relatively minor kerameikoi at Selinous or Lokroi Epizephyrii. Despite their large numbers, the excavated remains reveal little information regarding the organization of work and the scale of the output of individual Athenian workshops producing figured pottery. Moreover, the scale and organization of production as a whole, though probably quite large, remains hard to assess.[9]

From Numbers to the Social Reality of Workshops: Ancient Depictions

Even though Corinthian and Athenian painters (and a single Boeotian one) have left us images of potters in their working spaces, these depictions offer surprisingly limited useful information regarding scale of production of decorated pottery. Obviously, these depictions do not offer information beyond single workshops. Yet, more than a hundred scenes on votive plaques found at Penteskouphia near Corinth and ca. 16 scenes on Athenian plaques and pots represent a wide spectrum of the production cycle in detail, from digging out clay to firing and possibly selling pots.[10] Such evidence provides valuable insight into the technologies and the scale and organization of the production within workshops. Representativity is an issue however, since the votive purpose of the plaques and many of the pots involved is likely to have affected what these images show or leave out, and the generally small scale of visible operations may be partly related to the limitations posed by the medium used and the available drawing space. Much of what is shown regarding the organization of work and the hierarchies within workshops is therefore either ambiguous or rather self-evident. It is no surprise that one sees older supervisors and boys working as wheel-turners (fig. 2). In the scenes of painters at work, one can detect a possibility of labor division by seniority, but nothing more. And processes like serial work on parts of the decoration can hardly be visualized – and were not. At most, one could suppose that workshops which had hierarchical teams of two or three people firing kilns and turning the wheel, might also have had similar (or the same) combinations of experienced artisans and apprentices during the painting process.

From Numbers to the Social Reality of Workshops: Starting from Style and Attributions

This then brings me back to Beazley. As illustrated elsewhere in this volume, but also in several books and articles published over the last decades, there are various ways of using framework of stylistic attributions to reconstruct workshop organization. My own aproach is based on a series of monographs on 6th century BC mainly pre-525 BC Attic Black Figure makers, produced in Amsterdam, which offer the following list of hands and their outputs:

Tyrrhenian Group (Kluiver 1997)	8 hands	260 items
Komast cups (Brijder 1983; see also 1991; 2000)	10 hands	ca. 250 items
Siana cups (Brijder 1983; 1991; 2000; Stissi 2009)	ca. 40 hands	1.077 items
Little Master cups (Heesen 2009)	ca. 35 hands	ca. 5.400 items
Nikosthenes (Tosto 1999)	37 hands	ca. 200 items

Even excluding very minor hands, in all these studies many more stylistical units appear than in the Beazleyan corpus they started from, but a large number of them is represented by small numbers of pots. Nevertheless, if one spreads the 130 hands over 5 year blocks starting from dated vessels, there are over 25 hands per year for 565–540 BC, with a peak of 48. As these 48 hands produced a small proportion of the total Athenian output at the time, this again indicates the Beazleyan corpus is missing many artisans.

Zooming in, shapes like Siana cups and Little Master cups appear to have been made by groups of painters spread over (and possibly sometimes moving between) several workshops[11], but the Nikosthenic output seems to be connected to a single workshop, employing between 5 and 8 recognizable hands. The Tyrrhenian Group also looks like a closely connected unit of 4–7 painters, who were probably also doing some of the potting. These results can be repeated by considering other monographs on black or red figure painters. One example is the Shuvalov Painter's workshop which employed some 35 hands between ca. 460 BC and the early 4th century BC, of whom at least 4 were active in any 5-year period, with peaks of over 10 hands around 440–430 BC.[12]

Interestingly, most of these 'hands' come and go fairly quickly while long lasting, truly productive artisans, who constitute the core of the traditional Beazleyan framework, are remarkably rare. Of the 130 Black Figure hands mentioned above, 21 have left us more than 30 surviving pots, and 6[13] of those more than 100. The Shuvalov Painter arrives at about 150 items, but nobody else in the workshop surpasses 20, although a few of the employees have a substantial output elsewhere. In Beazley's original corpus, the proportions of more productive painters are somewhat higher (for about 10% of hands there are over 100 attributed pots, for about 20% more than 30, but for around 60% less than 10). It is therefore clear more intensive recent study has added relatively many 'minor hands'.

While we should probably assume that many small stylistic groups can be merged with others, and some are phantoms, there must be more to this phenomenon. There are certainly some painters moving between workshops, or starting their own workshop after working elsewhere – the Shuvalov workshop offers several cases. These, however, are a minority. Apparently, only a small proportion of potters and painters were regularly active for a long period, while most others either did not work long enough to be recognized by us, or perhaps combined potting and/or painting with other activities. Precisely these minor hands, which appear to form more than 80% of the stylistic units visible to us now, deserve some focused scholarly attention.

The fact that many can be connected to just a few items, often a single vessel, and that even the more visible minor hands usually seem to have been active for a short period only, needs explanation. Low survival rates play a role, in two significant ways: at 0.25%, every surviving vessel of an assistant (also doing other tasks) painting 50 vessels a year would represent 8 years of work. The mortality rate in the pre-modern world must also have affected the average total output of artisans: careers of twenty or thirty years as master, leading to a now well visible output, can perhaps be expected to have been exceptional.

Even those masters who died early in their careers should be visible to some extent during their training and formative years, and not appear suddenly as well-defined hands. The same could apply to many minor hands in the workshop staff who were not regularly engaged in painting. These craftsmen would have required an apprenticeship in painting.[14] Furthermore, one would expect some of them popping up at several moments over longer periods, which is not what we see – or perhaps goes unnoticed due to our way of seeing. Similar issues would arrise if one assumes that workshop staff moved around quickly, perhaps due to other occupations: this again would fit minor hands appearing several times during their working years, and not through single concentrated groups of vessels – unless the general staff turnover rate was high, but in that case training and formation are once more problematic. A final explanation may be found in migration, which could mean that a portion of the minor hands represent staff coming in from elsewhere and/or leaving to workshops in new areas. At least some of these, however, should be visible in their other workplaces as well as the migrant vase-painters we are occasionally able to trace.

Conclusions: Sketching 'Real' Workshops

Perhaps the high output combined with our small corpus are indeed so problematic that we have to stick to broad outlines: a major issue regarding all the hypothetical possibilities mentioned above is that they do not seem to fit any realistic model of workshop organization and operation – a model which should not only include a technical and practical labor division, but also take into account the social organization of work and workshop hierarchies. While it seems clear that the backbone of Athenian decorated pottery production, and the cores of actual workshops, were formed by a relatively small number of very active 'masters' (painters, potter-painters or potters), it is still difficult to envisage how the complete workforce was organized and placed in and around their workshops. While there must have been a flexible, dynamic and to us poorly visible group of minor hands around the core of masters, it is not easy to estimate how many minor hands existed, what their tasks were, and how they were connected to and moved through workshops.[15] A few well-studied workshops or groups of workshops, like those of the Shuvalov Painter, the Penthesileia Group or the painters of Siana cups, moreover, show a level of complexity and interaction between artisans that does not seem to fit a traditional master-centered model very well. Indeed, even some simpler looking groups, like the Tyrrhenian workshop with its handful of apparent 'masters' who seem to operate closely together but with no clear hierarchy, deviate from such a traditional organisational perspective.

In view of these, but also of the scale of production as estimated above, I would suggest that there was more labor division and specialization and a larger floating body of short term and/or part time staff than scholars often have thought. At the same time, since many 'minor hands' exhibit high levels of quality in painting and potting, barely distinguishable from what 'masters' achieved, we may need to consider that the basic skills required to be a fully qualified potter or painter were easier to develop than we have assumed.

It may be noted here that some of the criticism offered to my earlier workforce estimates by Sapirstein seems to conflate my lines of argumentation: first, the use of biographic studies: as it is evident also in this paper, I have used recent monographs to show that there are many more 'hands' than Beazley once recognized. However, I never stated that *all* these 'hands' correspond to *full-time* craftspeople – rather the opposite, as my point is that we should envisage a flexible workforce, and various kinds of employment; second, my estimation of the pottery workforce: as should be clear from my previous calculations[16] and the argumentation in this paper I do not think that the increased number of 'hands' (or known 'hands' with an increased recorded output) can all simply be added up to estimate the total size of the pottery workforce. Some hands should definitely be included and it is odd that many hands, such as the KX Painter or the Castellani Painter, which fulfill the quantitative criteria for inclusion in Sapirstein's model, are excluded. For others, however, we have to look for alternative approaches, as I think we do need to account for the output of these 'minor' artisans and cannot simply remove them either from an economic model or from historical reality; it is untenable that all these minor hands *together* were marginal, as Sapirstein argues.

To support this, I argue that not only the total group of producers but also our corpus of existing decorated pottery is considerably larger than that estimated by Sapirstein. The numbers I offer for the corpus are extrapolations from the total of items listed by the Beazley Archive Pottery Database (BAPD) which I based on a series of case studies of groups of material, including a corpus of about 30.000 published Athenian figured pots and fragments from regular excavations, few of which are included in the BAPD, that I have used in my dissertation.[17] If one finds extrapolations too risky, an alternative would be to start from a minimum number of published material, which I estimate at (far) above 200.000 items. Overall estimates can always be a matter of debate, but Sapirstein's model, based on 38.830 items, fails to address even this lowest possible estimate, which seems a clear bottom figure.

What we need is an integrated approach, combining data and avoiding uncertain individual detail. I provide two examples: the 5.400 Little Master cups listed above (based on Heesen 2009, a mere selection of the corpus) were produced in about 40 years (ca. 565–525 BC), so at a rate of 135 surviving vessels a year. Using Sapirstein's regular output figure for potter-painters, 27 full-time artisans would be needed to produce these pots. Of course, many (but not all!) Little Master cups are relatively small and simply decorated, so possibly a much higher output rate should be used in a workforce size reconstruction. Even so, it is difficult to reduce the total number of the makers of Little Master cups to a number (2, 3, even 5?) which, given the relative role of these cups in the total Athenian production of the period, would fit the 18–34 that form Sapirstein's total estimates for the size of the Athenian pottery workforce between 575 and 525 BC. In addition, the existing 2.700 Siana cups (pers. comm. H. Brijder, soon to be published) produced in an overlapping 50-year span (ca. 580–530 BC), would add 54 elaborate vessels to the yearly output of 135 Little Master cups just mentioned. The Siana cups alone then would have required 5–10 artisans, according to Sapirstein's model. Additional cases are easy to find, but I think the basic point is clear: the numbers of artisans suggested by Sapirstein are far too low to have produced the output as documented by published items.

If the number of skilled potters and painters potentially available was much higher than the masters we readily recognize, there must have been a large number of minor hands backstage, either doing generic work in the pottery or (un)employed outside, and only occasionally coming into the light – as we perceive the ancient reality. Some of these hands may have been young apprentices who never advanced further, dying early or moving to other occupations, others skilled hands on the background, others again potential masters who never managed to establish themselves properly or had to give up soon. Undeniably, it is difficult to know what exactly happened in each case. I would argue, however, that the availability of a large group of skilled craftspeople outside a core group of workshops and artisans would have kept the social and economic balance tense and could have been a major factor in the functioning of workshops, possibly stimulating high production figures and perhaps even keeping costs low.

This brings me to a final point. Our ideas or hypotheses about the organization of workshops are at least partly grounded in assumptions, which are also a foundation of our approach to attribution. Starting from the preserved images and ethnographic examples, it is generally assumed that workshops had a core of few potters and/or painters, usually even just one of each or a single potter-painter, surrounded by some assistants, who could well be family members (as also suggested by signatures). A similar image, partly based on a somewhat romantic view on early modern artists' workshops, is also the starting point of the attribution framework, centering on masters who have groups around them and train pupils. I am not quite sure this cosy image fits what I have sketched above: both the very large output and the dynamic body of invisible or partly visible minor hands suggest a much less romantic Kerameikos than we may like to recognize, with a large body of 'flex workers', and rather unstable workshop teams, producing large numbers of vessels.

Notes

[1] I want to thank E. Hasaki and M. Bentz for inviting me at this session, and particularly D. Cline for reading my paper when I could not attend, at the last minute. I should also note here that parts of this paper are based on Stissi 2016, which explores related issues, with a stronger focus on artisanal organization and less attention to quantities of production.

[2] <www.beazley.ox.ac.uk/xdb/ASP/default.asp> (09.4.2020). As Philip Sapirstein (this volume) rightly remarks, in earlier work I have been wrong to assume that non-"Athenian figured" material in the Beazley archive is negligible – it forms more than quarter of the entries. This difference does not significantly affect my argumentation. The number I now give is that of the entries for Athenian black and red figure in the database; this includes items which may not be considered as "figured" by some, but also excludes some potentially relevant material entered under different headings.

[3] See Bentz 1998, 17 f. n. 62; Stissi 2002, 24–31; Sapirstein 2013b, 9, all with references to earlier literature.

[4] According to Sapirstein 2013a, 506 f.; Table 1.

[5] See Sapirstein 2013a, 507; 2013b, 9.

[6] For overviews and lists of finds see Hasaki 2002, Stissi 2002, 35–73 and Appendix I; 2012; see also, for Athens, Baziotopoulou-Valavani 1994; Monaco 2000.

[7] For the workshop in Corfu (city) see Preka-Alexandri 1992; Kourkoumélis – Démesticha 1997; for the recent finds at Selinous Bentz et al. 2013, and this volume.

[8] Zachariadou et al. 1985.

[9] Stissi 2012 is an attempt. Hasaki 2011 offers an interesting different approach, bringing together ethnographic and archaeological data.

[10] A good recent overview with references can be found in Williams 2009; see also Stissi 2002, 75–95.

[11] This phenomenon is very nicely explored in the article by Hasaki and Cline in this volume.

[12] Lezzi-Hafter 1976.

[13] The C Painter, the Heidelberg Painter, the Taras Painter, Tleson/the Tleson Painter, the Centaur Painter and Nikosthenes.

[14] For an excellent overview of apprenticeship in ancient crafts, offering many insights relevant to the discussion here, see Hasaki 2013.

[15] The project started by Hasaki and Cline to map connections between makers in a network is a promising start, but is limited by its (understandable) rooting in Beazley's work, which misses many more recently defined makers.

[16] Stissi 2016, 50–51.

[17] See Stissi 2002, 24–27, Tables III.3.a-b-c.

Image Credits

Fig. 1: Based on Baziotopoulou-Valavani 1994, 48, fig. 2, with some modifications. – Fig. 2: from I.S. Mark, The Lure of Philosophy: Craft and Higher Learning in Ancient Greece, in: W.G. Moon (ed.), Polykleitos, the Doryphoros and Tradition (London 1995) 25–51. 26 fig. 3.1.

References

Baziotopoulou-Valavani 1994
E. Baziotopoulou-Valavani, Ανασκαφές σε αθηναϊκά κεραμικά εργαστήρια αρχαϊκών και κλασικών χρόνων, in: W.D.E. Coulson et al. (eds.), The Archaeology of Athens and Attica under the Democracy. Proceedings of an International Conference Celebrating 2500 Years since the Birth of Democracy in Greece, Held at the American School of Classical Studies at Athens, December 4–6, 1992, Oxbow Monograph 37 (Oxford 1994) 45–54.

Bentz 1998
M. Bentz, Panathenäische Preisamphoren. Eine athenische Vasengattung und ihre Funktion vom 6.–4. Jahrhundert v. Chr., AntK Beih. 18 (Basel 1998).

Bentz et al. 2013
M. Bentz – L. Adorno – J. Albers – J.M. Müller – G. Zuchtriegel, Werkstätten in Selinunt. Vorbericht über die Arbeiten 2010-2012, RM 119, 2013, 69–98.

Brijder 1983
H.A.G. Brijder, Siana Cups I and Komast Cups, Allard Pierson Series 4 (Amsterdam 1983).

Brijder 1991
H.A.G. Brijder, Siana Cups II: the Heidelberg Painter, Allard Pierson Series 8 (Amsterdam 1991).
Brijder 2000
H.A.G. Brijder, Siana Cups III, The Red-black Painter, Griffin-bird Painter and Siana Cups resembling Lip-cups, Allard Pierson Series 13 (Amsterdam 2000).
Hasaki 2002
E. Hasaki, Ceramic Kilns in Ancient Greece: Technology and Organization of Ceramic Workshops (Ph.D. diss. University of Cincinnati 2002).
Hasaki 2011
E. Hasaki, Crafting Spaces: Archaeological, Ethnographic, and Ethnoarchaeological Studies on Spatial Organization in Pottery Workshops in Greece and Tunisia, in: M. Lawall – J. Lund (eds.), Pottery in the Archaeological Record: Greece and Beyond (Aarhus 2011) 12–28.
Hasaki 2013
E. Hasaki, Craft Apprenticeship in Ancient Greece: Reaching beyond the Masters, in: W. Wendrich (ed.), Archaeology and Apprenticeship: Acquiring Body Knowledge in the Ancient World (Tucson 2013) 171–202.
Heesen 2009
P. Heesen, Athenian Little-Master Cups (Ph.D. diss. University of Amsterdam 2009).
Kluiver 1997
J. Kluiver, The 'Tyrrhenian' Group. Athenian Black-Figure Vases from ca 570/565–545 B.C. (Ph.D. diss. University of Amsterdam 1997).
Kourkoumélis – Démesticha 1997
D. Kourkoumélis – S. Démesticha, Les outils de potier de l'atelier de Figaretto à Corfou, BCH 121, 1997, 553–571.
Lezzi-Hafter 1976
A. Lezzi-Hafter, Der Schuwalow-Maler. Eine Kannenwerkstatt der Parthenonzeit, Kerameus 2 (Mainz 1976).
Monaco 2000
M.C. Monaco, Ergasteria: Impianti artigianali ceramici ad Atene ed in Attica dal protogeometrico alle soglie dell'ellenismo (Rome 2000).
Preka-Alexandri 1992
K. Preka-Alexandri, A Ceramic Workshop in Figareto, Corfu, in: F. Blondé – J.Y. Perreault (eds.), Les ateliers de potiers dans le monde grec aux époques géometrique, archaïque et classique. Actes de la Table Ronde organisée à l'École française d'Athenes (2 et 3 octobre 1987), BCH Suppl. 23 (Athens 1992) 41–52.
Sapirstein 2013a
P. Sapirstein, Painters, Potters, and the Scale of the Attic Vase-Painting Industry, AJA 117, 2013, 493–510.
Sapirstein 2013b
P. Sapirstein, Methodology, Bibliography, and Commentary for the Painters in the Study, AJA 117, 2013, online 1–47.

Stissi 2002

V.V. Stissi, Pottery to the People: The Production, Distribution and Consumption of Decorated Pottery in the Greek World in the Archaic Period (650–480 BC) (Ph.D. diss. University of Amsterdam 2002).

Stissi 2009

V.V. Stissi, Why Did They End up There? The Role of Iconography in the Distribution, Purchase and Use of Siana Cups, in: E. Moormann – V. Stissi, (eds.) Shapes and Images. Studies on Attic Black Figure Black Figure and Related Topics in Honour of Herman A.G. Brijder (Paris, Walpole MA 2009) 21–36.

Stissi 2012

V.V. Stissi, Giving the Kerameikos a Context. Ancient Greek Potters' Quarters as Part of the Polis Space, Economy and Society, in: A. Esposito – G. Sanidas, (eds.) "Quartiers" artisanaux en Grèce ancienne. Une perspective méditerranéenne (Villeneuve d'Ascq 2012) 201–230.

Stissi 2016

V.V. Stissi, Minor Artisans, Major Impact? in: N. Eschbach – S. Schmidt (eds.), Töpfer, Maler, Werkstatt: Zuschreibungen in der griechischen Vasenmalerei und die Organisation antiker Keramikproduktion, CVA Beih. 7 (Munich 2016) 47–53.

Tosto 1999

V. Tosto, The Black-Figure Pottery Signed ΝΙΚΟΣΘΕΝΕΣΕΠΟΙΕΣΕΝ, Allard Pierson Series 11 (Amsterdam 1999).

Williams 2009

D. Williams, Picturing Potters and Painters, in: J.H. Oakley – O. Palagia (eds.) Athenian Potters and Painters II (Oxford 2009) 306–317.

Zachariadou et al. 1985

O. Zachariadou – D. Kyriakou – E. Baziotopoulou, Σωστική ανασκαφή στον ανισόπεδο κόμβο Λένορμαν-Κωνσταντινουπόλεως, AAA 18, 1985, 39–50.

Production and Consumption of Ceramics at Selinous: A Quantitative Approach

Martin Bentz

Introduction

This chapter presents new evidence from Selinous to shed light on the role of ceramic production in the economy of the Greek city-states in Classical times. At this Western Greek metropolis, we have found an efficiently organized system of mass production previously unknown in Greece. As I argue here, this is one of the few cases where we are on a more solid ground to calculate and compare production and consumption numbers of ceramic products.[1]

The term "ceramics" covers all products made of fired clay: (1) building materials, mainly roof tiles; (2) a wide range of objects of different sizes and functions: from the large (e.g., altars, louteria and sarcophagi), to the very small (loom-weights, lamps); (3) pots of various sizes, shapes and functions from large pithoi to cooking and table ware; and (4) figurines, mostly of small size and other decorative objects in terracotta.[2]

The main aim here is to provide a detailed account of ceramic production and consumption in Selinous. On the production side, how many workshops existed, and what was their annual output? How many workmen were involved in the ceramic industry? And on the consumption side, how many ceramics does a city require? How many households used how many ceramics? How many ceramic objects were used in sanctuaries? How many local ceramic products were given as grave goods in how many graves? How many ceramic products were used in other public spaces?

An examination of these issues allows us to draw some conclusions about the economic importance of the ceramic industry at Selinous, asking for example what percentage of the population earned its living from working in the ceramic industry. Can the numbers help us characterize the city's economy in general: was it subsistence-based or export oriented?

While previous estimates of the production capacities of the Greek ceramic industry have been based largely on the output of painted Attic pottery, this is a particular case, significant mostly for Athens and not as relevant for the Greek polis economy in general as other ceramic products are.[3]

Many scholars, especially historians, doubt whether ceramics can be used at all for the reconstruction of ancient economies; as J.K. Davies recently stated: "And yet I have to be frank: from among the primary materials of all the specialist sub- disciplines of the Altertumswissenschaften, it is the ceramic material which I – and I suspect many others – find the hardest of all to use intelligently and constructively".[4] Archaeologists, however, are mostly convinced of the opposite viewpoint, expressed as follows by G. Fülle: "If the field of ancient economy is a battlefield, arguments based on pottery research certainly belong with the best of the weapons."[5] Even more skepticism exists –

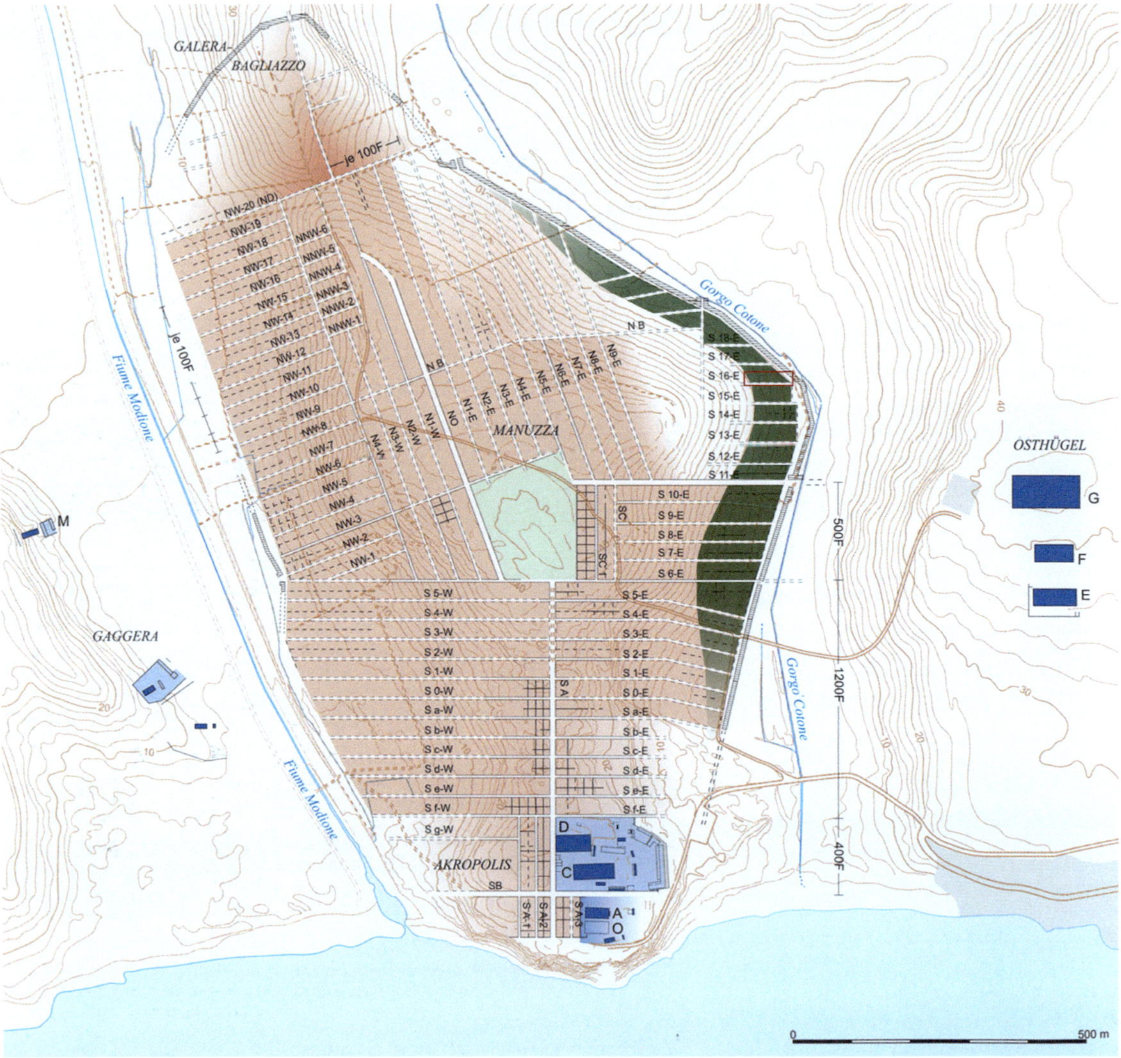

Fig. 1: Selinous with the potter's quarter (in green, to the right).

among archaeologists as well – concerning quantitative accounts: "to seek quantification is a pipe-dream".[6] The numbers presented here can undoubtedly be criticized in many details and should not be taken as absolute. The general picture they outline, and the proportions they suggest, however, are founded on many observations in the field, not merely on assumptions.

Selinous

Selinous was founded in 628 BC by its mother city, Megara Hyblaia and was destroyed by the Carthaginians in 409 BC. Thanks to geophysical prospection and studies by

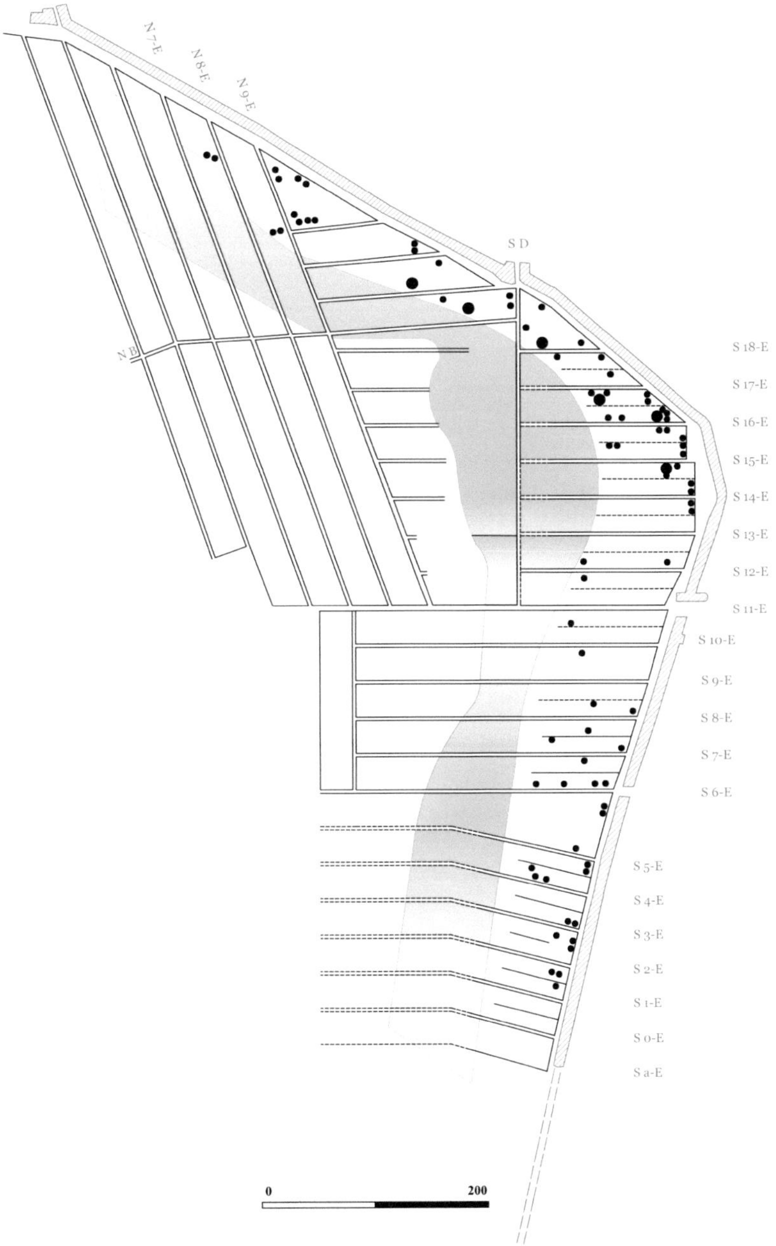

Fig. 2: Schematic plan of the potter's quarter.

Dieter Mertens,[7] we are able to reconstruct with a high degree of precision, the city map, including all streets, insulae, and houses (fig. 1).

Our understanding of the different functional parts of the town is well established: the sacred space with the central sanctuary on the acropolis with six temples; several extramural sanctuaries east and west of the city; the cemeteries bordering the town on the north and west; the agora, the political and economic city center; the residential areas; and

number of kilns	dimensions (diam.)	capacity single kiln	capacity all kilns
6	>= 5 m	40 m^3	240 m^3
55	2–3 m	10 m^3	550 m^3
23	< 2 m	4 m^3	92 m^3
84			**882 m^3**

Fig. 3: Potter's quarter in Selinous, kilns and their capacities.

Ceramic-Types	Dimensions and Weights of Single Vases	no./m^3	weight/m^3
Lekythoi, Aryballoi etc.	diam. 5,5 × h 11 cm; 0,175 kg	1536	256 kg
Bell krater	diam. 30 × h 28 cm; 2,3 kg	36	128 kg
Transport amphora	diam. 35 × h 60 cm; 7,2 kg	12	86,4 kg
Tile/stroter	57 × 80 cm; 24 kg	50	1200 kg
Tile/calypter	20 × 80 cm; 21 kg	100	2000 kg
Pithos	diam. 1,0 × h 90 cm	1	

Fig. 4: Dimensions and weights of different products.

the economic spaces, including the two ports located at the mouths of the two rivers and the potter's quarter in the east.

Geophysical prospection aided in the identification of an industrial zone or potter's quarter on the east edge of the city, inside the wall along the Cotone valley.[8] It is more than 1 km long and 84 kilns, clearly visible as black anomalies, can be dentified, 55 of which are larger than 2 m in diameter. All of these kilns date to the 5th century, as kilns in Archaic levels would not be visible in the prospection,[9] and all went out of use when the city was destroyed in 409 BC. This potter's quarter is separated from the residential areas by a strip of undeveloped land. The schematic map reveals further details about its layout (fig. 2): the larger kilns (with a diameter of about 5 m) are located in the north, while the smaller ones are concentrated in the south, towards the port. There was obviously a purposeful topographic distribution of workshops for different products. Another striking aspect of the layout is the preference for pairs or clusters of kilns situated near each other; only rarely do we find single kilns.[10] This points to a high degree of efficiency in the production process, as these kilns were clearly used for continuous, cyclic firing; that is, when the first kiln was fired, the second was prepared and was fired when the first was emptied, and so on. Here we can recognize an optimized efficient division of labor with specialists handling each phase of the production process: a potter, for example, only working clay, and a kiln master only concerned with the firing.

annual consumption	Basis for calculation
Houses: – roof tiles etc. – equipment from big storage jars to lamps	– 2.500 houses in Selinous – parallels from Himera, Attica, Olynthos, Halieis
Graves: – grave goods – terracotta sarcophagi	ca. 5.000 graves from Tusa excavations 1963–1967, absolute no. of graves/year according to population
Sanctuaries: – buildings – votive offerings	e.g. Malophoros sanctuary with 7.000 terracottas, 4.850 lamps, 5.000 vases (18% local)
public buildings, infrastructure	

Fig. 5: Basis for the calculation of the consumption of ceramic products.

To illustrate the usefulness of the geophysics' maps, we can compare observations based on the map against the results of excavations in one of the insulae where we found a workshop measuring about 1.200 m^2 built on four terraces.[11] The seven kilns, parts of which are well preserved, date to the 5th century. A wide range of products were made, or at least fired, here: the large circular kiln would have been used in the production of roof tiles, the rectangular kilns accommodated sarcophagi, pithoi, and louteria, while the smaller ones fired pots and table ware of different size and shape. This was a large workshop – one of the largest ever discovered – and it was designed for mass production: the big kiln alone (diam. 5.2 m) was able to fire up to 2.000 roof tiles at once. It is likely that about 18–20 men worked here (fig. 8).

In reality, the workshop was even more extensive, as the wall that limited the courtyard on the second level towards the north was pulled down in the early 5th century. This combined our workshop with the adjacent one creating a space of ca. 2.000 m^2 with a common central courtyard and at least six more kilns.[12]

Calculation

Production

The evidence allows us to make some estimates relating to ceramic production and consumption at Selinous. We begin with the production numbers from the potter's quarter. Altogether there are the 84 kilns of the 5th century: 6 with a diameter of at least 5 m, 55 of 2–3 m and 23 of 1–2 m. These should be viewed as minimum numbers as there may be smaller kilns that cannot be distinguished on the map from other structures. Given the diameter or length of the kilns it is possible to estimate their

	Pithoi	large (e.g., louteria, bathtubs)	medium (e.g., amphorae, bowls)	small (table-ware)	very small (e.g., loom-weights, lamps)	Terracotta figurines
Dema	5	2	29	53	6	1
Vari	2	27 (beehive)	40	81	2+x	
Halieis 7	1		56	202	11	
Halieis A	3		15	95	7	
Halieis C	3	1	27	101		
Halieis D	7		26	100		
Halieis E	?		27	87	16	x
Olynthos, Many Colours	4	2	19	75	150	19
Olynthos, Bronzes	3	3	4	>41	10	
Olynthos, A iv 9	2	5	6	32	112	5
Olynthos, D v 6	4	3	19	40	50	1
Himera III, VI, 2	3	9	11	59	34	35
Himera III, IV, 1	2	4	12	31	20	6
Himera II, I, 2–3	3	8	16	26	48	11
range	2–7	1–27	4–56	32–202	0–150	0–19
average	3	3	26	100	75	10
Selinous, × 2.500	**7.500**	**7.500**	**65.000**	**250.000**	**187.500**	**25.000**

Fig. 6: Ceramic products found in Classical houses.

volume/ capacity in cubic meters; exact numbers cannot be calculated, however, without knowing the height of the cupola, which differs according to kiln size (fig. 3).[13]

Fig. 4 lists products of varying sizes from small perfume vases or lamps up to large pithoi, and shows how many of them fit in a space of 1 m^3 and how much they weigh. These considerations become important for calculating consumption numbers.

I consider that a kiln was fired once per month (a firing cycle takes about two weeks and the pairs of kilns were used in the alternating manner discussed above).[14] I suppose that these specialized workshops operated year-round,[15] but due to variations in weather conditions production levels were probably not always consistent; therefore I assume an average number of nine months a year. These calculations yield a result of nearly 8.000 m^3.

We must keep in mind that not all kilns detected by geophysics would have been in use at the same time. In our excavated workshop, for example, four of the seven 5th

	total no. all houses	per year	sanctuary	grave	total no.	m³	kg/ m³	fuel kg
replacement rate	*+ 100%*							
pithoi	15.000	164		2	164	150	100	4.065
louteria etc.	15.000	164	2		164	80	100	2.170
replacement rate	+ 800%							
mid-size	520.000	5.715			5.715	160	128	5.550
small	2.000.000	22.000	112	1.800	40.000	30	256	2.080
very small	1.550.000	16.500						
terracottas	200.000	2.200	190	?	2.400			
replacement rate	+ 20%							
tiles (stroter)	1.000.000	11.000	?		11.000	220	1200	71.500
tiles (calypter)	1.000.000	11.000	?		11.000	110	2000	59.600
						750	**3.800**	**145.000**

Fig. 7: Consumption of ceramics in Selinous.

century kilns were used contemporaneously. So, to avoid inflation of the numbers, I divide the maximum capacity by two, arriving at 4.000 m³ per year. This would represent about 2.000 tons of clay, if we take the average weight of all products per cubic meter.

Consumption

Calculations relating to consumption must take into account all parts of the city (fig. 5). First, we must consider all local products used in an average house, from roof tiles for the covered spaces,[16] to pithoi, amphorae, table ware, loom weights, and so on. This number can then be multiplied by the number of the existing houses (2.500). To reconstruct the number of ceramic objects found in houses, I compare the evidence from Selinous[17] to that from other Classical sites, including the well-published Himera on Sicily[18] and other better- excavated examples from Greece (fig. 6).[19] Houses used solely for residential purposes present a different picture from houses that were also dedicated to commercial activities. Still, the average result seems quite homogeneous: ca. 3 pithoi, 3 louteria, about 25 amphorae, and hundreds of small objects.

These numbers seem quite reliable, but there are other unknown factors, such as how often objects needed to be replaced. For example, how long would a roof tile last? Roofs were never entirely replaced; instead, individual damaged tiles were repaired as needed.[20] Wikander's addition of 10% to account for repairs over a 100-year period[21] seems a bit low to me; accordingly, I have doubled this number, to 20%. For most other objects I figure on a substitution roughly every decade in the 5th century, which at Selinous lasted only until 409. Pithoi are only doubled whereas

human resources/ production steps	one big workshop (half insula)	whole potter's quarter (24 insulae)
clay extraction		25
clay transport		20
clay processing		25
fuel producing and transport		50
provision of other materials (e.g., colors)		20
potter assistant	3 3	288
painter	3	144
kiln master assistant	3 3	288
unskilled labor	3	144
organization/sale	2	96
	20 (× 48 ?)	**ca. 900–1.200**

Fig. 8: Human resources involved in the ceramic production.

mid-size vessels are multiplied by 8 in the 5th century. Finally, the total of products is divided by 91 to reach a yearly average (fig. 7).

We know the average numbers of grave contents very well as thousands of 5th century examples were excavated by Vincenzo Tusa in the 1960s. This number is not really relevant to questions about production, because only a few objects in the graves (one or two) were made of local clay.[22] There was, however, a limited production of terracotta sarcophagi at Selinous.[23]

In sanctuaries, mostly small objects, such as terracotta figurines or miniature vases, were deposited. The Malophoros sanctuary yielded thousands of objects, giving us some idea of the quantities involved.[24]

If we translate all of the numbers (fig. 7) from the different areas of the city into m^3, in order to compare them with the kiln capacities, we reach a figure of 760 m^3 for the total consumption of ceramic goods.

The main conclusion to be drawn from these calculations is that annual ceramic production of the workshops (4.000 m^3) would have resulted in a large surplus. At least five times more ceramics were produced than were consumed, meaning that a major part of the production was to be sold outside the city.

Another important aspect of the pottery industry's impact on the city's economy is the size of its workforce: the workers involved in the 40–50 workshops in the Kerameikos of

Selinous, plus the workmen engaged in extracting and delivering raw material and fuel, mostly wood. A workshop like ours may have employed 18–20 people; the ceramic business as a whole, about 900–1.200 (fig. 8).[25] If we consider only some these men as responsible for the support of a whole family we can estimate that the number of people living on ceramic production was between 2.500 and 4.000, a considerable segment (15%–25%) of the population of Selinous, which had between 14.000 and 19.000 inhabitants in the 5th century.[26] If we also take into account the building sector with its consumption of millions of mudbricks, the number of people living on clay products in general is much higher.

In conclusion, Selinous offers a unique opportunity to attempt to quantify both production and consumption of ceramics. The city's potter's quarter, an efficiently organized and specialized cluster of workshops with no residential features, was certainly dedicated to full-time production. Looking at the whole of products, it is possible to calculate production and consumption rates. Two or three workshops like the one we excavated would have been sufficient to meet the demands of the city alone, so it is clear that the annual production of all workshops resulted in a large surplus. The pottery industry with its required workforce, was an important part of the city's economy, supporting a significant part of its population. And while the demonstrable wealth of the city, which boasted a dozen templs, was more likely derived from agricultural products[27], Selinous seems to have been a major ceramic production center, at least for Western Sicily. We cannot say whether Selinous, with its emormous surplus production and large workshops is a typical example or an exception. It is evident however, that the familiar concept of smaller, family-based workshops working mostly to satisfy local demand is not the only model for Classical ceramic production.[28]

Notes

[1] This short paper focuses on production scale and does not provide a thorough description of the results of the excavations at Selinous. For a more detailed version, with more evidence and discussion of the implications on economic questions in general, see Bentz 2017, or the overview in Bentz 2018. All dates are BC.

[2] I exclude unfired clay products such as the millions of mudbricks used in the building sector.

[3] Cook 1959 was the first to attempt a detailed account; the most recent (and much more reliable) estimates can be found in Sapirstein 2013; Sapirstein 2014; and in this volume.

[4] Davies 2013, 11.

[5] Fülle 1997, 111.

[6] Davies 2013, 12. Cook (1959, 120) had already abandoned his quantitative considerations citing Beloch 1912, 88 who talks of houses of cards: "Er kann dabei sehr viel Scharfsinn und Gelehrsamkeit zeigen, aber was er baut, sind Kartenhäuser, die beim leisesten Hauch umfallen". Stissi 2002, 5–66, likewise remains very skeptical.

[7] Mertens 2003.

[8] Bentz et al. 2013; Bentz et al. 2016; Bentz 2017; Bentz 2018; the final publication of the results of the seven fieldwork seasons from 2010 to 2016 is in preparation.

[9] This is a result of our excavations; the measures of the excavated 5th century kilns correspond exactly to the geomagnetic plan where even the praefurnia of the bigger kiln can be seen.
[10] Bentz 2017, 21–24 with references and a detailed list in fig. 4.
[11] Space does not permit me to describe this space in greater detail; in addition to the references given in note 8, see panel 3.2 "Organization of space and work: potter's workshops in the Greek World" in the congress proceedings.
[12] Bentz 2017, fig. 5.
[13] On the basis of iconographic evidence, better-preserved excavated examples and ethnographic parallels, it is generally assumed that the height of the cupola matches the diameter of the kiln. This rule, however, does not apply to larger kilns (2–5 m in diameter); a mudbrick cupola 5 m high, for example, cannot be realized. In these cases I assume a cupola height equal to one-half of the diameter. See Stissi 2002, 59–60; Cuomo di Caprio 2007, 510–512. 516–521; Manacorda – Pallecchi 2012, 287–292; Barra Bagnasco 1989, 30 with different approaches.
[14] There exists a consensus on this point: Cuomo di Caprio 1974; Barra Bagnasco 1989; Hasaki 2002, 271; Manacorda – Pallecchi 2012, 471–474.
[15] There are ethnographic parallels for this assumption: Hampe – Winter 1965, 199: "Die Töpfer und Ziegler Süditaliens müssen meist ganz von ihrem Handwerk, dem Töpfern und Ziegelmachen leben; sie arbeiten das ganze Jahr hindurch in ihrer Werkstatt, im Sommer pausenlos, im Winter gemächlicher, weil das Trocknen der Gefäße oder der Ziegel dann langsamer vonstattengeht. Oder, soweit Töpferei und Ziegelei in einer Werkstatt vereinigt sind, arbeiten sie in der warmen Jahreszeit vorwiegend als Töpfer, in der kalten hauptsächlich als Ziegler." See also Manacorda – Pallecchi 2012, 472 f., who refer to the evidence of the monthly stamps from Scolacium with a break of only two months.
[16] The house plots measure 220 m^2 and we must consider that on average one-quarter was not roofed, there are overhangs etc., therefore, I count 330 stroters and calypters per house.
[17] To date, no inventory of a Classical house in Selinous has been completely published.
[18] Allegro 1976; Allegro 2008; Harms 2010.
[19] Attica, Dema House: Jones et al. 1962; Vari House: Jones et al. 1973; Halieis: Ault 2005; Olynthos: Cahill 2002.
[20] For example, one better-preserved workshop space in the Selinous workshop is roofed with 7 different types of stroters.
[21] Wikander 1993, 137–139.
[22] The Buffa necropolis contained more than 1.200 graves of the 5th century: Meola 1996, 14–16; Meola 1997, 520 pl. 5 with list of pottery; Meola 1998; Manicalunga-Timpone Nero-Necropolis: Leibundgut Wieland 1994, Leibundgut Wieland 1997; Manicalunga-Gaggera-Necropolis: Kustermann Graf 2002, 55–58. 260–271.
[23] Bonanno 1998, 40–41. 210–212 pls. 95–107 with the published examples.
[24] See Hinz 1989, 152 f. for an overview; Dewailly 1992, 33 lists 7.000 terracottas, 5.000 lamps and 1.250 local vases from the old excavations from 1888–1918; Dehl-von Kaenel 1995, 417, lists nearly 5.000 Archaic vases, 20% of which were locally produced. If you halve these numbers, to separate the 6th from the 5th century, and multiply the 5th century number by 10, to take into account the later excavations, the result is more than 500 statuettes and vases per year – which is irrelevant for the overall production.

[25] We do not know if these were mainly slaves or free citizens.
[26] Zuchtriegel 2011 with references, recently followed by De Angelis 2016, 197. These numbers depend on how many persons we consider to be part of a family and living in one house, the estimates range from 4,6 to 10 depending on how many slaves each family had.
[27] Bentz 2017, 36 with references.
[28] Acton 2014 and Acton 2016 on the "small-scale business" model which theoretically is the most efficient.

Image Credits

Fig. 1: after Mertens 2006, 174 Abb. 303 with modifications by the author. – Fig. 2–8: by the author.

References

Acton 2014
P. Acton, Poiesis. Manufacturing in Classical Athens (Oxford 2014).

Acton 2016
P. Acton, Industry Structure and Income Opportunities for Households in Classical Athens, in: E.M. Harris – D.M. Lewis – M. Woolmer (eds.), The Ancient Greek Economy. Markets, Households and City-states (Cambridge 2016) 149–165.

Allegro 1976
N. Allegro (ed.), Campagne di scavo 1966–1973, Himera 2 (Rome 1976).

Allegro 2008
N. Allegro (ed.), L'abitato. Isolato II. I blocchi 1–4 della zona 1, Himera 5 (Rome 2008).

Ault 2005
B.A. Ault, The Houses. The Organization and Use of Domestic Space, The Excavations at Ancient Halieis 2 (Bloomington 2005).

Barra Bagnasco 1989
M. Barra Bagnasco, Aspetti di vita quotidiana a Locri Epizefiri, in: M. Barra Bagnasco (ed.), Cultura materiale e vita quotidiana, Locri Epizefiri 3 (Florence 1989) 5–40.

Beloch 1912
K. Beloch, Griechische Geschichte 1, 2 [2](Straßburg 1912).

Bentz et al. 2016
M. Bentz – L. Adorno – J. Albers – A. Miß – J.M. Müller, Das Handwerkerviertel von Selinunt – Vorbericht zu den archaischen Strukturen der Kampagnen 2010–2016, KuBA 6, 2016, 59–74.

Bentz 2017
M. Bentz, Zur Rolle der Keramikproduktion in der griechischen Stadt klassischer Zeit. Ein quantitativer Ansatz am Beispiel von Selinunt, KuBA 7, 2017, 17–44.

Bentz 2018
M. Bentz, The Role of Ceramic Production in the Classical Greek City, in: M. Bentz – T. Helms (eds.), Craft Production Systems in a Cross-Cultural Perspective, Studien zur Wirtschaftsarchäologie 1 (Bonn 2018) 101–112.

Bonanno 1998
C. Bonanno, I sarcofagi fittili della Sicilia (Rome 1998).

Cahill 2002
N. Cahill, Household and City Organization at Olynthus (New Haven 2002).

Cook 1959
R.M. Cook, Die Bedeutung der bemalten Keramik für den griechischen Handel, JdI 74, 1959, 114–123.

Cuomo di Caprio 1974
N. Cuomo di Caprio, Fornaci per ceramica a Locri, Klearchos 16, 1974, 43–66.

Cuomo di Caprio 2007
N. Cuomo di Caprio, Ceramica in archeologia. Antiche tecniche di lavorazione e moderni metodi di indagine ^{2}(Rome 2007)

Davies 2013
J. K. Davies, Ceramics and the Economic Historian: Mixed Messages and Unharmonised Agendas, in: A. Tsingarida – D. Viviers (eds.), Pottery Markets in the Ancient Greek World (8th–1st centuries B.C.) (Brusssels 2013) 11–17.

De Angelis 2016
F. De Angelis, Archaic and Classical Greek Sicily (Oxford 2016).

Dehl – von Kaenel 1995
C. Dehl – von Kaenel, Die archaische Keramik aus dem Malophoros-Heiligtum in Selinunt: die korinthischen, lakonischen, ostgriechischen, etruskischen und megarischen Importe sowie die "argivisch-monochrome" und lokale Keramik aus den alten Grabungen (Berlin 1995).

Dewailly 1992
M. Dewailly, Les statuettes aux parures du Sanctuaire de la Malophoros à Sélinonte: contexte, typologie et interprétation d'une catégorie d'offrandes (Naples 1992).

Fülle 1997
G. Fülle, The Internal Organization of the Arretine Terra Sigillata Industry: Problems of Evidence and Interpretation, JRS 87, 1997, 111–155.

Hampe – Winter 1965
R. Hampe – A. Winter, Bei Töpfern und Zieglern in Süditalien, Sizilien und Griechenland (Mainz 1965).

Harms 2010
A. Harms, Wohnhäuser in Himera. Untersuchungen zur Stadtentwicklung, Raumorganisation und -funktion (Ph.D. diss. University of Hamburg 2010).

Hasaki 2002
E. Hasaki, Ceramic Kilns in Ancient Greece: Technology and Organisation of Ceramic Workshops (Ph.D. diss. University of Cincinnati 2002).

Hinz 1989

V. Hinz, Der Kult von Demeter und Kore auf Sizilien in der Magna Graecia (Wiesbaden 1989).

Jones et al. 1962

J.E. Jones – L.H. Sackett – A.J. Graham, The Dema House in Attica, BSA 57, 1962, 75–114.

Jones et al. 1973

J.E. Jones – A.J. Graham – L.H. Sackett – M.I. Geroulanos, An Attic Country House below the Cave of Pan at Vari, BSA 68, 1973, 355–452.

Kustermann Graf 2002

A. Kustermann Graf, Selinunte: necropoli di Manicalunga. Le tombe della contrada Gaggera (Catanzaro 2002).

Leibundgut Wieland 1994

D. Leibundgut Wieland, Selinunt, Nekropole Manicalunga, Gräber im Gebiet Timpone Nero (Zürich 1994).

Leibundgut Wieland 1997

D. Leibundgut Wieland, Beobachtungen und Gedanken zu Grabbeigaben. Importierte und lokale Keramik aus der Nekropole Manicalunga von Selinunt, AntK 40, 1997, 3–19.

Manacorda – Pallecchi 2012

D. Manacorda – S. Pallecchi (eds.), Le fornaci romane di Giancola (Bari 2012).

Meola 1996

E. Meola, Buffa, Necropoli di Selinunte I, 1 (Palermo 1996)

Meola 1997

E. Meola, Buffa, Necropoli di Selinunte I, 2 (Palermo 1997)

Meola 1998

E. Meola, Buffa, Necropoli di Selinunte I, 3 (Palermo 1998)

Mertens 2003

D. Mertens et al., Die Stadt und ihre Mauern, Selinus 1 (Mainz 2003).

Sapirstein 2013

P. Sapirstein, Painters, Potters and the Scale of the Attic Vase Painting Industry, AJA 117, 2013, 493–510.

Sapirstein 2014

P. Sapirstein, Demographics and Productivity in the Ancient Athenian Pottery Industry, in: J.H. Oakley (ed.), Athenian Potters and Painters III (Oxford 2014) 175–186.

Stissi 2002

V. Stissi, Pottery to the People. The Production, Distribution and Consumption of Decorated Pottery in the Greek World in the Archaic Period (650–480 BC) (Ph.D. diss. University of Amsterdam 2002).

Wikander 1993

Ö. Wikander, The Roof Tiles. Typology and Technical Features, Acquarossa VI, 2 (Stockholm 1993).

Zuchtriegel 2011

G. Zuchtriegel, Zur Bevölkerungszahl Selinunts im 5. Jh. v. Chr., Historia 60, 2011, 115–121.

The Economy of the Ancient Pavements. Prices and Contracts of Marble Floors and Mosaics in the Ancient Greek World

Niccolò Cecconi

Introduction

This study aims to discuss some archaeological and epigraphic documents related to the prices, contracts and economy of flooring of the ancient Greek world. The analysis will focus on financial operations relating to marble floors registered in the building accounts of the Greek sanctuaries of the Classical and Hellenistic age. In particular, four main aspects of the documentation will be analyzed:

1. The prices of materials for the production of marble floors and mosaics.
2. The payment of craftsmen involved in the construction of marble floors and mosaics.
3. The relationships between craftsmen and buyers involved in the construction of marble floors.
4. The financing models related to the fabrication of mosaics and marble floor.

The information inferred from research, compared with the archaeological data, could provide an initial framework of the economic, financial and productive processes of the floors of the ancient Greek world.

Epigraphic Documentation

The data considered here comes from Eleusis, Delos and Epidauros, and is dated to the Classical and Hellenistic periods.[1]

A building account from Eleusis, dated to the middle of the 4th century BC (*IG* II², 1672), mentions the activity of five artisans (Table 1): Demetrios, Ergasios, Kyprios, Euarchos and Milakos, who were entrusted to extract 304 blocks of breccia-stone to cover the floor of the tower (στρῶμα τῶι πύργωι) and courtyard (ἐδάφους τῆς αὐλῆς) for the price of 1 dr. for each extracted block (lines 48–50).

A description of the payment to the craftsman Neokleides from Kifissia follows. He was commissioned to pave the floor of the tower with 304 blocks (as mentioned above) at the price of 1 dr. for each piece set up (line 51). The craftsman is also mentioned in relation to the supply of 34 blocks of stone from Aegina (Αἰγιναῖοι λίθοι), which were to be placed above the breccia blocks of the tower floor at the price of 1 dr. per block (lines 52–53).

In the following lines, Pistias from the demos of Sphettos and Douriktonides from the demos of Kolonos are mentioned, who each received 270 dr. to remove the breccia rubble (ἐξαγωγὴ τῶν λίθων) from the floor of the tower (lines 51–52).

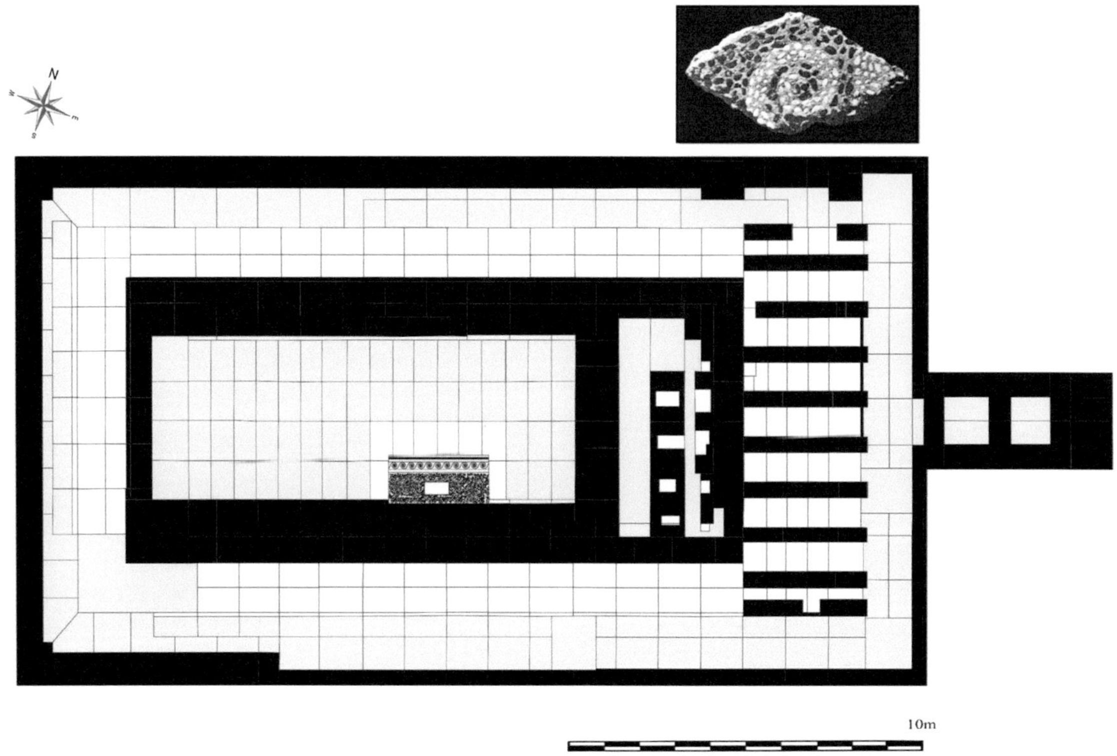

Fig. 1: Epidauros. Temple of Asklepius. Plan with mosaic.

The payments to Damasias, son of Kypragoras from Paros, who built the floor of the temple of Apollo in 297 BC, are registered at Delos (*IG* XI, 2 150 A, 1. 6–8).

The artisan Aristokles, who constructed the floor of the stoa of the Artemision for 36 dr., is also mentioned in the same document (*IG* XI, 2 199 A, 1. 81–82). Ten dr. out of 36 dr. were retained by the *hieropoioi* as a guarantee.

At the Asklepieion of Epidauros[2] important information is offered by the epigraphic documentation concerning the Aphrodision (or Artamition), the Asklepieion (fig. 1), and the Tholos (fig. 2). In this document (*IG* IV^2, 1 106), Damophilos, who supplied five paving slabs of mottled stone (λίθων ποικίλων) at the price of 14 dr. and 2 ob., is mentioned. (lines 96–98).

Additional information is provided by the *Rationes Aedificatiorum* of the Temple of Asklepius (*IG* IV^2, 1 102). In this inscription the following craftsmen involved in the construction of the pavement for the building are documented (379–378 or 374–373 BC): Lysikrates, who was entrusted for transporting and assembling the poros blocks of the foundation floor (στοιβὰν τῶι στρώματι) for 843 dr. and 2 ob. (lines 33–34); Mnasillos, for extracting and transporting blocks for the floor and for the ramp-pavement for 4.320 dr. (lines 40–41); Echetimos, for assembling the floor (στρῶσιν) for 759 dr. (lines 52–53); Kallis, for smoothing the floor of the pronaos and the interior of the temple (στρώματος τοῦ ἔνδοι καὶ τοῦ προδόμου) for 150 dr. (lines 70–71); and finally, Gorgias, for cleaning

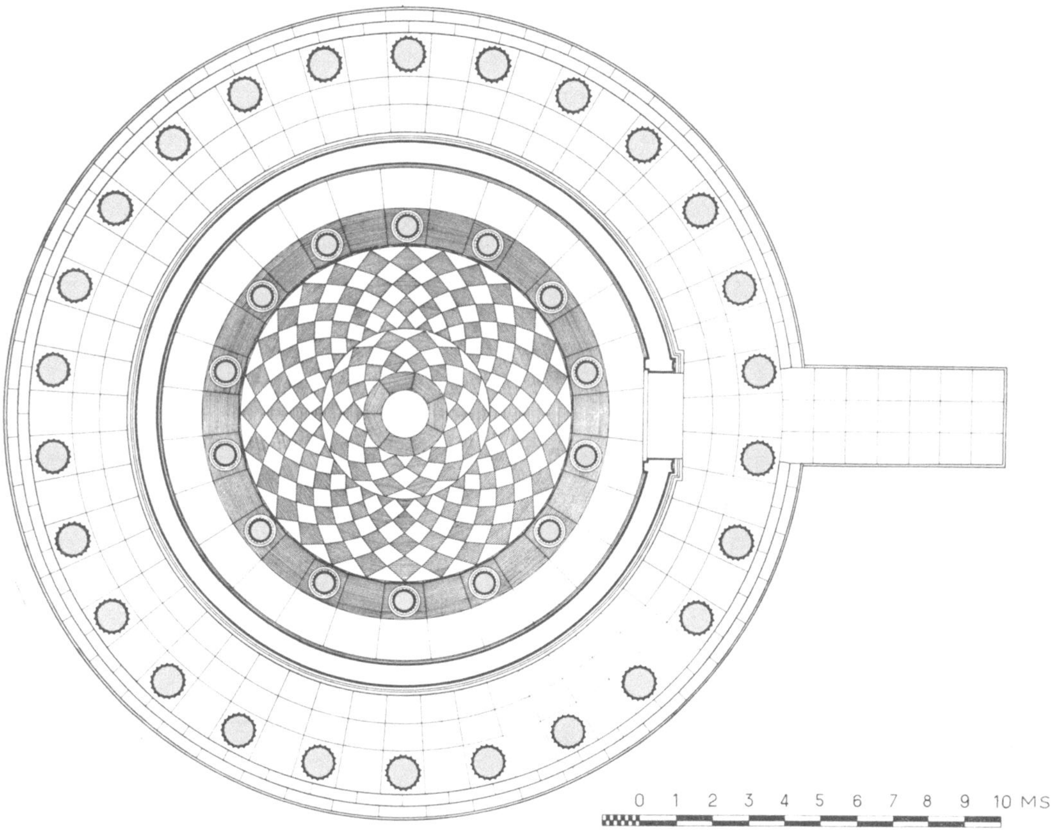

Fig. 2: Epidauros. Plan of Tholos.

the external floor (ἐπιξοὰν τοῦ στ [ρ] ώματ [ος]) and the external walls of the sekos, for 821 dr. and 20 ob. (lines 84–86).

The craftsman Lakrines also appears in this document, elsewhere identified as the sponsor of Lysikrates and Mnasillos, as mentioned above. He was paid 11 dr. for providing stones for the treasury of the cella (BII, II. 243–244), which can be interpreted as the pebbles of the mosaic that covered the floor of *bothros*.[3]

The documentation provides a detailed picture of the fitting procedures, and of the expenditure (about 6.000 dr.) which *hieropoioi* and *epistates* considered for the construction of the temple floor. The data can be related, furthermore, to the materials used for the construction of the pavement: poros for foundation blocks; white limestone with red and gray inclusions (ποικίλος λίθος) for floor coverings.

Financial operations related to the construction of floors can also be identified in the *Rationes Aedificatiorum* (*IG* IV^2, 1 103) of the Tholos. The paving operations are registered in the final parts of the B-side and the C-side of the stele (years 27 and 28).

The ὠνήματα of the document show that the construction of the floor was entrusted to a number of contractors, who supplied, transported, and set a variable number of σελίδες. Each σελίς was formed by two blocks of limestone, at a cost of 260 or 130 dr. for each block.

The inscription of the B-side is interrupted at the base of the stele, where 33 of the 52 σελίδες are mentioned, and continued on the C-side, which is almost illegible. Roux suggests the payment of the pavement of cella was recorded, which consists of a chessboard pattern of Pentelic marble and black stone probably from Argos.[4]

Craftsman	Site	Building	Type of pavement	Chronology	Duties	Amount	Price	*IG* document
Demetrios	Eleusis	Tower	στρῶμα	mid 4th c. BC	extraction of 304 blocks of breccia-stone	304 pieces of stone	1 dr. per piece of stone	II², 1672, 1. 48–50
Ergasios	Eleusis	Tower	στρῶμα	mid 4th c. BC	extraction of 304 blocks of breccia-stone	304 pieces of stone	1 dr. per piece of stone	II², 1672, 1. 48–50
Kyprios	Eleusis	Tower	στρῶμα	mid 4th c. BC	extraction of 304 blocks of breccia-stone	304 pieces of stone	1 dr. per piece of stone	II², 1672, 1. 48–50
Euarchos	Eleusis	Tower	στρῶμα	mid 4th c. BC	extraction of 304 blocks of breccia-stone	304 pieces of stone	1 dr. per piece of stone	II², 1672, 1. 48–50
Milakos	Eleusis	Tower	στρῶμα	mid 4th c. BC	extraction of 304 blocks of breccia-stone	304 pieces of stone	1 dr. per piece of stone	II², 1672, 1. 48–50
Pistias and Douriktonides	Eleusis	Tower	στρῶμα	mid 4th c. BC	cleaning operations	N.S.	270 dr.	II², 1672, 1. 51–52
Damasias	Delos	Temple of Apollo	[στ]ρῶμα	297 BC	construction of floor	N.S.	N.S.	XI, 2 150 A, 1. 6–8
Aristokles	Delos	Stoa of Artemision	στρῶσαι	274 BC	construction of floor	N.S.	36 dr.	XI, 2 199 A, 1. 81–82
Damophilos	Epidauros	Aphrodision (or Artamition)	στρώματος	4th c. BC	providing spotted limestone	5 slabs	14 dr. 2 ob. 5 ch. per slab	IV²,1 106, 96–98
Euxenidas	Epidauros	Domestic space		4th c. BC	providing spotted limestone	295 medimmi	1 dr. 4 ob.	IV²,1 109 III, 102–109
Lysikrates	Epidauros	Asklepieion (foundation)	στοιβὰν ... τῶι στρώματι	first third of 4th c. BC	transport and assembly of limestone blocks	N.S.	843 dr. 2 ob.	IV²,1 102, 33–34
Mnasillos	Epidauros	Asklepieion (pavement and ramp)	στρώματος	first third of 4th c. BC	transport and assembly of spotted limestone blocks	N.S.	4.320 dr.	IV²,1 102, 40–41
Echetimos	Epidauros	Asklepieion	στρῶσιν	first third of 4th c. BC	construction of floor	N.S.	759 dr.	IV²,1 102, 52–53

Table 1: Specific work assignments to the craftsmen involved in the construction of floors recorded in the *Rationes Aedificatiorum*. N.S. = Not Specified.

Kallis	Epidauros	Asklepieion (pronaos and cella)	στρώματος	first third of 4th c. BC	sanding of the floor	N.S.	150 dr.	IV²,1 102, 70–71
Gorgias	Epidauros	Asklepieion (external floor)	στρώματος	first third of 4th c. BC	cleaning of the floor	N.S.	N.R.	IV²,1 102, 84–86
Lakrines	Epidauros	Asklepieion (treasure)	N.S.	first third of 4th c. BC	provision of stone	N.S.	11 dr.	IV²,1 102, 243–244
Apollonidas	Epidauros	Tholos (peristasis)	στρῶμα	last third of 4th c. BC	provision of σελίδες	13 σελίδες (26 blocks)	3.330 dr.	IV²,1 102, 166–169; 173; 175–176.
Kleomilos and Philonidas	Epidauros	Tholos (peristasis)	στρῶμα	last third of 4th c. BC	preparation and provision of σελίδες	20 σελίδες (40 blocks)	5.200 dr.	IV²,1 102, 164–166; 169–170; 176–177.

Table 1 *(continued)*

The Financing Models

The documents discussed above allow us to explore some aspects related to public and private financing. The relationship between workers and clients is certainly one of the most influential aspects in the economy of floors of ancient Greece and helps demonstrate two main financing models: a) financing by the sanctuary and b) private financing.

Financing by the Sanctuary

Regarding the financial responsibilities of the sanctuary, the examined reports provide a detailed picture of the economic relations between the workers and the *hieropoioi*, *naopoioi* and *epistatai*, entrusted to supervise the work of the sanctuary. In this case, the financing practices were simplified, and the provisions benefitted both the sanctuary, which would not have been linked to any obligation for contract payments, and the craftsmen, who could have clarified the methods of remuneration prior to the beginning of the work.

In the case of the craftsmen involved in the construction of floors, it was possible to verify at Eleusis that the payments were made once the work was completed.

At Delphi, on the other hand, the *naopoioi* applied a more complex remuneration procedure. The contractor received, in one or more payments, the fixed sum of the contract before the end of the work. A tenth of this payment was subtracted as a guarantee and was returned when the work was completed and verified.

At Epidauros the financing systems were much more flexible. In the Asklepieion, for example, the floor was commissioned to a few craftsmen who were in charge of transporting and/or setting huge portions of the floor. In the case of the Tholos and Aphrodision (or Artamition), instead, payments were divided by increasing the number of craftsmen involved in the construction of the pavement.

Fig. 3: Delos. Inscriptions on the floor of the Sanctuary of the Syrian Gods.

Fig. 4: Eretria. Mosaic at the Sanctuary of the Egyptian Gods.

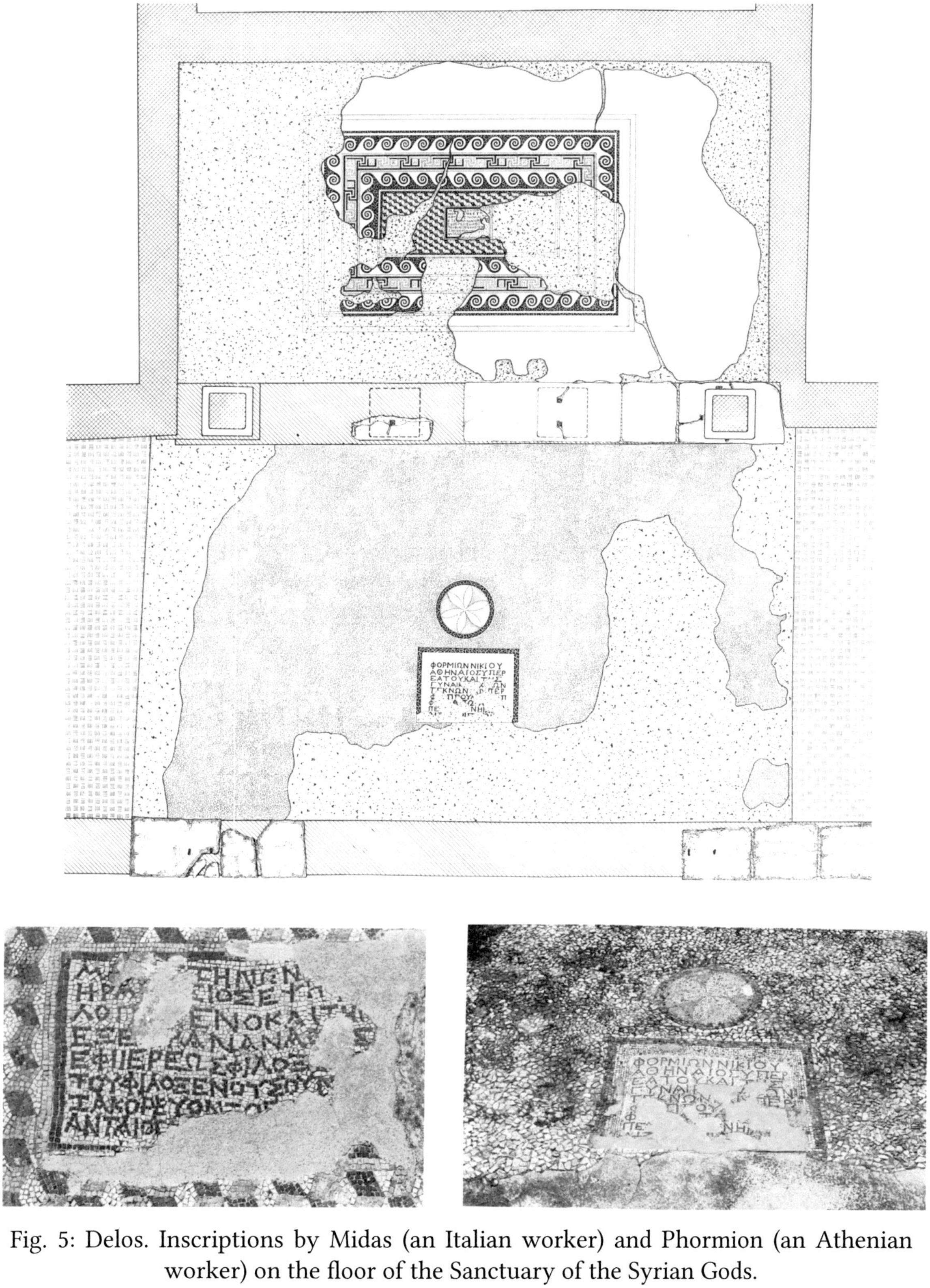

Fig. 5: Delos. Inscriptions by Midas (an Italian worker) and Phormion (an Athenian worker) on the floor of the Sanctuary of the Syrian Gods.

Private Financing

The second model concerns private funding. Our information is provided by the dedications, which were inscribed directly on the mosaics or on a stele (fig. 3). In this regard, the epigraphic documentation testifies to the various backgrounds of the clients, ranging from local, connected with the city where the mosaic was put in place, such in the case of Alexippos and Klearetes, who dedicated a mosaic in the sanctuary of the Egyptian gods of Eretria[5] (fig. 4) to foreign, as evidenced by the rich mosaic repertoire on Delos[6] (fig. 5).

Conclusion

The examination of the epigraphic evidence, related to the archaeological data, has demonstrated some aspects of the economy of flooring in the Greek sanctuaries of the Classical and Hellenistic age.

In particular, it was possible to demonstrate five main points: first, the most important information concerning the workers and the economy of the floors and mosaics of the Classical and Hellenistic age comes from the epigraphic documentation of the sanctuaries at Eleusis, Delos and Epidauros; second, at Eleusis the operations were divided between those who constructed the floors and those who cleaned them; third, at Delos there is evidence of public contracts for architects and artisans. The winners of these public contracts were subjected to a complex contractual system, characterized by the retention of one-tenth of the payment to the *hieropoioi* as a guarantee; fourth, the Epidauros documents, instead, show different forms of payment, in particular for the transport of raw materials. The floor of the Asklepieion, for example, was commissioned to a few craftsmen who transported huge amounts of stones. In the case of Tholos and Aphrodision, on the other hand, the preferred payment method was to divide the payments by increasing the number of craftsmen involved in the transportation and construction of the floor; finally, two financing models can be reconstructed: one managed by the sanctuary, and another based on funding from private individuals. The first was mostly associated with the construction of marble floors, while the second model mostly concerned mosaic floors.

In conclusion, this research can be viewed as a starting point for new important studies on the economy of the marble floors and mosaics in the ancient Greek world.

Notes

[1] The most important information about the economy of marble pavements are offered by the Rationes Aedificatiorum of the Classical and Hellenistic periods. For recent research on this topic, see Feyel 2006 and Prignitz 2014.

[2] For general information on the builders and contract at Epidauros, see Burford 1969.

[3] For more detailed information, see Cecconi 2017.

[4] Roux 1961, 176.

[5] Bruneau 1975, 120.

[6] Bruneau 1972, 115.

Image Credits

Fig. 1: Roux 1961 pl. 27 and Salzmann 1982, pl. 56.6. – Fig. 2: Roux 1961, pl. 38, rieal. aut. – Fig. 3: Bruneau 1972, fig. 153. 154. – Fig. 4: Bruneau 1975, pl. 12. – Fig. 5: Bruneau 1972, figs. 155. 157. 159.

References

Bruneau 1972
Ph. Bruneau, Les mosaïques de Délos, EAD 29 (Paris 1972).

Bruneau 1975
Ph. Bruneau, Le sanctuaire et le culte des divinités égyptiennes à Erétrie (Leiden 1975).

Burford 1969
A. Burford, The Greek Temple Builders at Epidauros (Liverpool 1969).

Cecconi 2017
N. Cecconi, Tappeti musivi nei templi della Grecia continentale e insulare tra età arcaica e proto-ellenistica, in: E. Greco (ed.), Atti dei primi Dialoghi sull'Archeologia della Magna Grecia e del Mediterraneo – Paestum 7–9 settembre 2016 (Paestum 2017) 1255–1264.

Feyel 2006
C. Feyel, Les artisans dans les sanctuaires grecs aux époques classique et hellénistique à travers la documentation financière en Grèce (Athènes 2006).

Prignitz 2014
S. Prignitz, Bauurkunden und Bauprogramm von Epidauros (400–350): Asklepiostempel – Tholos – Kultbild – Brunnenhaus, Vestigia 67 (München 2014).

Roux 1961
G. Roux, L'architecture de l'Argolide aux IVe et IIIe siècles a. J.C. (Paris 1961).

Salzmann 1982
D. Salzmann, Untersuchungen zu den antiken Kieselmosaiken (Berlin 1982).

Commentary

Peter Acton

My comments on the papers in this volume reflect my limited expertise in archaeology and my strong interest in economic interpretations of the production of artifacts and monuments. Such questions as I raise about the analyses are intended to suggest alternative interpretations rather than problems with the findings themselves. In particular I have tried to propose hypotheses and further research that might make the lines of enquiry put forward in the papers still more revelatory about ancient society.

Comparing the Labor Investment and Production of Early and Late Bronze Age Ceramic Roofing Tiles in Mainland Greece. Kyle Jazwa

Jazwa's paper on early and late Bronze Age ceramic roofing tiles provides an excellent example of how understanding the way a product was manufactured can provide important insights into expenditure choices and labor conditions in an ancient society. By reverse engineering tiles to see how they were made, he has been able to estimate relative resource consumption and skill levels for different roofing options.

He draws two important conclusions: first, through comparing the finished tiles, he shows that the level of skill required to make Early Bronze Age (EH) ones was very limited and they could probably have been made in any household, whereas the higher skills required for Late Bronze Age (LH) tiles suggest they would have been made by an experienced potter. Second, that the resources required to roof one's house with LH tiles suggest it was a luxury and an example of conspicuous consumption.

On the first point, he is almost certainly correct in saying that the tiles were made by the household in which they were to be used. He notes that the technology is very similar to brick-making of the period. Even in classical Athens, there is no evidence of a specialized home building trade and it is logical to conclude that the labor involved in constructing a house was provided by the site owner's family and slaves, ideally helped by friendly neighbours who had done it before. It is likely the same arrangements prevailed in the Early Bronze Age and covered roofing as well as walls.

A little more questionable is Jazwa's inference that LH tile makers were generalist potters who made many other items as well as tiles. This might well be the case, as the detritus of later pottery kilns shows a wide variety of decorative and utility items, and Jazwa posits that there would not have been enough demand for roofing in a small community to permit specialisation. On the other hand his analysis shows that the forming and firing required to tile the roof of a reasonable sized house might occupy a potter and his kiln for an entire growing season. Allowing for accidents, dilapidation and some population growth, it might not have needed a very large community to generate enough demand to keep one or more specialist potters busy, though there might have been limited benefit from specialisation. In terms of pottery economics, this does not affect Jazwa's conclusion. He infers correctly that, if tiles had to compete with alternatives for a generalist potter's efforts, the cost of tiles would not have been less than the potter could have made by working on other products. If the potter was a specialist, he would still have demanded a price-point that would bring in the same income as he could make with other products. From the point of view of social history, though, the development of specialisation within an industry is informative about social workings and relationships, and it will be interesting to see if future kiln discoveries throw more light on the specialist/generalist question.

Jazwa's second point is well supported by his energetic analysis that shows that both EH and LH tiles consumed far more resources than the more primitive flat clay or thatched roofs, and that LH consumed considerably more than EH. His view that this cost, together with the visibility of the projects, shows that LH tiled roofs were an example of conspicuous consumption is plausible – even probable – but would be best supported by any data that can be accessed or estimated about the relative wealth of the sites in question, the distribution of that wealth within the community, and expenditure on other costly items. All of these are hard to know or infer, but to the extent new information can be adduced that touches on these points, Jazwa's cost-based analysis will provide a robust foundation for understanding LH roofing tile customer dynamics.

Crossing Thresholds and Building States: Labor Investment, Tomb Construction, and Early State Formation in the Bronze Age Argolid. Rodney D. Fitzsimons

It is always reassuring to see scholars of the ancient world give economics some prominence in their explanation of events. Fitzsimons bases his analysis on the premise that control of what might be considered a polity's most important resource, non-specialized labor, is a powerful indicator of social organisation – an important truth but one that does not seem to have been pursued very much by others. His own pursuit is another confirmation of the benefits that can accrue to archaeological interpretation from adopting techniques from other disciplines, in this case architectural energetics and network theory.

The former approach demonstrates beyond doubt that different periods of tomb construction show very significant increases (multifold) in the amount of labor required, from cists through shaft graves to tholos tombs and ultimately to the huge engineering feats of the Mycenaean state. He calculates the minimum labor simultaneously required from the size of the largest block that needed to be transported, which makes perfect sense. On the other hand, I would encourage Fitzsimons to put more emphasis on the fact that the values he generates represent the minimum, number employed on the project, thereby avoiding assumptions of that assumes consecutive working and that of all laborers were being interchangeable, moving from one task to the next. This might not have been the case; Adam Smith would have pointed out that, provided there was a single point of authority in overall charge of the project, they wouldn't have taken long to figure out that, even for the most basic tasks, higher productivity can be achieved by specialisation. Laborers might have been working on different tasks in parallel, the total numbers employed might have been higher and time to completion shorter.

If this was, in fact, the case, it only reinforces Fitzsimons' findings from his second approach. Network theory provides an experimentally supported way of calculating the degree of social complexity in a society based on the number of individuals being co-ordinated in some manner. If the numbers turn out to have been higher than otherwise thought at a point in time, then the complexity was greater. Interestingly this process feeds back into Fitzsimons' observation about grave groupings that suggests the existence of elites within elites and the emergence of new ones, and it would be interesting to see if this element of network theory can explain some of the chronology of these changes in social hierarchy.

The development of social complexity in early societies is one of the most important questions in ancient history and Fitzsimons has produced a powerful methodology for identifying inflection points. May it continue to be developed.

Relations among Workshops and Craftsmen in Protoattic Vase-painting: Limits and Perspectives in Quantifying the Production. Giulia Rocco

Making sense of the scale of operations, the activities of particular workshops and the relationships between potters and painters, never simple in any period, appears especially difficult in Protoattic pottery. Rocco's painstaking analysis of commonalities of shapes among the output of various ergasteria sheds new and important light on the subject. I am far from qualified to critique Rocco's analysis of shapes, but her approach reflects some important truths about the industry and leads to some interesting questions about the relative status of potters and painters in different eras.

She rightly distinguishes between the output of potter-painters and that of master potters working with specialist painters, and notes that some small pieces appear to have been painted by apprentices while others might be "the hasty executions of an expert painter". She sensibly protests at identifications of individuals that imply impossibly lengthy careers and attributes commonalities over periods greater than 20–30 years to further generations educated in the same long-standing workshop traditions. She analyses collaborative work on commissions to establish that the best painters were mobile in Protoattic times just as they were in the classical period.

Her potter-centric approach also offers an intriguing take on hierarchies within the industry. By her account, master potters engaged the best painters to decorate their best works – a reversal of the usual assumptions about painter-potter relationships later on. If she is correct, it suggests that the scarce skill and the one most in demand in the marketplace was vase formation and that those who possessed this skill in a high degree could get the best painters to work for them. This also implies (although Rocco does not say so) that the real value of a special piece would have been captured by the potter while painters would have been obliged to accept the potter's terms of payment, perhaps even in a bidding competition. In later periods it is generally thought that the proven mobility of painters indicates that the best painters captured the value of their work, using whatever potter they were comfortable working with (or who offered the best terms subject to quality standards), if they didn't make the pot themselves. If this temporal reversal is correct it can only mean that between 700 and, say, 400 BC skill in painting became more valued than skill in forming, or, to put it another way, sophistication in painting developed much faster than in forming. There would not have been a simple point-in-time transition and there would have been a period – possibly of several decades – when the relative claim to value would have been unclear and might even have differed between different workshop groups or for different types of vases at the same time.

Whether or not this speculation has substance does not affect the importance of Rocco's shape-based analysis, but I very much hope that she will pursue this line of thinking and see if it is possible to identify inflection points (such as the transition from Black to Red Figure or a change in the expectations of those commissioning large and complex ritual vessels) in which the skills of the painter came to outweigh those of the potter.

Social Network Analysis and Connoisseurship in the Study of Athenian Potters' Communities. Eleni Hasaki and Diane Harris Cline

This paper is another demonstration of how the complexities and uncertainties inherent in interpreting archaeological discoveries can be illuminated by adopting techniques from other disciplines. The application of Social Network Analysis (SNA) to relationships identified in the Beazley corpus provides a novel and dynamic view of relationships and interactions in the Athenian Kerameikos. The paper refers to an enormous advance in this respect between Boardman's 1974 work and Osborne's of 2004, which used the same data and a slightly more sophisticated version of Boardman's basic approach. SNA is an order of magnitude more powerful. As the authors recognize, using Beazley's unverified classifications as they have is fraught with methodological problems that Beazley himself did not help to resolve, but the approach will certainly be robust when applied to alternative identifications of commonalities in output.

In fact, exactly how many different hands can be identified is not very important for understanding how the Kerameikos actually worked (except in the unlikely event that a large number of relationships identified turn out to be between units that are actually the same person). What matters is the patterns of relationships. By exposing intermediate connections between groups of craftsmen it provides a picture of how people went about their business in a much more relatable manner than traditional tendencies to isolate identifiable groups. Particular findings of interest in this respect are that some nodes of artists were central to a large number of relationships, while others were relatively isolated, connecting to just one other node, and that there was a mix of large and small "clusters". The picture is intuitively plausible. With no advantages in cost of production or price realization to be derived from collaboration, and with all or most workshops based around a household unit, relationships were likely to have been based on family ties, friendships, common artistic interests, and energy for socializing rather than pragmatic concerns over production economics, and the result would be as shown here: somewhat random and chaotic.

The analysis also identifies a new class of player: those such as the Cactus Painter whose own output was modest but seem to have had some kind of linkage to a large number of other hands. It is fascinating to speculate how such intermediaries operated and how they made a living. Brokers of potter-painter arrangements? Resellers? Entrepreneurs? Educators?

The authors' plan to pursue the analysis in time slices to ensure that the relationships posited were chronologically possible will be an important further step. Even if some relationships need to be redefined it might provide new insights into apprenticeships and workshop traditions over time.

Productivity of Athenian Vase-painters and Workshops. Philip Sapirstein

Sapirstein's revision of Cook's analysis of painter output is welcome and 8.2 pots per year for "productive painters" seems much more plausible than Cook's figure of less than half that. His numbers are carefully calculated and his use of the data wisely discriminating, but irrespective of the accuracy of the answer, it is the variability from the norm that is of most interest.

The analysis makes clear that there were a large number of decorators, including some very good craftsmen, whose output was far less than the norm and were probably doing something else with their time than decorating vases. Sapirstein suggests various possibilities within the workshop, including but not limited to throwing pots. He might also consider the range of activities open to Athenian citizens outside the workshop. A household might choose only to operate a workshop for a few weeks a year when other activities such as managing their small farm or military service permitted. Some might be spending most of their time playing roles in the Athenian democracy. Some might simply have been quite satisfied with a modest income from a few weeks work; after all the accumulation of wealth beyond one's basic needs was not a major objective for all Athenians. One of the great attractions of making pots to part-timers was that all resource costs (labor and materials) varied directly with output so a small occasional producer would have the same costs as a larger full-time operation. And of course, if the small occasional producer was a good enough painter to get a premium for his work, he'd probably try.

In contrast to Stissi (see below), Sapirstein's analysis brings him to a much lower estimate than Cook of the number of people working in decorated pottery and he explains why he questions Stissi's conclusion. This debate seems likely to be productive and is not one I am in any way qualified to adjudicate, but I offer the following observations:

- Apart from the lifestyle choices mentioned above, the evidence for a reasonable number of painters not being full-time is very strong, and Sapirstein is right to question a calculation of total employment based on all identified hands being Full Time Equivalents.
- He also seems justified in questioning a calculation based on an estimate of the percentage completeness of the Beazley Archive Pottery Database, especially if it contains irrelevant material.
- It would be interesting to know to what extent Sapirstein's readiness to dismiss the possibility of there being a large number of "minor hands" takes into account likely survival bias in the archaeological record. The less distinguished a piece was, the more likely it would have been to be used in a way that might destroy it altogether.

Sapirstein rightly observes that to estimate the population engaged in making utility ware requires a different approach. A special challenge is that archaeological finds suggest that many, probably most, workshops made both decorated and utility ware – which would have been economically sensible as it would take a very long time for a painter to fill a kiln. Irrespective of what they were making, there is no reason to suspect workshops needed much more than the five people Sapirstein posits – perhaps six if they used a specialist clay-preparer and a wheel spinner.

From Counting Pots to Counting People: Assessing the Scale of Athenian Pottery Production and its Impact on Workshop Staff. Vladimir Stissi

Stissi's paper provides an excellent exploration of the complexities of trying to estimate workshop scale, organisation of labor, and employment arrangements in Athenian potteries and his conclusion that there was more specialisation and casual labor than the usual static picture of small workshops with stable staffing is almost certainly correct. His estimate of annual production of pots in Athens at one to two million a year, derived from other estimates of survival rates and the incompleteness of the Beazley Archive, is necessarily tenuous but plausible. His conclusion that the number of active potters at any one time in the Kerameikos was much higher than traditionally believed is more open to challenge.

Stissi's analysis of monographs, together with Sapirstein's work which he cites and the inevitable impact of survivor bias, gives strong support to his conclusion that there were many more "minor hands" in action than has generally been thought, but his inference about total numbers depends upon taking a view on the average annual production per active hand. He shows that the conventional estimate of 130 potters applied to a conservative calculation of the volumes he thinks were produced suggests output per person per year of 1.770 items per year "which seems on the high side." This is debatable, as potting can be done very fast and much depends on time needed for painting. I would suggest it may in fact be very low. I have seen a potter in England make a nicely shaped vase in two and a half minutes and one in Rajasthan, using a single ball of clay and with a single hand-spin of a heavy wheel, form three ornamental vases of different shapes, each about 25 centimetres high and 15 in diameter, one with a separate lid, in just over two minutes. Of course some of the vases in the archive are much more complex and of finer finish and would have taken longer, and the larger ones were thrown in more than one part, but for the vast majority of shapes, a potting output per person of several thousand units a year might well be possible.

Similar considerations apply to decoration. Stissi recognizes that most potters spent some of their time painting, but one suspects that what most of them painted tended to be repetitive, simple and copied, taking only a short time. Highly decorated pots with novel scenes carefully planned and executed would have taken much longer – possibly a few days but nothing like the four months Cook suggested. In any event, for the best painted pots, painting was certainly the production bottleneck and probably divorced from the standard potting firing chain, not least because the best pots seem to have been fired separately to avoid the risk of other vessels exploding.

One hopes that Stissi's admirably creative approach to estimating volumes from analysis of the Beazley Archive and monographs can be applied to estimating the relative output of products with very different forming or decorating requirements. To achieve more confident conclusions about productivity would require a careful segmentation of products according to the likely time they took to produce, distinguishing especially:

- Shapes that really do take more than a few minutes for an experienced potter
- Painting that would have taken several hours or days and a genuine master as against simple or copied decorations that could be churned out quite quickly by an experienced potter.

This is not an easy segmentation given the limitations and biases in the data we have, but perhaps further finds, together with the application of artificial intelligence in pattern recognition and manipulating big data, will make it more achievable. Stissi's approach should underlie such developments.

The paper raises two other issues of great interest to social and economic historians. First is the question of employment arrangements. Stissi shows there was a fair amount of mobility between workshops, not only among young artisans finding their niche but also among recognized "masters". It is interesting to speculate on the relevant economic arrangements. One would expect that the best decorators could command a premium for their work in a way that other painters could not. They needed a workshop in which to base themselves – at least for raw materials and firing, even if they formed the pots themselves. Their presence would also have shed some lustre on the workshops they used and might well have helped the education of apprentices. Their bargaining power would have been considerable. This perhaps explains why there was considerable mobility. Perhaps they just set themselves up with whatever workshop offered the best terms season to season. Were they actually engaged in the economics of the workshop they used or did they just outsource the rest of the process to the lowest bidder offering acceptable quality standards?

A second question is around the size of average workshops in Athens. Stissi seems suspicious of the data that suggest that all or most workshops in Athens were small and, though he does not really challenge it, he does note that much larger ones have been discovered at Selinous and Corfu. I believe the reason Attic workshops were small was purely economic: there was no financial advantage and a considerable risk in getting larger. An interesting question, and one addressed in relation to Bentz's paper, is what markets Selinous served that made scale beneficial.

Production and Consumption of Ceramics at Selinous: A Quantitative Approach. Martin Bentz

Bentz's paper on discoveries at Selinous presents a fascinating challenge to those of us who like to try to explain industry structures through economics. It is pretty universally accepted now that workshops in 6th and 5th century Athens were small and largely based around households, and the reasons are not far to seek. Scale brought no cost or price advantages for utility ware and premiums for decorated pieces could be achieved in any size of workshop. Expansion therefore brought risk and no economic benefit.

The pottery industry in Selinous was very different. Bentz draws particular attention to the remarkable size of the potters' quarters, the large number of kilns, the presence of some very large kilns and the pairings of them which imply, at least, co-operative working, if not common ownership.

To calculate output and local demand, Bentz uses whatever sources he can find and applies them boldly. Output calculations rest on assumptions about product mix, firing cycles, contemporaneity and seasonality. Local demand calculations start with a reasonably firm quantification of the needs of households, graves and sanctuaries. The former requires an estimate of replacement rates (a notoriously contested topic) and the items in the latter two, though generally small, were large in number, meaning errors might be significant. Nevertheless, there is no reason to think the account is more likely to err in one direction than the other and it would take inconceivably large errors to undermine Bentz's conclusion that the amount produced greatly exceeded local demand and much of it must have been aimed at another market.

We must question how this occurred. Cases of one location exporting a wide variety of pottery items, as seems to have been the case here, are thought to be extremely rare and for the very good reason that, if you had access to a reasonable clay deposit, you could make the products yourself consuming no more materials or labor than anyone else – and there would be no cartage to pay. Pottery exports we know of tended to be items of a single class, decorated vases from Attica being the most notable example. The substantial movement of amphoras in the Northern Aegean at the time was certainly due to the contents rather than the vessels. The most notable examples we have of major exporting centres in Roman times also specialized: terra sigillata from Arretium and "Samian" red terracotta ware from Graufesenque, for example.

Bentz's important paper raises many questions. Two stand out to me. Why did whoever was buying pottery from Selinous not make their own? Despite Selinous' scale, the nature of pottery cost structures is such that I cannot believe it would have been cheaper to bring in product from there. Was their home deficient in good clay deposits? Did they have some exchange arrangement whereby they specialized in something else that Selinous imported from them? Were defence alliances involved? Improbable as some of these ideas may seem, the answer must lie in something of that nature.

The second question involves the ownership structure of the kilns. Were they independents who found it convenient and efficient to work together or were the kilns owned by a few individuals and the rest of the workers employees? Or was it a public utility, perhaps with firemen on regular duty, that potters could choose to use when it suited them? If so, what were the governance and maintenance arrangements? Such speculations are intriguing, far though we seem from being able to answer them at present. If anything can throw more light on such matters, it will probably be Bentz's rigorous yet creative approach to quantification.

The Economy of the Ancient Pavements. Prices and Contracts of Marble Floors and Mosaics in the Ancient Greek World. Niccolò Cecconi

Cecconi's analysis of contractual payments for the construction of public works in Eleusis, Delos and Epidauros builds on and refines the efforts of scholars such as Feyel to establish payment values and arrangements. By focusing on marble and mosaic flooring, he is able to dig deep into the data available and identify different contract types for different locations and for different buildings within the same location, as well as what may be an important difference between marble and mosaic construction contracts.

The limited number of observations in the surviving epigraphy where both volumes and prices are given shows, as one would expect, the same price per extracted block of breccia stone in 5 contracts at Eleusis. It would be interesting to see if the cost of spotted limestone at Eleusis varied between public and private uses but this would require estimating how many medimnoi there were per "slab" which Cecconi wisely does not attempt. One wonders if data from other sites might show some basis for one or two hypotheses to be tried. An estimate of labor time required to deliver on the extraction or cleaning contracts – and hence earnings per day per person – would be another interesting continuation of the analysis.

More important though, are Cecconi's observations on financing. For marble flooring, financed by the sanctuary, Eleusis offered simple contracts, engaging different individuals for extraction and cleaning, while Delos's contracts were much more complex and Epidauros did a bit of both. Presumably this variability was a pragmatic response to circumstances and it is interesting to speculate on what those circumstances might have been. Labor market variations in different trades? Different priorities or risk-preferences among the commissioners or their communities? Time constraints?

A final question raised by this intriguing piece of research is the motivation of private individuals to finance mosaic floors. For local benefactors like Alexippos and Klearetes, was it a liturgy or a political gambit or a bit of both? And what was driving foreigners to be so kind to Delos?

Printing and Binding
Books on Demand GmbH, Norderstedt